CHRISTIANITY, DEMOCRACY, AND THE SHADOW OF CONSTANTINE

ORTHODOX CHRISTIANITY AND CONTEMPORARY THOUGHT

SERIES EDITORS
George E. Demacopoulos and Aristotle Papanikolaou

This series consists of books that seek to bring Orthodox Christianity into an engagement with contemporary forms of thought. Its goal is to promote (1) historical studies in Orthodox Christianity that are interdisciplinary, employ a variety of methods, and speak to contemporary issues; and (2) constructive theological arguments in conversation with patristic sources and that focus on contemporary questions ranging from the traditional theological and philosophical themes of God and human identity to cultural, political, economic, and ethical concerns. The books in the series explore both the relevancy of Orthodox Christianity to contemporary challenges and the impact of contemporary modes of thought on Orthodox self-understandings.

CHRISTIANITY, DEMOCRACY, AND THE SHADOW OF CONSTANTINE

GEORGE E. DEMACOPOULOS
AND ARISTOTLE PAPANIKOLAOU
EDITORS

FORDHAM UNIVERSITY PRESS
New York • 2017

Fordham University Press has no responsibility for the persistence or accuracy of URLs for external or third-party Internet websites referred to in this publication and does not guarantee that any content on such websites is, or will remain, accurate or appropriate.

Fordham University Press also publishes its books in a variety of electronic formats. Some content that appears in print may not be available in electronic books.

Visit us online at www.fordhampress.com.

Library of Congress Cataloging-in-Publication Data

Names: Demacopoulos, George E., editor. | Papanikolaou, Aristotle, editor.
Title: Christianity, democracy, and the shadow of Constantine / George E.
    Demacopoulos and Aristotle Papanikolaou, editors.
Description: First edition. | New York : Fordham University Press, [2017] |
    Series: Orthodox Christianity and contemporary thought | Includes
    bibliographical references and index.
Identifiers: LCCN 2016027219 | ISBN 9780823274192 (cloth : alk. paper) | ISBN
    9780823274208 (pbk. : alk. paper)
Subjects: LCSH: Church history. | Constantine I, Emperor of Rome,
    –337—Influence. | Christianity and politics. | Democracy—Religious
    aspects—Christianity.
Classification: LCC BR145.3 .C455 2017 | DDC 261.7—dc23
LC record available at https://lccn.loc.gov/2016027219

Printed in the United States of America

19 18 17   5 4 3 2 1

First edition

In Memory of Michael J. Jaharis (1928–2016)
Friend, Philanthropist, and Visionary
"Well done, good and faithful servant; you have been faithful over a little, I will set you over much; enter into the joy of your master."
(Matthew 25:23)

CONTENTS

CONSTANTINE'S SHADOW:
HISTORICAL PERSPECTIVES

AN APOPHATIC APPROACH

CHRISTIANITY, DEMOCRACY, AND THE SHADOW OF CONSTANTINE

OUTRUNNING CONSTANTINE'S SHADOW

Aristotle Papanikolaou and George E. Demacopoulos

Whatever one may mean by "political theology," or even whether, as Stanley Hauerwas questions,[1] there can be such a thing as political theology, it is fair to assert that the discussion on these themes has followed primarily a Protestant-Catholic trajectory. The post-Communist situation has thrust the Orthodox into these debates, though there appears little evidence in the literature of any mutual influence between the centuries-long Protestant-Catholic conversation and that emerging within the Orthodox world. It was this lack that we hoped to address at the Patterson Conference, "Christianity, Democracy, and the Shadow of Constantine," sponsored by the Orthodox Christian Studies Center at Fordham University.

The question of the relation of Christianity to democracy is especially acute in the post-Communist Orthodox countries. Although Orthodox theological engagement with modern liberalism is evident in nineteenth- and early twentieth-century Russia, it was in relation to the existing imperial structures and was interrupted by the Communist Revolution. The traditional Orthodox countries are now not empires, and even though one sees movements toward totalitarianism within some of these Orthodox countries, there is no way for the Orthodox countries to avoid engagement with the challenge of modern political liberalism. Even in Greece, where church-state relations have been a national public issue since Greece's liberation from the Ottomans in the early nineteenth century, the complicated relation to the European Union manifests how an East-West divide shapes Orthodox thinking on the political. There is not an Orthodox

Church in the world that would disavow democracy, but they do argue that the particular shape of church-state relations is not uniform and must take into account a nation's particular religious history. Fr. Capodistrias Hämmerli supports this claim, drawing on the now landmark case of *Lautsi v. Italy*, and shows how most of the twenty countries participating in Italy's appeal to the case were traditional Orthodox countries. Kristina Stoeckl further elucidates this East-West rhetoric by analyzing the discourse on human rights in the Russian Orthodox Church (ROC). Although the ROC supports human rights, it advances an understanding of human rights that counters that of the Western liberal tradition. In effect, it uses a Western notion to claim a diametrical opposition between East and West by arguing for a particular Eastern notion of human rights and, by extension, of democracy. In so doing, it forms alliances with Western conservatives, with whom the ROC shares an antiliberal rhetoric. It is unclear to what extent the ROC influences the Russian state or particular legislation; but Vladimir Putin is using Russia's Orthodox history and cultural traditions in order to forge a new East-West ideological divide. In this sense, the ROC's own ambivalence toward modern Western liberalism indirectly contributes to such seemingly un-Christian legislation as the laws against "gay propaganda."

Given this new global reality, it is timely for a new ecumenical discussion to occur where Protestant and Catholic theologians reflect on these questions in light of both the Orthodox situation and Orthodox sources; and, conversely, where Orthodox theologians reflect on the unprecedented global reality within Orthodoxy in dialogue with the already-existing debate among Protestants and Catholics. This theological exchange occurs, of course, in light of the larger discussions within political philosophy about the relation of religion to the state, society, and culture.

Mount Athos is to many the heart of the Orthodox world, and Luke Bretherton appeals to what some refer to as the holy mountain and the experience of living between liturgical and "worldly" time as a bridge to the consociational model of democracy, which pluralizes political sovereignty across different overlapping associations. He argues that Orthodox should think about politics in terms of consociational democracy, which he connects to Orthodox understandings of the Trinity and eschatology. Thinking in consociationalist and eschatological terms would further help the Orthodox resist the temptations of *phyletism* and ethnonationalism because it would challenge the claims to undivided sovereignty by any worldly political authority or association.

A seminal moment within the Roman Catholic tradition regarding its relation to liberal democracy is Vatican II, and Mary Doak writes on the Council's description of the Church as a "sign and instrument" of divine-human communion and ties it to the Orthodox teaching on *theosis*, arguing that Catholics can learn from the Orthodox how to better show Catholic social thought's rootedness in central Christian teachings. Orthodox teaching on communion can help resist globalization, rampant individualism, and social atomism, while helping to promote justice and inclusion. In continuity with this theme of divine-human communion, or *theosis*, Eric Gregory identifies the need for both East and West to better relate the world-affirming incarnational dimension of political theology to redemption history and the awareness of sin. The Orthodox are often accused of overstressing the former, leading to uncritical alliances with political institutions, while political Augustinians tend to overstress the latter, leading to pessimism about earthly politics. Gregory calls on both traditions to think about the importance of political action *in time* as a way of navigating the dialectic tensions between political confidence and pessimism.

One of the most challenging, if not basic, questions Orthodox theologians must confront is the compatibility between the Orthodox tradition and liberal democracy. Perry Hamalis argues for such a compatibility through highlighting the affinities between Orthodox thinkers and Thomas Hobbes on the dynamics of death. Orthodoxy and the liberal tradition founded on Hobbes both see the modern political order grounded in the dynamics of death, and Hamalis argues that such a notion allows for a bridge between disparate traditions in ways not possible with the theological notion of divine-human communion.

Nathaniel Wood focuses our attention on late nineteenth and early twentieth-century Russia, where one sees one of the few substantive debates on liberal democracy within the Orthodox tradition prior to the post-Communist situation. As Wood illustrates, the notion of divine-human communion was central to this discussion. He further argues that Russian theologians, such as Sergius Bulgakov, viewed the secular liberal order through the lens of divine-human communion in a way that was critically appreciative, as such an order allows for a divinization of the created order in freedom, and not through force. Finally, Emmanuel Clapsis, like Doak, sees the Orthodox understanding of the Church in terms of the Eucharist as enabling it to act as an agent for promoting human solidarity and communion. While the pluralism of liberal democracies has posed a challenge to the ways in which the Church has functioned within traditional Orthodox countries, members of Eucharistic communities—Church—should engage as connected critics, promoting solidarity and communion within the public sphere, while testifying also to the limitations of the age and to the world's eschatological future.

These theological discussions on political theology are ultimately haunted by the shadow of the Emperor Constantine's conversion to Christianity (312 CE), which has left its indelible stamp on Christian thinking of the political; his shadow even extends to the pre-Constantinian era, as it is impossible for scholars of Christianity to interpret the pre-Constantinian Christian response to the question of the political without being cognizant of what occurred after Constantine. In the fourth century, Constantine's turn to Christianity was simultaneously the constitution of a dualism in Christian political theology between Constantinianism and pre-Constantinianism that continues to haunt Christian theological reflection on the political.

At the time of Constantine's conversion, Christians were not yet the majority within the Roman Empire and it was not necessarily inevitable that they would succeed in Christianizing the Roman Empire. In hindsight, it is clear that the emperor's conversion facilitated this Christianization and, in the process, forged a new relation of the still-evolving institutional Church to the imperial state, as well as to the culture and traditions of Roman civilization. To say that what emerged was a caesaropapist model would be inaccurate and would better describe tsarist Russia after the eighteenth-century tsar Peter the Great. Even after Constantine, Christians maintained a pre-Constantinian critical distance between church and state. One way to interpret the well-known model of *symphonia*, enshrined in Justinian's *Sixth Novella*, is to see the "established" Church, even with all of its growing privileges, as distinct from the state. From the fourth century up until the fall of Constantinople, there are numerous examples, including writings of patristic thinkers, monastic protestations, and emperor-bishop squabbles, that testify to the continuation of a pre-Constantinian Christian consciousness as a community distinct from the political. If "Constantinianism" is meant to characterize an absolute accommodation of the Christian Church to the state, then that does not describe the post-Constantinian Roman Empire; and, in fact, one would be hard-pressed to find a moment in Christian history where this Christian consciousness is ever eviscerated. Inasmuch as Constantine's shadow looms large over Christian political discourse, so does that of Augustine. As Peter Kaufman demonstrates, even though Augustine made use of state power against the Donatists, unlike the state, the Church is a community that restores sinners and combats pride through its stories and memories.

One might be more sympathetic to the charge of "Constantinianism" if it pointed to the kinds of possibilities opened to the Christian Church as a result of Constantine's conversion, and the kinds of exclusions it enabled. It would be difficult to dispute that after Constantine, the Christian Church suffered from the temptation of using state power to advance what is determined to be Christian objectives, and this temptation plagued the Christian Church even during the formation of the modern nation state. The use of state power ultimately leads to the violent exclusion of not simply those who are not Christian, but those who might interpret Christianity differently. Constantine also opened the door for state power to influence the institutional life of the Christian Church, to the point, as Timothy Barnes has proven, of the election of the archbishop of Constantinople being determined by the will of the emperor, even if the latter did not formally meddle in the official process of electing him. During the later years of the Empire, James C. Skedros describes how "Orthodoxy" transitioned from being a theological concept to one appropriated as "political Orthodoxy" in order to affirm a superior political and cultural identity over and against Latin Christians and the Ottomans, in a way that is similar to Vladimir Putin's appropriation of Orthodoxy against the liberal West. Constantine did enable new ways of envisioning the relation of Christians and the institutional church to the political, which Christians have not been able to resist even up to our current moment.

The greatest challenge to this symphonic model was the emergence of modern political liberalism, which has as one of its core principles the separation of the state from the church. Even though there always existed Augustinian voices attempting to remind Christians that they are a community distinct from and in critical relation to the political, the history of Christian political theology in both the East and the West has been one form or another of Justinian *symphonia* in which the Church feels it is justified to use the power of the state to advance Christian objectives, and where the state makes use of the institutional church and appropriates Christian discourse to advance the interests of the state. Modern political liberalism challenged that relationship, but not without resistance from the Christian churches. Eventually, one sees the growing Christian acceptance of democratic structures, from Walter Rauschenbusch's Social Gospel to Vatican II's affirmation of democracy. As detailed by J. Bryan Hehir, the Catholic Church has had and continues to have a complicated relationship with democracy, even if it now unequivocally supports democracy. The complication entails the liberal presuppositions that seemingly structure modern democratic institutions, processes, habits, attitudes, and modes of subjectification. It is fair to say that given the Ottoman and Communist occupations of traditional Orthodox countries, the Orthodox have not had the luxury to confront the challenge posed to Christianity by modern liberalism, except for a strain of political thinking in nineteenth-century Russia. Up until the fall of communism, one cannot detect a vociferous critique of democracy by Orthodox thinkers. In fact, Orthodox Christians in the diaspora seemed to thrive within the European, American, and Australian democracies within which they found themselves. Even if ambivalent, there seemed to be an emerging Christian consensus around democracy; it appeared as if Constantine's shadow had finally receded.

As the Christian world was making its peace with modern liberal democracy, and as secular liberal political philosophers from John Rawls to Jürgen Habermas were finally conceptualizing a way for religion to participate in the public sphere, Christian theologians started to critically examine the relation between Christianity and democracy. Theologians from the movement known as Radical Orthodoxy argued that the presuppositions of modern liberal political philosophy are antithetical to those inherent in a Christian participatory ontology. Hauerwas has been one of the most vocal critics of the Christian accommodation to liberal political philosophy, arguing, in part, that the Christian endorsement of any particular structuring of the political is still a form of Constantinianism insofar as such an endorsement tends toward absolutizing the political. There are even nontheologians who would indirectly agree with Hauerwas, such as Talal Asad, Saba Mahmood, and Giorgio Agamben, insofar as they interpret the "secular" as simply an extension of Christianity and, thus, of some form of Constantinianism, even if Hauerwas would interpret the secular as a distortion of the Christian Gospel. There is a strange and ironic alliance between certain Christian theologians and nontheologians in rejecting the categories of the "secular," "public square," and "liberalism." The question of Christianity's relation to democracy has returned to the center of Christian political theology, and in this discussion, Constantine's shadow once again looms large.

We are living in an age where just as it seemed there was increasing acceptance for the role of religion in the public square, Christians started again to question their relationship to modern liberal democracy, and non-Christian thinkers started to question their relationship to the secular. The state of the question is a state of confusion, which makes the question of religion and politics, of political theology even more urgent. Although the tide of the academic discussion has shifted toward imagining that religion should participate in the public sphere, the liberal left is on the defense globally. What remains to be seen, especially in Orthodox countries, is whether what will emerge will be a distinctive Christian politics or a resurgence of rightist, exclusionary politics.

The conference from which this book emerges would not have been possible without the generous support of Solon and Marianna Patterson, whose generous gift has endowed the Patterson Conference Series on Orthodox-Catholic Dialogue. Words simply cannot express our gratitude for their unwavering support of the work of the Orthodox Christian Studies Center at Fordham University. The conference was also funded by grants received from the Archbishop Demetrios Chair in Orthodox Theology and Culture at Fordham University (which was graciously established by Mary and Michael Jaharis through the Jaharis Family Foundation, Inc.), the Kallinikeion Foundation, the Virginia H. Farah Foundation, members of the Orthodox Christian Studies Center Advisory Council, the Interdisciplinary Center for Hellenic Studies at Stockton University, and the Michael G. and Anastasia Cantonis Chair of Byzantine Studies at Hellenic College and Holy Cross. We are also thankful to Gregory Tucker and Nathaniel Wood, graduate students at Fordham University, for the editorial and administrative work that facilitated the production of this volume. Finally, we would like to express our thanks to the indefatigable Valerie Longwood, who has taken the Orthodox Christian Studies Center to another level.

Note

1. When we mention particular authors, we are referring to their essays for this volume.

THE POST-COMMUNIST SITUATION

Moral Argument in the Human Rights Debate of the Russian Orthodox Church

Kristina Stoeckl

Introduction

Over the last decade and a half the Russian Orthodox Church has conducted an intense debate on human rights, initiated by today's patriarch and former metropolitan of Smolensk and Kaliningrad, Kirill.[1] In an article published in *Nezavisimaya Gazeta* on 26 May 1999, Kirill expressed the conviction that human rights are a natural result of the Western cultural development that he outlined as follows: The Renaissance (i.e., the return of ancient paganism) triggered a chain of subsequent cultural changes leading to the Reformation, the Enlightenment, materialism, and atheism, which finally led to the Universal Declaration of Human Rights, the ultimate codification of anthropocentrism. Since the Russian Orthodox tradition did not share this history, ran Kirill's argument, it could not share the concept of "human rights."[2] Shortly after the appearance of this rather pointed article, Kirill apparently felt the need to express his position in more detail. Thus, on 16 February 2000, he published a second article in *Nezavisimaya Gazeta*, which began as follows:

> A fundamental contradiction of our time and also a major challenge to the human community in the twenty-first century is the confrontation of liberal civilization standards, on the one hand, and the values of national cultural and religious identity. The study of the genesis of the contradiction between these two crucial factors of modern

development and the search for ways to overcome it should take, as it seems, an important place in Orthodox theological studies. Since this is a problem whose solution will largely determine the future shape of the human civilization, it is clear that the very formulation of the problem and attempts to settle its primary definition [here Kirill refers to his previous article] are not only the fruit of a sincere interest, but no less of sincere anger. Anger about those who out of ideological convictions reject the very idea of raising these issues for fear of a possible correction or revision of the liberal ideas which today underpin the attempts to shape the human community into a "melting pot" of cultures and civilizations. Anger also about those zealots and religious and cultural fundamentalists who have made up their mind on these problems long ago and are deeply convinced that the only way to move further is to tightly close the door of their house.[3]

Kirill concluded that critical and creative engagement with liberal values was among the most important tasks of Orthodox theology.[4] It is quite symbolic that *Nezavisimaya Gazeta* printed this article alongside a reproduction of a nineteenth-century woodcut by the romantic artist Julius Schnorr von Carolsfeld entitled *The Healing of the Two Blind Men*. The symbolism of the image underlined the argument of the article—namely, that there is a conflict between two sides blinded by their ideological fervor.

What Kirill did in this article was to distance himself from both forms of "blindness": He did not think that Russia should unconditionally adhere to the Western modern and secular trajectory, as liberal secularists would argue, nor did he want to find himself on the side of the religious zealots, who would not even consider the question of human rights because they condemn the intellectual universe that has created them in the first place. In contrast, Kirill argued for the need to find a third way. But of what should this third way consist? In this article, I look at three important documents—*The Basis of the Social Concept of the Russian Orthodox Church* from the Synod of the Russian Orthodox Church, the *Declaration on Human Rights and Dignity* by the Tenth World Council of Russian People, and the *Russian Orthodox Church's Basic Teaching on Human Dignity, Freedom and Rights*—in order to show how the shaping of an ideological middle ground in the Church's confrontation with human rights took place. A keyword in this process is "morality," and I will therefore pay particular attention to the way in which the moral argument developed in the official discourse of the Moscow Patriarchate in the period from 2000 to 2008. Before that, however, I will devote some words to the theoretical challenges related to the study of the relationship between religion and human rights.

Religion and Human Rights

How are we to conceptualize the relationship between religion and human rights in the modern secular world? Louis Henkin has described human rights and religion as two separate ideological worlds with good reasons for mutual suspicion. Religions are suspicious of human rights because they

> are much older than the human rights idea and have seen no need for that idea. Religions laid claim to conceptions of the good, of the good society, long ago, without any idea of rights. . . . They do not welcome the ideological independence of human rights, its insistence on nontheistic support for the idea, its resistance to the higher law of society and even to divine law. [Religions] have not had confidence in an ideology that does not claim divine origin and inspiration and has no essential place for the Deity. Spokesmen for religion have declared secular foundations for human rights to be weak, unstable, and doomed to fail and pass away. Some religions resist what they see as the concentration on, indeed the apotheosis of, the individual and the exaltation of individual autonomy and freedom. The emphasis of religion, of religions, was not upon the individual but upon the community.[5]

The human rights ideology, in turn, is suspicious about religion because it

> does not see human rights as integral to a cosmic order. It does not derive from any sacred text. Its sources are human, deriving from contemporary human life in human society. Human rights is a political idea and ideology that claims to reflect a universal contemporary moral intuition. Human institutions have adopted the idea to serve the purpose of the good life within national political societies in an international political system.[6]

The quotations from Henkin are helpful in framing the problem of the religious perspectives on human rights that I want to address in this article, not least because Henkin is slightly overstating the contrast between the two sides. Henkin rejects those theories according to which the human rights idea grew from religious inspiration: "Though some Christian theologians have argued that Western human rights theory is grounded in religious faith, human rights morality is, in fact, autonomous."[7] He also denies any kind of connection between the concept of "human dignity" as it is used in human rights covenants and a religious understanding of human dignity. In his view, the

> contours of the religious morality developed around this concept [of human dignity] are not congruent with human dignity as commonly conceived in the domain of human rights . . . [because] religions have defined human dignity so that it will coincide with a morality rooted in particular theological foundations and in its historic-sociological manifestations over centuries of life in particular religious societies.[8]

From Henkin's perspective, no real dialogue or engagement is possible between secular approaches to human rights and traditional religious positions; all that is possible is pragmatic adaptation and division of tasks. Religions should recognize that their interests can be advanced by the human rights idea, not least because, "if only in self-defense . . . [they have] had to develop attitudes toward modern society and modern political authority."[9] Human rights, on the other hand, are not a substitute for religion, but "a supplemental 'theology' for pluralistic, urban, secular societies."[10]

Henkin's sketch of the problem of religion and human rights contains four elements that are important for my interpretation of the contemporary Russian Orthodox approach to human rights: (1) the idea that from a human rights perspective the individual is, first and foremost, endowed with *rights*, whereas from a religious perspective what comes first are the *duties* of every single person; (2) the idea that from the human rights perspective the *individual* comes first, whereas from a religious perspective the *community* comes first; (3) the fact that "human dignity" has become a contested term that is used both in human rights and in religious discourses, but is endowed with different meanings; (4) the argument that religions adapt to the modern language of human rights out of a pragmatic calculation in order to claim their stake in secular societies, as well as the opposite view that their engagement with the modern world is a sign of genuine modernization.

These four elements—rights vs. duties, individual vs. community, human dignity, and pragmatic calculation vs. genuine modernization—are leitmotifs for the Russian Orthodox discussion of human rights in this article, but I will show that the ascriptions of the different positions to either religion or the human rights regime are not always as clear cut as Henkin suggests. I do not subscribe fully to Henkin's description since he presents religion and human rights as two closed and unchangeable systems of reasoning. This, I think, is wrong. It is wrong from the perspective of religions, because religious traditions and theologies evolve with time, even if very slowly, and their capacity to confront new topics is not only a matter of self-defense but also of human creativity and, from the perspective of the religious mindset, divine inspiration. It is also wrong from the perspective of human rights, because the human rights regime is continuously changing; human rights treaties and legislation have evolved since the Universal Declaration of Human Rights was signed in 1948, and religions are among those actors trying to take an active role in influencing human rights definitions today.

A theoretical perspective that I find more fruitful for structuring the debate on religion and human rights is the idea of "the sacralization of the person" put forward recently by Hans Joas.[11] Joas tries to show both that human rights do not belong to an exclusively secularist terrain, and that they do not sprout from a purely religious soil. He suggests that the modern human rights idea is a genuinely new development, related to religious and secular intellectual traditions and practices, but not reducible to either of them alone: He calls this new development "the sacralization of the person." Joas provides an excellent summary of the fruitless debate between secular and religious attempts to legitimize human rights. Conventional lay wisdom (not necessarily shared by academics), he writes, holds that human rights emerged from the spirit of the French Revolution, which is in turn considered a political expression of the anticlerical and antireligious Enlightenment: "From this perspective, human rights are clearly not the fruit of any religious tradition, but rather the manifestation of resistance to a power alliance linking state and (Catholic) church, or to Christianity as a whole."[12] The alternative narrative asserts that the notion of inalienable human rights was able to take root because it could build on an understanding of the human being as cultivated in the Christian tradition. This perspective became prevalent in the course of the twentieth century when the Catholic Church moved from its initial condemnation of the concept of human rights to its endorsement.[13] Both of these narratives, Joas concludes, are untenable, and he suggests an alternative in which the focus of his analysis is the notion of "sacredness." He interprets the belief in human rights and universal human dignity as the result of a specific process of sacralization of the human being, "a process in which every single human being has increasingly, and with ever-increasing motivational and sensitizing effects, been viewed as sacred, and this understanding has been institutionalized in law."[14]

In the early years of the 1990s, the New School professor Adamantia Pollis unequivocally stated:

> Individual human rights cannot be derived from Orthodox theology. The entire complex of civil and political rights—freedom of religion, freedom of speech and press, freedom of association, and due process of law, among others—cannot be grounded in Orthodoxy, they stem from a radically different worldview.[15]

This statement is correct insofar as it is indeed difficult to "derive" liberal individual human rights from Orthodox theology. However, it would be equally difficult to derive these rights in a straightforward manner from any other religious tradition. The Christian churches for most of their history existed untroubled by torture and other abuses, rejected the human rights declarations of the eighteenth century, and were even skeptical about the Universal Declaration of Human Rights of 1948.[16] Even today, most Christian churches in the United States are not moved to protest the continuing practice of the death penalty in many American states. Joas is correct, therefore, when he points out that it is erroneous to imagine human rights as something that inevitably springs up from the roots of some traditions and not of others. Traditions as such "generate nothing"[17]—what matters is how specific actors, belonging to certain traditions, in a specific moment of time and under specific institutional circumstances, set themselves in relation to the innovative idea of universal human rights or the process of the sacralization of the person, as Joas terms it. He writes:

> As a novel form of the sacralization of the person, the rise of human rights represents a challenge to Christianity—and to other religious and even to secular value traditions and worldviews—in light of which their adherents must inevitably reinterpret them.[18]

This is especially true for the Orthodox churches, which are somewhat delayed among Christians in engaging with the idea of human rights.

In a recent article, Vasilios Makrides mapped the Orthodox theological engagement with human rights on a continuum from "complete rejection" to "accommodation." At the "complete rejection" end of the scale he situates theologians including Christos Yannaras and Vigen Gurojan, and at the "accommodation" end he identifies writers and churchmen such as Anastasios Yannoulatos and Konstantinos Delikostantis. In the middle, he situates the *Russian Orthodox Church's Basic Teaching on Human Dignity, Freedom and Rights.*[19] This middle ground is characterized by what Makrides, with reference to Alexander Agadjanian, calls a strategy of "acceptance-through-rejection"—an acceptance of the human rights language paired with a rejection of the definition and aims of modern human rights ideologies.[20] My own findings regarding the function of moral arguments in the human rights debate in the Russian Orthodox Church confirm the assessment given by Makrides and Agadjanian. However, I have also found that the middle position is not stable: It took shape as a theological and moral strategy over a relatively short period of time from 2000 to 2008, but was then immediately incorporated into the larger and purely political category of "traditional values." In the remainder of this article I will describe this development and, in the conclusion, offer some ideas on why I think that the middle ground identified by Makrides is destined to remain theologically and intellectually barren.

Human Rights in the *Social Concept of the Russian Orthodox Church*

In 2000, the Synod of the Russian Orthodox Church approved a document, *The Basis of the Social Concept of the Russian Orthodox Church* (*Osnovy Sotsial'noi kontseptsii Russkoi Pravoslavnoi Tserkvi*; hereafter, *Social Concept*), which constituted a novelty in the Orthodox world. In this document, the Church laid out its position on a number of issues: church-state relations, law, family, society, biotechnology, and globalization. When *Social Concept* was published in 2000, many commentators interpreted the mere fact of its formulation as an important step of Russian Orthodoxy on its way toward modernization.[21]

Social Concept addressed members of the Russian Orthodox Church and Russian society as a whole. Though it also found resonance outside of

Russia, especially in the Catholic world, its intended audience was domestic. With this document, the Church quite clearly reacted to the social upheaval in Russian society since the breakdown of the Soviet Union, which had brought many freedoms but also many social and economic problems and, in the eyes of the Church, moral decline. In the document, the Church offered guidelines for Orthodox believers on questions such as abortion, contraception, euthanasia, genetic engineering, and environmental protection. In particular, the political agenda of *Social Concept* constituted a novelty: The Church defined itself as independent from the Russian state and government. Drawing a lesson from the history of subordination under the Tsarist state and of suppression by the Soviet state, the Church positioned itself as a potential counter-player to the government and an independent force in civil society.[22] This commitment to a separation of church and state was, as I have shown elsewhere,[23] not necessarily liberal in nature, but did constitute a break with the long tradition of the symphonic model of church-state relations, characteristic of Orthodox Christian politics.

Human rights are treated in Section IV: Christian Ethics and Secular Law of *Social Concept*, wherein they are associated with the rise of secularism and self-sufficient humanism:

> As secularism developed, the lofty principles of inalienable human rights turned into a notion of the rights of the individual outside his relations with God. In this process, the freedom of the personality transformed into the protection of self-will (as long as it is not detrimental to individuals) and into the demand that the state should guarantee a certain material living standard for the individual and family. In the contemporary systematic understanding of civil human rights, man is treated not as the image of God, but as a self-sufficient and self-sufficing subject.[24]

Social Concept presented human rights as the product of a Western secular legal positivism, which started to influence the Russian legal space after the breakdown of the Soviet Union, but was essentially alien to the national legal culture. The document clearly remained on a confrontational and ideologically closed plane vis-à-vis the concept of human rights. Though the document is, over considerable stretches, a text of moderation, the section on human rights departs sharply from this trend. Rather, it represents the nationalist and anti-Western viewpoint on human rights that was apparently dominant inside the Church at that time.

The *Declaration on Human Rights and Dignity* of the Tenth World Council of Russian People

In 2006, a second document concerning human rights emerged from the Moscow Patriarchate. To be precise, the *Declaration on Human Rights and Dignity* by the Tenth World Council of Russian People (*Vsemirnij Nardognij Russkij Sobor'*, hereafter often referred to as the *Russian Declaration of Human Rights* to distinguish it from the Universal Declaration of Human Rights) was not strictly speaking a Church document, but the fact that it was issued by the World Russian People's Council, a nongovernmental organization chaired by the patriarch, with its seat on the premises of the Patriarchate, makes it clear enough that the document was produced with the full knowledge of the hierarchy of the Church. In retrospect we can interpret the *Russian Declaration* as an intermediate step on the path of the Russian Orthodox Church toward the formulation of the *Basic Teaching*. In 2006, however, when the *Russian Declaration of Human Rights* was published, its decidedly anti-Western and antiliberal attitude escalated the reception of the ideas expressed in *Social Concept* six years earlier.

The *Russian Declaration* established a link between human rights and morality. In the Russian original this connection is expressed in the rather convoluted phrase "the content of human rights cannot not be connected with morality (*ne mozhet ne byt' svyazano*)," simplified in the English translation as "human rights essentially involve morality." The authors of the *Russian Declaration* offered a theological argument for this link—they drew a distinction between human worth (*tsennost'*) and human dignity (*dostoinstvo*), claiming that the attainment of the latter depends on morally dignified life-conduct: "Each person as image of God has singular unalienable worth, which must be respected by every one of us, the society and the state. It is by doing good that the human being gains dignity. Thus we distinguish between human worth and dignity. Worth is given, while dignity is acquired."[25]

The distinction between "human worth" and "human dignity" was theologically untenable, however, and it is no surprise that the Russian Orthodox Church's *Basic Teaching on Human Dignity, Freedom and Rights* published two years later corrected this distinction and dropped the term "human worth" altogether. But the very fact that this distinction was made in the document of the World Council of Russian People demonstrates that the Russian Orthodox Church was first and foremost interested in the link between dignity and morality, and not in a theological clarification of dignity as such.

The 2006 *Russian Declaration of Human Rights* made reference to a "clash of civilizations" as the justification for why the Orthodox world must defend its position in the international human rights debate. The first sentence of the *Russian Declaration* states: "Aware that the world, passing through a crucial point in its history, is facing a threat of conflict between the civilizations with their different understanding of the human being and the human being's calling, the Tenth World Council of Russian People, on behalf of the unique Russian civilization, adopts this Declaration."[26] A comparison of this passage with the *Basic Teaching on Human Dignity, Freedom and Rights* published by the episcopal Synod two years later shows an ideological shift inside the Patriarchate between 2006 and 2008. The *Basic Teaching* depicts a very different scenario:

> Without seeking a revolutionary reconstruction of the world, and acknowledging the rights of other social groups to participate in social transformations on the basis of their own worldview, Orthodox Christians reserve the right to participate in building public life in a way that does not contradict their faith and moral principles. The Russian Orthodox Church is ready to defend the same principles in dialogue with the world community and in cooperation with people of other traditional confessions and religions.[27]

The approach of these two documents is completely different: In the *Russian Declaration*, Orthodox tradition is described as a culture endangered by the clash of civilizations; in the *Basic Teaching*, the Russian Orthodox Church recognized that there is a public debate about values and rights in which all social groups and individuals are called to participate, and in which they are permitted to defend their respective positions. With regard to the significance of the moral argument, in 2006 the Russian Orthodox Church presented itself as a bulwark of morality against the immoral and corrupted West, whereas by 2008, though the same Church still perceived itself as a bulwark of morality, it was now willing to enter into a dialogue with what it described as a crisis-ridden and morally confused West. Though this may be a limited change in approach, it nonetheless required considerable argumentative and rhetorical efforts from the hierarchs of the Moscow Patriarchate, as I will now show.

The Moral Argument in the Russian Orthodox Church's
Basic Teaching on Human Dignity,
Freedom, and Rights

From 2005 onwards, the Church's standpoint on human rights shifted from mere rejection to a strategy of acceptance-through-rejection. This strategy consisted in both the acceptance of the human rights language in principle and the rejection of concrete human rights regulations in practice. A new feature of the discourse was a more intimate knowledge of the Western human rights regime, of its history, and of existing tensions in human rights legislation. This approach was inaugurated around 2005 by Metropolitan Kirill when he cited for the first time Article 29 of the Universal Declaration of Human Rights, a text to which he has subsequently returned many times. Article 29 states (in part):

(1) Everyone has duties to the community in which alone the free and full development of his personality is possible.

(2) In the exercise of his rights and freedoms, everyone shall be subject only to such limitations as are determined by law solely for the purpose of securing due recognition and respect for the rights and freedoms of others and of meeting the just requirements of morality, public order and the general welfare in a democratic society.[28]

The "discovery" of Article 29 had an important effect on the human rights debate in the Russian Orthodox Church, because it provided the means through which the Church no longer had to place itself in opposition to a Western individualistic understanding of human rights, but instead might actively present itself as the vanguard of a more original understanding of human rights according to Article 29—an understanding that emphasizes the importance of morality and duties to the community. This new approach is visible in several of Kirill's speeches in the years leading up to the publication of the *Basic Teaching*.

At a seminar entitled "The Evolution of Moral Principles and Human Rights in Multicultural Society" held at Strasbourg on 30 and 31 October 2006, Kirill said:

I am convinced that the concern for spiritual needs, based moreover on traditional morality, ought to return to the public realm. The upholding of moral standards must become a social cause. It is the mechanism of human rights that can actively enable this return. I am speaking of a return, for the norm of according human rights with traditional morality can be found in the Universal Declaration of Human Rights of 1948.[29]

The same view was expressed in his speech to UNESCO on 13 March 2007: "The Orthodox Church invites the world to return to the understanding of the role of human rights in social life that was established in 1948. Moral rules can put limits to the realization of human rights in public life."[30]

The same point was reiterated by Patriarch Alexei II in a speech to the Parliamentary Assembly of the Council of Europe on 2 October 2007, in which he made reference both to the Universal Declaration of Human Rights and to the European Convention on Human Rights:

> There occurs a break between human rights and morality, and this break threatens the European civilization. We can see it in a new generation of rights that contradict morality, and in how human rights are used to justify immoral behavior. In this connection, I may note that morality, with which any human rights advocacy has to count, is mentioned in the European Convention for the Protection of Human Rights and Fundamental Freedoms. I am convinced that the makers of the European Convention on Human Rights included therein morality not as something ambiguous but rather as an integral element of the whole human rights system.[31]

The point was corroborated once more, two years after the publication of the *Russian Orthodox Church's Basic Teaching on Human Dignity, Freedom and Rights*, by Metropolitan Hilarion Alfayev:

> It should be noted that the post-war human rights instruments did reflect the connection between freedom and moral responsibility. The Universal Declaration of Human Rights from 1948 and the European Declaration on Human Rights and Fundamental Freedoms from 1950 speak about the connection between human rights and morality. It is in later international acts such as the Charter of Fundamental Rights of the European Union from 2000 that the connection between human rights and morality is not mentioned. Freedom is therefore completely divorced from morality.[32]

This series of quotations shows that during the period in which the *Basic Teaching* was being drafted, the leadership of the Russian Orthodox

Church acquired an increasingly clear understanding of contemporary human rights politics and legislation. Alexei II even spoke about "a new generation of rights," a term that is habitually used in human rights literature.[33] The Church's position was no longer determined by the vague inclination toward rejection that informed debates up until the mid-2000s. The Department for External Church Relations of the Moscow Patriarchate had acquired a precise view on the problem and a concrete sense of how to approach it. They saw their mission as affirming the link between human rights definitions and morality.

The *Russian Orthodox Church's Basic Teaching on Human Dignity, Freedom and Rights*, published in 2008, provided the script for this mission. It dedicated the entire first chapter to the question of human dignity as a religious and moral category. In this chapter, we read that, from the Orthodox Christian perspective, human dignity is related to the creation of the human being "in God's image and likeness" (see Genesis 1.27). God's image in man is described by the document as the source of human dignity that remains "indelible . . . even after the fall"—even man's susceptibility to sinfulness cannot erase his God-given dignity. With this sentence, the *Basic Teaching* corrected the distinction made by the authors of the *Russian Declaration of Human Rights* between "worth" as something given and "dignity" as something acquired. Furthermore, the concept of human dignity does not go unqualified in the *Basic Teaching*: Divine-human likeness becomes, for the Church, the source for a precise understanding of how human beings should strive to overcome sin and "restore human life in the fullness of its original perfection."[34] Furthermore,

> dignified life is . . . achieved through God's grace by efforts to overcome sin and to seek moral purity and virtue. . . . What is dignified and what is not are bound up with the moral or amoral actions of a person and with the inner state of his soul. Considering the state of human nature darkened by sin, it is important that things dignified and undignified should be clearly distinguished in the life of a person.[35]

The restoration of human life to the fullness of divine likeness is called, in the Orthodox theological tradition, *theosis* (deification).

In these terms, the authors of the *Basic Teaching* explained what effectively constitutes a "good life" according to "God's design for human beings and their calling":[36]

Moral norms [are] inherent in humanity just as moral norms set forth
in the divine revelation reveal God's design for human beings and
their calling. These norms are guidelines for a good life worthy of
God-created humanity.[37]

Knowledge of these moral norms derives from revelation (scripture and the
example of Jesus Christ) and from conscience. Human nature is a problematic source for morality because of its potential for sin—"life according to the law of the flesh."[38] For this reason the document puts a special
emphasis on repentance: "The patristic and ascetic thought and the whole
liturgical tradition of the Church refer more to human indignity caused
by sin than to human dignity."[39] Chapter I concludes: "According to the
Orthodox tradition, a human being preserves his God-given dignity and
grows in it only if he lives in accordance with moral norms because these
norms express the primordial and therefore authentic human nature not
darkened by sin."[40]

The Russian Orthodox Church thus established a direct link between
human dignity and morality, to the point that critics have read the chapter as saying that the Church is making the moral behavior of the individual a condition for recognizing his or her human dignity.[41] I suggest
that this is a slightly unfair interpretation of the *Basic Teaching*. It was true
of the *Russian Declaration of Human Rights* by the Tenth World Council
of Russian People, which drew a distinction between human worth and
human dignity, but the *Basic Teaching* corrected this view and expressed,
in principle, a commitment to human dignity as such. However, this commitment remains ambiguous, and it is this ambiguity that I will now
address.

My sense is that one partial reason for the continuing dissatisfaction
among observers with the Church's equation of "dignified life" and
"morality" is the use (and translation) of the word "morality." The Russian
version of the *Russian Orthodox Church's Basic Teaching on Human Dignity,
Freedom and Rights* uses the word *moral'* three times, but more commonly
the term used is *nravstvennost'* or *nravstvennyj* (employed over forty times).
In the English translation, both words are rendered as "morality" or "moral,"
with the exception of the title of the first chapter, for which *nravstvennyj* is
translated "ethical." What are we to make of this difference, and why is it
relevant?

For ordinary Russian speakers, the words *moral'* and *nravstvennost'* do not have the same meaning. *Moral'* is understood to mean a "socially formed set of norms and principles" whereas *nravstvennost'* appears to reflect primarily a type of "inner ethical judgment."[42] I interpret the prevalence of the term *nravstvennyj* in the *Basic Teaching* as indicative of the intention of the authors of the document to define moral behavior in a comprehensive, individual, and social sense, and not merely as obeying rules.

That a real tension exists here is highlighted by the fact that the distinction between "morality" and "ethics" is a topic addressed by several Orthodox theologians throughout the twentieth century, notably Christos Yannaras. Yannaras dedicated an entire book to the difference between ethics and morality, in which he distinguishes between free ethical choice and moral dictate, and accuses the churches of his time of having become moral dictators instead of places for the growth of a free ethos.[43] Another Orthodox theologian, Anastasios Yannoulatos, has defined the moral meaning of the Church's human rights discourse in terms of the inner makeup and ethical orientation of religious life, rather than in terms of public morality.[44] He calls the churches to their vocation as "centres of moral and spiritual inspiration, nurseries of integrated and sanctified personalities, workshops of selfless love."[45] The *Russian Orthodox Church's Basic Teaching on Human Dignity, Freedom and Rights* has been criticized by liberal Orthodox commentators precisely on the grounds of this theology, which is said to lack emphasis on free ethical choice. Marina Shishova has pointed out that there is a tension in the *Basic Teaching*: Does the Church engage in human rights out of commitment to human dignity as seen from the perspective of eternal life, or out of an interest in the community defined in terms of the Russian state?[46]

The document, not least because of the semantics of *nravstvennost'*, remains ambiguous, but in the final analysis, it seems to me, the balance tips from dignity as a religious and ethical category to dignity defined in terms of compliance with a narrow public morality. I think it is not by chance that the Church's discourse has changed over the last few years since the publication of the *Basic Teaching*, shifting from an emphasis on "morality" to "traditional values." Tradition is invoked by the Church today as a source for rules of social and moral behavior and for limitations of individual human rights. When "traditional values" are invoked as the source of public morality, the inner-outer duality of ethical judgment contained in the word morality/*nravstvennost'* is lost.

Conclusion

Let us now conclude this analysis of the place of morality in the human rights debate in the Russian Orthodox Church prior to 2009. First, we have to recognize that this debate was as much a sign of the strength of Russian Orthodoxy, as it was a sign of self-defense. Why engage at all with the human rights question, if not because the Church felt affected by this new reality and new understanding of the "sacredness" of the person? Second, the human rights debate within the Church was characterized by a shift from total rejection to a more complex stance of acceptance-through-rejection. This stance was chiefly the fruit of the efforts of Metropolitan Kirill, now patriarch of Moscow, and his collaborators in the Department of External Church Relations. The outcome of this engagement was the *Russian Orthodox Church's Basic Teaching on Human Dignity, Freedom and Rights*, published in 2008, and a well-defined agenda of human rights and morality in the Church's external relations. But since then, and in particular in Russian domestic affairs, the key term for the Church appears no longer to be "human rights," nor even "morality," but "traditional values." My suspicion is that the "tradition" being invoked here is not the theological tradition, but a Russian cultural tradition.

Why is this invocation of cultural tradition problematic? In reference to the Roman Catholic Church, José Casanova once observed that tradition can never be an argument for uniformity but only for pluralism, because "tradition" has always been the sum total of a multiplicity of visions of religious life and teaching, all gathered under the umbrella of the Church.[47] In theological terms "tradition" does not appeal to doctrinal certainty but rather the opposite—openness. Along these lines, the Greek theologian Pantelis Kalaïtzidis has pointed out that the term "tradition" in Orthodox theology should not be understood in a historical sense:

> A certain version of theology has turned Tradition into traditionalism and taught us to associate the identity of the church mainly—
> or even exclusively—with the past, making us accustomed to an Orthodoxy that is permanently out of step with its time and history in general.[48]

Instead, the Eastern Orthodox tradition should be conceived in the light of eschatology: "The fullness and identity of church is not located in the past or the present . . . but in the future."[49] And he quotes John Meyendorff:

> Without eschatology, traditionalism is turned only to the past: it is nothing but archaeology, antiquarianism, conservatism, reaction, refusal of history, escapism. Authentic Christian traditionalism remembers and maintains the past not because it is past, but because it is the only way to meet the future, to become ready for it.[50]

If one takes this criticism seriously, then, paradoxically, the Russian Orthodox treatment of human rights falls short of its potential not because of an excess of tradition, but because of a lack of it—a lack of tradition in an eschatological sense.

Notes

1. This article draws on material from my book *The Russian Orthodox Church and Human Rights* (London: Routledge, 2014).

2. Kirill (Gundyayev), Metropolitan of Smolensk and Kaliningrad, "Obstoyatel'stva novogo vremeni," *NG-Religii* (26 May 1999): http://www.ng.ru/specfile/2000-12-15/14_obstoyatelstva.html (last accessed 24 June 2013).

3. Kirill (Gundyayev), Metropolitan of Smolensk and Kaliningrad, "Norma very kak norma zhizni I," *Nezavisimaya Gazeta* (16 February 2000): http://www.ng.ru/ideas/2000-02-16/8_norma.html (last accessed 24 June 2013).

4. Kirill (Gundyayev), Metropolitan of Smolensk and Kaliningrad, "Human Rights and Moral Responsibility: Part I," *Europaica Bulletin* 97 (2006), http://orthodoxeurope.org/page/14/97.aspx#3 (last accessed 6 December 2009).

5. Louis Henkin, "Religion, Religions, and Human Rights," *The Journal of Religious Ethics* 26, no. 2 (1998): 229–39, here 232.

6. Henkin, "Religion," 231.

7. Henkin, "Religion," 229.

8. Henkin, "Religion," 231.

9. Henkin, "Religion," 236.

10. Henkin, "Religion," 239.

11. Hans Joas, *The Sacredness of the Person: A New Genealogy of Human Rights* (Washington, D.C.: Georgetown University Press, 2013).

12. Joas, *Sacredness*, 4.

13. Joas, *Sacredness*, 4.

14. Joas, *Sacredness*, 5.

28 KRISTINA STOECKL

15. Adamantia Pollis, "Eastern Orthodoxy and Human Rights," *Human Rights Quarterly* 15, no. 2 (1993): 339–56, here 353.

16. Joas, *Sacredness*, 140.

17. Joas, *Sacredness*, 140.

18. Joas, *Sacredness*, 141.

19. Vasilios Makrides also identifies a fourth group, which defies easy categorization along this continuum: He defines the group by "pragmatic acceptance and self-critique" and includes there authors such as Pantelis Kalaïtzidis and Konstantinos Delikostantis. I would add also Aristotle Papanikolaou. See Vasilios Makrides, "Die Menschenrechte aus orthodox-christlicher Sicht—Evaluierung, Positionen und Reaktionen," in *Schwierige Toleranz: Der Umgang mit Andersdenkenden und Andersgläubigen in der Christentumsgeschichte,* ed. M. Delgado, V. Leppin, and D. Neuhold (Stuttgart: Kohlhammer): 293–320.

20. See Alexander Agadjanian, *Russian Orthodox Vision of Human Rights: Recent Documents and their Significance,* Erfurter Vorträge zur Kulturgeschichte des Orthodoxen Christentums 7 (Erfurt: Universität Erfurt Religionswissenschaft [Orthodoxes Christentum], 2008), 26.

21. Rudolf Uertz, "Menschenrechte, Demokratie und Rechtsstaat in der Sozialdoktrin—eine politikwissenschaftliche Betrachtung," in *Beginn einer neuen Ära? Die Sozialdoktrin der Russisch-Orthodoxen Kirche vom August 2000 im interkulturellen Dialog,* ed. Rudolf Uertz and Éduard Afanasiev (Bonn: Konrad-Adenauer-Stiftung, 2004): 77–96; Konstantin Kostjuk, "Die Sozialdoktrin—Herausforderung für die Tradition und die Theologie der Orthodoxie," in *Beginn neuen Ära? Die Sozialdoktrin der Russisch-Orthodoxen Kirche:* 67–74; Alexander Agadjanian, "Breakthrough to Modernity, Apologia for Traditionalism: The Russian Orthodox View of Society and Culture in Comparative Perspective," *Religion, State and Society* 31, no. 4 (2003): 327–46.

22. Hilarion (Alfeyev), "Prospects for Catholic-Orthodox Relations: Paper delivered at the University of St. Thomas (Minnesota, USA) on 7 October 2002 and the Catholic Church of America (Washington DC) on 9 October 2002," *Europaica Bulletin* 24 (October 2003); available online at http://orthodoxeurope.org/page/14/24.aspx#4 (last accessed 26 June 2013).

23. Kristina Stoeckl, "Political Hesychasm? Vladimir Petrunin's Neo-Byzantine Interpretation of the Social Doctrine of the Russian Orthodox Church," *Studies in East European Thought* 62, no. 1 (2010): 125–33.

24. Russian Orthodox Church, *The Basis of the Social Concept of the Russian Orthodox Church* (2000), Department for External Church Relations of the Moscow Patriarchate, http://www.mospat.ru/en/documents/social-concepts/ (last accessed 6 December 2009), IV.7.

25. Vsemirnij Nardognij Russkij Sobor' [World Council of Russian People], *Deklaratsiya o pravakh i dostojnstve cheloveka [Declaration on Human Rights and Dignity]* (2006), http://pravovrns.ru/?p=430 (last accessed 24 June 2013).

26. World Council of Russian People, *Declaration*.

27. Russian Orthodox Church, *The Russian Orthodox Church's Basic Teaching on Human Dignity, Freedom and Rights* (2008), Department for External Church Relations of the Moscow Patriarchate, http://www.mospat.ru/en /documents/dignity-freedom-rights/ (last accessed 24 June 2013).

28. Universal Declaration of Human Rights, Article 29, http://www.un.org /en/documents/udhr/ (last accessed 30 July 2014).

29. Kirill (Gundyayev), Metropolitan of Smolensk and Kaliningrad, "The Experience of Viewing the Problems of Human Rights and their Moral Foundations in European Religious Communities: Presentation at the Conference 'Evolution of Moral Values and Human Rights in Multicultural Society' at Strasbourg, 30 October 2006," *Europaica Bulletin* 6 (November 2006): 108, http://orthodoxeurope.org/page/14/108.aspx#1 (last accessed 24 June 2013).

30. Interfax Religion, "Vystuplenie mitropolita Smolenskogo i Kaliningrad-skogo Kirilla na mezhdunarodnom seminare UNESCO na temu 'Dialog tsivilizatsii: prava cheloveka, nravstvennye tsennosti i kul'turnoe mnogoobrazie,'" *Interfax Religion* 108 (13 March 2007), http://www.interfax-religion.ru /?act=documents&div=604 (last accessed 24 June 2013).

31. Alexei (Ridiger), Patriarch of Moscow and All Russia, "Address to the Parliamentary Assembly of the Council of Europe," *Europaica Bulletin* 128 (7 October 2007), http://orthodoxeurope.org/page/14/128.aspx (last accessed 3 March 2013).

32. Hilarion (Alfayev), "Выступление митрополита Волоколамского Илариона на презентации польского издания книги Святейшего Патриарха Московского и всея Руси Кирилла 'Свобода и ответственность: в поисках гармонии. Права человека и достоинство личности'" http://www.patriarchia.ru/db/text/1186072.html (last accessed 6 December 2009).

33. See Karel Vasak, "Human Rights: A Thirty-Year Struggle: The Sustained Efforts to Give Force of Law to the Universal Declaration of Human Rights," *UNESCO Courier* 30 (1977): 11.

34. Russian Orthodox Church, *Basic Teaching* I.1.

35. Russian Orthodox Church, *Basic Teaching* I.2.

36. Russian Orthodox Church, *Basic Teaching* I.3.

37. Russian Orthodox Church, *Basic Teaching* I.3.

38. Russian Orthodox Church, *Basic Teaching* I.4.

39. Russian Orthodox Church, *Basic Teaching* I.5.

40. Russian Orthodox Church, *Basic Teaching* I.1.

41. Aristotle Papanikolaou, *The Mystical as Political: Democracy and Non-Radical Orthodoxy* (Notre Dame, Ind.: Notre Dame University Press, 2012); Community of Protestant Churches in Europe, "Menschenrechte und Christliche Moral: Eine Antwort der Gemeinschaft Evangelischer Kirchen in Europa (GEKE)—Leuenberger Kirchengemeinschaft—auf die Grundsätze der russisch-orthodoxen Kirche über 'menschliche Würde, Freiheit und Rechte,'" (2009), http://leuenberg.net/sites/default/files/doc-9805-2.pdf (last accessed 15 April 2013).

42. Agata Ładykowska, "Post-Soviet Orthodoxy in the Making: Strategies for Continuity Thinking among Russian Middle-Aged School Teachers," in *Multiple Moralities and Religions in Post-Soviet Russia*, ed. J. Zigon (Oxford: Berghahn, 2011): 27–47, here 40.

43. Christos Yannaras, *The Freedom of Morality* (Crestwood, N.Y.: St. Vladimir's Seminary Press, 1984).

44. Anastasios Yannoulatos, "Eastern Orthodoxy and Human Rights," *International Review of Mission* 73 (1984): 454–66.

45. Yannoulatos, "Eastern Orthodoxy," 466.

46. Marina Shishova, "Spiritual and Political Dimensions in the Conception of the Russian Orthodox Church Concerning Dignity, Freedom and Human Rights," in *Orthodox Christianity and Human Rights*, ed. E. Van der Zweerde and A. Brüning (Leuven: Peeters, 2012): 351–64; see also Papanikolaou, *Mystical as Political*, 87–130.

47. José Casanova, "The Contemporary Disjunction between Societal and Church Morality," in *Church and People: Disjunctions in a Secular Age*, ed. C. Taylor, J. Casanova, and G. McLean (Washington, D.C.: Council for Research in Values and Philosophy, 2012): 127–36.

48. Pantelis Kalaïtzidis, *Orthodoxy and Political Theology* (Geneva: World Council of Churches, 2012): 89–90.

49. Kalaïtzidis, *Orthodoxy*, 111.

50. See Kalaïtzidis, *Orthodoxy*, 89.

Post-Communist Orthodox Countries and Secularization

The Lautsi Case and the Fracture of Europe

Father Capodistrias Hämmerli

Introduction

This essay explores how the accession of post-Communist and Orthodox countries to the European Union and the Council of Europe during the last two decades has impacted the process of secularization in Europe. Post-Communist Orthodox countries provide an alternative approach to secularization that has come to play a significant role in today's political debates concerning the role and place of religion in modern society in Europe.

I shall illustrate my argument with reference to the case of *Lautsi v. Italy*. In 2009, the European Court of Human Rights (ECHR) ruled that the Italian government was in violation of the European Convention on Human Rights by permitting crucifixes to be displayed in public school classrooms, arguing that it broke from the principle of the confessional neutrality of the state. Twenty of the forty-seven member states that comprise the Council of Europe intervened in the case, supporting the appeal of the Italian government against the ECHR decision. The majority of those twenty states are post-Communist countries, and predominantly traditionally Orthodox countries. They contested the ECHR's authority to impose the principles of *laïcité* and confessional neutrality on countries, in contradiction to their national culture and religious traditions. This essay argues that *Lautsi v. Italy* revealed a division between Eastern and Western Europe over the role of Christianity in Europe's political and cultural identity.

This paper will examine some historic and religious specificities pertaining to post-Communist and Orthodox countries that explain their different approaches to secularization. The historical experience of radical, forced secularization under Communism provides a solid basis for the critical approach of post-Communist countries to the increasing secularization of Europe. I shall also argue that close church-state relationships and a strong bond between religious and national identities are some of the characteristics of Orthodox cultures that are leading several Eastern European countries to a different stance on secularization. I will explore this point further with reference to recent political developments in Russia.

The Crucifix Case: Background

The local conflict that was to become known across the whole of Europe as "the Crucifix Case" began in Northern Italy in 2002, in the small town of Abano-Terme near Venice. Mrs. Soile Lautsi contested the presence of crucifixes on the classroom walls of the public school attended by her two sons, then aged thirteen and eleven. In making her case, she appealed to the principle of *laïcité*[1] which is recognized by Italian constitutional jurisprudence.[2] Lautsi is a member of the Associazione Nazionale del Libero Pensiero "Giordano Bruno" (the Giordano Bruno National Association of Free Thought), whose main political endeavor is to obtain a complete separation between church and state. The Associazione Nazionale supported Lautsi during the lengthy juridical procedures she underwent. It is on the ground of her philosophical convictions, rather than on the ground of any substantial moral damage that would have been inflicted upon her sons by the public school, that Lautsi began the juridical struggle that was to last almost a decade. During the several proceedings, she consistently focused on trying to prove that the principle of *laïcité* was being violated by the presence of religious symbols in public schools.

First Ruling of the European Court of Human Rights

In 2006, after the Italian courts had eventually rejected her arguments and appeals,[3] Lautsi filed a petition with the European Court of Human Rights.[4] On 3 November 2009, the Chamber of the Second Section of the ECHR issued its ruling concerning *Lautsi v. Italy*.[5] In its argumentation, the court introduced formally for the first time the principle of the confessional neutrality of the state:

> The State's duty of neutrality and impartiality is incompatible with any kind of power on its part to assess the legitimacy of religious convictions or the ways of expressing those convictions. In the context of teaching, neutrality should guarantee pluralism.[6]

Formally, the court concluded that both the right of Mrs. Lautsi (as mother) and her children to education (Protocol 1, Article 2 of the European Convention on Human Rights) and to religious freedom (Article 9 of the convention) had been violated.[7] A close analysis of the structure of the argument of the court shows that pluralism, rather than the right to education and to religious freedom per se, is the key principle that the court sought to uphold. The jurisprudence of the court considered pluralism as a fundamental aspect of democracy. According to the Chamber of the Second Section, since the displaying of crucifixes in Italian public schools could not be interpreted as contributing to educational pluralism, the practice should not be accepted.

The court argued that, since pluralism is vital to democratic societies, it is necessary to guarantee it through the confessional neutrality of the state, in order to prevent an unjust domination of the majority religion over other religions and convictions—a situation that would disrupt the equality of religions in the state. The court's argument in favor of neutrality is founded on an induction, as is made clear by the ruling itself, already quoted above: "In the context of teaching, neutrality should guarantee pluralism."[8]

The implied consequences of the ruling were far reaching: Italy should remove all crucifixes from all public schools. Moreover, since the ruling on *Lautsi v. Italy* was a decision of the ECHR, all member states of the Council of Europe, from Portugal to Russia, could be expected to comply with the newly enforced legal principle of the confessional neutrality of the state. All countries in Europe would be obliged to remove religious symbols from public school classrooms.

The court, through the first *Lautsi v. Italy* ruling, was trying to establish *laïcité* as a political norm that would be binding upon all the states that signed the European Convention on Human Rights. However, *laïcité* is not mentioned by, and therefore not guaranteed by, the convention, and in fact many countries in Europe have juridical systems that do give a particular privileged place to their own historically and sociologically dominant religious tradition.[9] The implicit idea in the chamber's ruling is that European identity and unity can only rest on secular values, and not on Europe's Christian heritage.

Reactions and Political Implications

The ECHR's ruling provoked strong public reactions in Italy and several other European countries. The Vatican, together with representatives of many major ecclesiastical institutions, condemned the court's decision. The Patriarchate of Moscow was a major voice on behalf of the Orthodox Church and took an active role in responding publically to the court's decision.[10]

The Italian government contested the decision and lodged an appeal with the Grand Chamber of the ECHR.[11] The appeal was accepted and the proceedings resumed, with unprecedented media coverage. The Italian government's argument was grounded on premises very different from those exhibited in the first ruling of the ECHR:

> The Republic of Italy, though secular (*laïque*), has freely decided to preserve a tradition which dates back almost a century. . . . [This decision] is motivated by the distinctive national characteristic expressed by the close relation between state and the people, and Catholicism, at the historical, traditional, cultural, and territorial level, as well as by the fact that Catholic values have always been deeply rooted in the feelings of the majority of the population.[12]

The strongest argument adduced by Italy was that the government, i.e., the state (which holds political power), must take account of the character of the nation. Political power (*kratia*) must represent the people (*demos*). This is the very definition of *demo-cracy*. In other words, the Italian government claimed that it could not apply the court's principle of confessional neutrality of the state in Italy without showing contempt for the majority of its own population and for its historical and cultural traditions.

Lautsi v. Italy acquired its real political significance with the intervention of other states. Ten member states of the Council of Europe constituted themselves officially as third-party interveners, standing against the decision of the court.[13] These countries participated in the proceedings, each submitting to the Grand Chamber a written argument for the display of religious symbols in public schools or public spaces maintained by the state. They also took part in a session of the court on 30 June 2010. Eight states were represented by Joseph H. H. Weiler, who delivered a rhetorically brilliant speech arguing that it is Europe's unique characteristic to have juridical pluralism, in which each country is permitted to have its own church-state model.[14] This pluralism is secured by the court's acceptance of the Margin of Appreciation, which acknowledges that the European Convention on Human Rights will be interpreted differently in individual member states. The Margin of Appreciation was also at the center of the written submissions of the ten countries intervening on behalf of the Italian government.[15]

The written statements submitted to the ECHR Grand Chamber are of great significance. Ten member countries of the Council of Europe wrote to defend the importance of Christianity in the cultural and political future of Europe. Such a third-party intervention, by states not directly involved in the case, contesting a decision of the ECHR, was totally unprecedented, as Grégor Puppinck noted:

> This is really an important precedent in the practice of the Court because, usually, member States abstain from intervening, or intervene only when the case affects a national of their State as permitted by Article 31(1). The Lautsi case is unique and unprecedented. Ten States are in fact explaining to the Court what is the limit of its jurisdiction; what is the limit of its ability to create new "rights" against the will of the member States. This can be viewed as a kind of counterbalancing power.[16]

In addition, ten other governments made public declarations in favor of the Italian government, opposing the ruling of the ECHR. In total, twenty-one of the forty-seven member states of the Council of Europe contested the Second Section Chamber's initial decision.

Who Were the Intervening Countries?

It is interesting to analyze which countries constituted the opposition to the court's initial ruling. Two characteristics emerge among those states that determined to intervene. The first is political: The strongest resistance to the court's secularism came from post-Communist countries; the second is religious: Orthodox countries represented the majority of the opposition.

The other opposing countries were Roman Catholic. No traditionally Protestant country contested the ruling.

Taking into account these two criteria we can categorize the twenty-one countries that opposed the *Lautsi v. Italy* ruling (which includes Italy) into four classifications:

 1. *Post-Communist and Orthodox*, representing approximately 232 million people—by far the largest and most significant group:
   a. *Third-Party Interveners:* Armenia, Bulgaria, Romania, and Russia;
   b. Public declarations in opposition to the ruling: Macedonia, Moldova, Serbia, and Ukraine;[17]
 2. *Post-Communist and Roman Catholic,* representing approximately 61 million people:
   a. *Third-Party Interveners*: Lithuania;
   b. *Public declarations:* Croatia, Hungary, Poland, and Slovakia;
 3. *Orthodox (and not formerly Communist),* representing approximately 12 million people: Greece and Cyprus (both third-party interveners).
 4. *Roman Catholic (and not formerly Communist),* representing approximately 70 million people:
   a. *Third-Party Interveners:* Malta, Monaco, and San Marino;
   b. *Public declarations*: Austria;
   Italy also belongs in this category, and accounts for 61 million people.
   Albania (approximately 3 million people) is difficult to classify by religion, but should also be counted as a post-Communist country.

In order to achieve a more meaningful comparison, I have taken account of the population of each country. Through the analysis that follows, my aim is to give an impression of the importance of the reaction against the court's ruling, and to demonstrate conclusively that political history (the experience of having been Communist) and religion (being Orthodox) did indeed play a major role in the decision to intervene in the legal proceedings of the ECHR in the case of *Lautsi v. Italy*.

The population of all the member states of the Council of Europe combined is approximately 800 million people. The twenty-one countries that contested the initial ruling of the court represent approximately 378 million people or 47 percent of the population of the member states of the Council of Europe. In other words, the countries that contested the secular ruling of the court account for half the population of the constituent states of the Council of Europe.

Collectively the post-Communist countries that contested *Lautsi v. Italy* (leaving aside their religious affiliations) stand for approximately 296 million people, representing 78 percent of the population of the twenty-one countries contesting the court's first ruling. If we exclude Italy and take into account only the countries that defended her, the proportion of the contesting populations drawn from post-Communist countries rises to 92 percent.

Turning now to the religious criterion, it is clear that Orthodox countries were dominant in the reaction against the *Lautsi v. Italy* ruling: They represent 64.5 percent of the opposition to the ECHR's decision, or 77 percent, if we exclude Italy.

Half of Europe contested the secularist ruling of the ECHR: Three-quarters of the protesters were from post-Communist states; two-thirds of the protesters were from Orthodox countries—formerly Communist and Orthodox countries represent three-fifths of all the protesters. These impressive figures prompt us to investigate the reasons for such a configuration and the meaning of Communist history and Orthodox religion as factors strengthening resistance against the *laïcité* political model.

The Fracture of Europe

Lautsi v. Italy revealed a fault line in Europe caused by the question of the societal legitimacy of Christianity. It has made manifest the strength of the popular opposition to the secular political line that the European Court of Human Rights has been following during the last decades. The *Lautsi v. Italy* case has revealed a legal and political conflict in Europe concerning the way states should deal with the religious dimension of their own national identities. This fracture divides Western and Eastern Europe. The countries that took the unprecedented step to constitute themselves as third-party interveners in the case of *Lautsi v. Italy* are almost all from Eastern Europe.

The Chamber of the Second Section certainly did not anticipate such a determined reaction to its ruling—had it, the court would have given a much more detailed argument and would have addressed the application of the Margin of Appreciation, which later became the crux of the case. The importance of *Lautsi vs. Italy* lies precisely in the fact that it has revealed this difference between East and West. During the seventy years of the Communist era, Europe was divided. During the last two decades, all European post-Communist countries have become members of the Council of Europe, and many of them have also joined the European Union.[18] This long series of adhesions is extremely significant in the history of the Council of Europe and the European Union. Both institutions had, until then, developed exclusively in Western Europe after the Second World War.[19] Post-Communist countries, with an Orthodox majority among them, represent now more than one-third of the population of the member states of the Council of Europe.[20] This means that the Council of Europe, as well as the European Union, has integrated countries with a very different historical, political, and religious background. During the 1990s, post-Communist countries were in a period of transition and most of their political elites welcomed Western values and political models with enthusiasm. This situation has now partly changed in some countries.[21] The colossal media interest in *Lautsi vs. Italy* played a role in strengthening the perception among post-Communist Christian countries (whether Roman Catholic or Orthodox) that they share a common position against a juridically imposed secularization of the state and public sphere. The ECHR, which may have regarded the employment of the principle of *laïcité* as self-evident progress, has come to realize through the appeal over *Lautsi vs. Italy* that the new Eastern post-Communist member states will not willingly follow the current secular Western political trend, but rather challenge it.

The Grand Chamber Ruling

The Grand Chamber gave its final judgment on 18 March 2011.[22] The judges declared (by a majority of fifteen to two) that Italy had not violated the European Convention on Human Rights by allowing crucifixes to be displayed in public schools. This ruling appeared to be a complete reversal of the situation established by the Chamber of the Second Section, which made the initial ruling unanimously.

At the juridical level, the key element that led the Grand Chamber to revise the first judgment was taking into account the principle of the Margin of Appreciation.[23] Although it is a well-established principle in the jurisprudence of the ECHR, the Chamber of the Second Section did not even mention it in its analysis, or in its deliberation of the case. The principle of the Margin of Appreciation allows the state a discretionary freedom to legislate religious matters, provided there is no European consensus on the issue at stake. In its final judgment, the Grand Chamber declared that it understood Mrs. Lautsi's discomfort with crucifixes, but also underlined the subjective nature of this discomfort and concluded that the Italian state was not guilty of indoctrination (which is clearly prohibited under the convention).[24] Therefore, exposure to crucifixes in public schools was not interpreted by the court as a violation of the applicant's rights, or those of her children.[25]

Since there was no doubt that the principle of the Margin of Appreciation exists in the court's jurisprudence and has played a significant role in many similar cases, the key remaining question was: How is it that the judges of the Chamber of the Second Section did not take this principle into account at all (dismissing its importance by ignoring it—not even giving arguments against its use in this specific case), while the Grand Chamber made it the key element on which to base its revised ruling?

Considering the importance of the political reactions outlined above, it seems difficult to contest the hypothesis that the opposition of twenty-one countries, representing almost half of the population of the Council of Europe's member states, to the first ruling by the Chamber of the Second Section played a decisive role in the final decision of the Grand Chamber. Since, in fact, the court does not have any power to enforce its decision within the borders of any individual country, with so many countries contesting the legitimacy of the court to impose a secular model over the whole of Europe, the court would have lost credibility and moral authority by confirming the first ruling.[26]

However, the ruling of the Grand Chamber cannot be considered as a straightforward victory for the Italian government and her allies. At the level of juridical concepts, the Grand Chamber has maintained—although with some limitations—the principle of the confessional neutrality of the state.[27] The ruling of the Grand Chamber is paradoxical, since the very principle that was introduced by the Chamber of the Second Section, according to which Italy was first condemned, has been confirmed by the Grand Chamber, and yet the Italian government was no longer considered to have contravened the European Convention on Human Rights. In other words, on the one hand, Italy was granted freedom to act according to her own wisdom and to organize the relationship between church and state according to local circumstances, but on the other hand, the court established the principle of confessional neutrality as a norm everywhere in Europe.

The most obvious explanation for this lack of coherence in the Grand Chamber's ruling is that the court had to accommodate two contradictory stances: On the one hand, there was its own preference for political *laïcité* and a clear separation between state and church; and on the other hand, there was the pressure of the unexpectedly robust support for the appeal lodged by the Italian government. Thus, the court did not condemn Italy (to satisfy the opponents of the first ruling) but nonetheless upheld the secular norm of the confessional neutrality of the state, moving its jurisprudence in the direction it wished.

Two Conflicting Interpretations of Human Rights

The debate took place in the context of the acceptance of pluralism as a legitimate foundation for contemporary democracy, itself viewed as the best and most legitimate political system. During the hearing before the ECHR, Prof. Weiler attempted to show that allowing crucifixes to be displayed in Italian public schools, and at the same time permitting France to have a political model grounded on strict *laïcité*, was a sign of the authentic pluralism. According to Weiler, the European model of tolerance, allowing juridical pluralism, is a most precious part of Europe's heritage.[28]

Confessional neutrality of the state was necessary, according to the Chamber of the Second Section, to protect pluralism. In his defense for the Italian government, Grégor Puppinck commented on the use of the word "pluralism" in the Second Section ruling: "This constituted a misinterpretation of the second sentence of Article 2 of Protocol 1, which merely stands for the principle that in a democracy, the educative offerings should be pluralistic, not the teaching itself."[29] Puppinck further notes the paradoxical use of the principle of pluralism by the judges of the Second Section and the secularists: "This 'pluralism' ironically results in exclusion of the very possibility of plurality by imposing the monopoly of secularism."[30] *Lautsi vs. Italy* showcases a conflict of interpretation between two groups, which agree on some basic terminology—human rights, democracy, and pluralism—but give different meanings to each of these key terms, according to the role and significance religion is accorded in public life.

At the heart of the conflict is the question: Does the Italian state have the right to give visibility to the religious dimension of its national identity in its public spaces? In other words, must the state renounce its national identity in order to respect human rights? The straightforward consequence of the first ruling was that the modern state should be removed from the continuing influence of the nation's history and from the majority religious intuition of the people. This is a model in which the state imposes a secular norm based on a doctrinal principle, rather than one derived from the democratic will of the majority of its people. Secularists believe that excluding religion from the public sphere will prevent further religious conflict; they perceive this prescriptive norm as democratic, even when it contradicts the intuition of the majority, because it helps achieve the equality of religions under the law. The state has to remain external to any religious matters, because were it to adjudicate on religious norms or values, it would establish an unjust difference between people belonging to different confessions or professing no confession at all. This was the case made by Mrs. Lautsi: The fact that one child would see the symbol of their religion in the classroom and another one would not constitutes unjust discrimination—a violation of the principle of equality.

Defenders of the presence of religion in the public sphere perceive this type of equality as an excuse for the complete domination of secularism. Indeed, removing crucifixes in Italy means that the dominant religion will be reduced to the same status as other religions—a status of almost nil public and political influence. The Italian government and its supporters were unable to accept this logic of equality, since they desire religion to play a role in public life and to be part of the identity of the state. Therefore, religious symbols displayed by the state in schools and other public spaces are fundamental, because they show that the government of the state is true to the nation's culture and tradition. From this perspective, democracy is not a secularist political ideology, but one that preserves the etymological meaning of "democracy" as a political system that is rooted in the will of the *demos*, the people. Thus the will of a local or national majority should prevail over both universal abstract principles (in this case, the secularist ideals of the ECHR) and excessively individual claims (those of Mrs. Lautsi).

Imposing a Nationless State?

Another significant dimension of the secularist argument for the confessional neutrality of the state is the unity of Europe. Secularists consistently argue that European integration requires coherent legislation to regulate religion.[31] Nationalism is traditional by nature, because it inherently tends toward the preservation of an identity that is historically constituted: Since the history and religious traditions of Europe are predominantly Christian, patriotism almost always includes a Christian dimension. To be patriotic in Europe usually entails sympathy for the Christian identity of one's own nation and of the continent—therefore contemporary Western secularism cannot count on nationalism as an ally in the construction of a unified Europe.

The identity and values of a state are reflected in the symbols it adopts publicly, so the idea of symbolic neutrality is impossible. Were England, Switzerland, or Greece to remove the cross from their national flags, it would certainly not be perceived as a "neutral" decision. An empty wall in a classroom in the countryside in Italy achieves neither neutrality nor equality. A state *must* have a flag, a national anthem, a constitution, state-funded museums, etc.—these are symbolic of the state—but they cannot be religiously neutral since national history is never religiously neutral. The meaning of state symbols is rooted in national history, and thus those symbols cannot be neutral.

For this reason, to say that states should be religiously neutral implies that they should be detached from the nation they govern. In order to be perfectly neutral, a state should become nationless, disconnected from its history and culture, supremely indifferent to the religious feelings of the majority of its own people. It is this that the Italian government could not accept in the first *Lautsi v. Italy* ruling.[32] It was agreement with this challenge that led to so many vehement reactions, especially from Orthodox countries for which it is unthinkable to erase the constitutive role of religious traditions in the identity of the state.

A nationless state would enforce only individual rights, based on a principle of human equality. Philosophically, such equality entails the exclusion of national identity, grounded in the will and sentiment of the majority, since democratic laws (i.e., those that accord with the preference of the majority) are necessarily less favorable for minorities. One of the key roles of human rights is to counterbalance the power of the democratic majority, to ensure that minorities will still preserve their most fundamental rights.

But if individual rights are permitted to overrule the will of the people, can the society still properly be called "democratic"? While the Italian government and Italian laws do indeed accept the notion of individual rights, those rights need to be balanced by collective societal rights. Many supporters of the Italian government in this case insisted on that the European Convention on Human Rights does not establish the confessional neutrality of the state or *laïcité* as political principles.

Post-Communist Countries

Radical secularism in Communist countries was grounded in an atheistic philosophy that interpreted religion as oppressive and superstitious. According to Marx, religious superstitions had always played a political role and were the means through which the capitalist oligarchy could dominate the people and hold them in captivity. In the political philosophies that led to Communism in Eastern Europe, religion was viewed as a tool of political and economic domination, and the key factor that hindered the development of an equal and just society. Thus, a liberating state had the duty and responsibility to free the minds of its people from religious superstitions, which hitherto were restricting them to inferior social status and unjust living conditions. It became the mission of the Communist state to cleanse religion from society. The social structures and habits connected with the Church, as well as public practices and regulations directly inspired by Christianity, had to be suppressed.

In the context of my argument, it is important to emphasize that the programmatic eradication of religion from public life involved an attentiveness to the symbolic world. In the states that became Communist, religious symbols had previously been endorsed and used by the government. Therefore, the only action that a Communist state could undertake to achieve its new political end was the removal of those symbols altogether. With important nuances in form and intensity, the Communist programs used a familiar method to achieve this aim: Church buildings were either destroyed, reassigned to secular use, or hidden behind new buildings, and streets, squares, even entire cities, which had Christian names were renamed (so, for example, St. Petersburg became Leningrad). But since public spaces cannot be deprived of symbols entirely, the Communist governments created new statues, names, and slogans to fill the void created by the eradication of Christian symbols and to promote their own philosophy.

This extended period of forced de-Christianization—which entailed social and physical persecution, as well as the eradication of religion from public life—has left a deep trauma in the consciences of those who now live under post-Communist regimes in Eastern Europe. There are solid reasons to believe that the first *Lautsi v. Italy* ruling, in which an international court attempted to force a state to suppress the traditional presence of religious symbols in schools, awoke painful memories for those who had recently experienced just that. It is not surprising, therefore, that the most determined supporters of the Italian government's appeal to the ECHR were formerly Communist countries. The key factor that makes the first *Lautsi v. Italy* ruling similar (although much softer) to Communist policies is the fact that the Court claimed that it is the duty of the state to remove religious symbols not because the majority had democratically decided on such a course of action, but for the sake of a political ideology—secular pluralism.

I believe that a thorough reflection on the role of secularism in the future of Europe must take into account the political history of post-Communist countries, for whom their past provides a solid basis for their critical response to this trend. And this position must be taken very seriously, since more than a third of the current population of the member states of the Council of Europe is now living in these countries. It is undeniable that the Communist experience will remain engraved in the conscience of Eastern Europe for a long time to come, and it is thus to be expected that the reactions triggered by the first *Lautsi v. Italy* ruling are only the symptom of what will certainly prove to be a long-lasting disagreement concerning the place and role of secularism and Christianity in Europe's destiny.

Orthodox Countries

Since Eastern European Orthodox countries are also post-Communist, it is difficult to distinguish and evaluate separately the respective weight of political and religious factors in their rejection of the Court's decision. However, in the written statements from the traditionally Roman Catholic and Orthodox countries acting as third-party interveners, the defense of the Christian inheritance of Europe appears as a strong motive for their reaction.[33] As we shall later see, religion and politics are deeply intertwined in Orthodox countries.

All the countries that contested the first ruling on *Lautsi v. Italy* are either Roman Catholic or Orthodox.[34] Both insist on the value of a good and fruitful relation between the state and the church, the latter having a public and active role to play in the life of the nation. This common feature distinguishes them from postmodern Protestantism, which insists that religion is a private affair and therefore that public law should not be molded according to specifically Christian principles. Even so, the fact that the governments of traditional Orthodox countries represent two-thirds of the opposition to the Second Section Chamber's decision needs further investigation. Orthodox countries have several political, historical, and theological aspects to their identity that account for their strong stand against the Court's secularism.

Orthodox countries have not passed through the long historical process of the privatization of religion that took place in the West, which brought to the fore the principle of *laïcité* in the wake of Enlightenment and the French Revolution.[35] Romania, Bulgaria, Serbia, and Greece (to name the most prominent) became independent nation states only during the nineteenth century, with the collapse of the Ottoman Empire. In the past their territories and important parts of their populations had been part of "Romania"—the Christian Roman Empire (which lasted from 382 to 1453) centered on Constantinople, the New Rome.[36] In the Christian Roman Empire, the "Roman" identity was one and the same with the "Christian" identity.[37] This Roman/Christian identity was preserved during the Ottoman rule through the *Rum millet* system, which established the Orthodox Patriarch of New Rome (which came to be known as Istanbul) as an *ethnarch* for all the Romans (i.e., the Christians) living in the Sultan's empire.[38] When the Ottoman Empire dwindled, new nation states on a Western model became independent and once more proclaimed traditional Christianity as their national religion, around which much of their respective national identity came to coalesce. The Church played a major role in the preservation of a continuous ethnic and religious identity defined against that of their Muslim rulers during centuries of Ottoman subjugation. When the Orthodox countries we know today became independent in the nineteenth century, the Orthodox Church played an important role in their reorganization as newly established states.[39] This Orthodox national history, which antedates the coming of Communism in the twentieth century, plays again—since the fall of the Berlin Wall—a very important role in the formation of the national identity of those countries. Russia was never part of the Roman Empire, but the successors of Saints Cyril and Methodius's missions to Bulgaria from New Rome played a major role in the conversion of Russia to Christianity. After the fall of Constantinople, Russia often interpreted herself as the heir to the Christian Roman Empire and the guardian of Orthodox Christianity.[40]

I want to underscore four major differences between post-Communist Orthodox countries and Western countries, which help explain their strong rejection of the secular political model promoted by the ruling of the Chamber of the Second Section.

First, in the West, the public function of Christianity gradually declined over a long period, which was still not complete in the 1950s when Christian democrats (mostly Roman Catholics) began their project to unite the states of Europe.[41] In contrast to this process, Communist revolutions represented a sudden and radical breach with the past, without gradual transition. Immediately, traditional monarchical Christian societies had to adjust to the new values and political principles of radical international socialism. When Communism collapsed, religion won back its social position in a context in which a clear separation between the state and the church, and the confinement of religion to the private sphere, were naturally felt to belong to the recent Communist past, which was viewed very negatively. Western observers may be misled by the solemn declarations of *laïcité* or separation of state and church in some constitutions of former Communist countries. The texts of these laws may very well have been inspired by Western standards, but in the minds of the majority of the populations, as well as politicians, a clear and well-established separation of state and church does not exist, and is not recognized in practice.

Secondly, after the fall of Communism, religion has found again a public voice, as well as social and even political influence. There is a public and social revival of Christianity in both Romania and Russia: In these countries, the whole society has once more become Christian. The fact of Christianity gaining importance and public influence on such a vast scale is unheard of for more than two centuries in the West, where there has been only a long decline of Christianity and no sign of a revival.

Thirdly, there is a strong relationship between Orthodox faith and national identity in most (if not all) Orthodox post-Communist countries. This goes back to the nineteenth century, when the Ottoman Empire was losing its power and the present nation states were being created. Each new country established—not without religious debates and even schismatic situations with the Patriarchate of Constantinople—a national church. It is common in Orthodox countries that a citizen of that country would consider themselves an Orthodox Christian, even if they do not believe in God, and even if they are not baptized. Orthodoxy and national identity are deeply tied together.

The fourth point may certainly be the most surprising for someone from a Western point of view. In post-Communist countries, the institution of the Church is well respected. Anticlerical feelings, which are very common in the contemporary West, do not have any equivalent in mainstream public opinion in Eastern Europe. Orthodox parish priests are almost always married and there is often an organic relationship, especially in rural areas, between the laity and the clergy. Without a pope, Orthodoxy is not a centralized international institution. The authority of its hierarchy, now as always, entails the voluntary reception of that authority by the people. In Orthodox countries, it is not uncommon to find nonbelievers who are critical of aspects of Orthodoxy but who nonetheless respect the Church as an institution.

These four points, (1) no clear separation of state and church, (2) the contemporary revival of Christianity, (3) the strong relationship between religious and national identity, and (4) trust and respect for the Church as an institution, lead to an interpretation of democracy and human rights that differs from that in the secular West. The idea that democracy must be grounded in the traditions and will of a people understood as a whole, with its religious and cultural traditions, is resilient. The democratic principle according to which it is the privilege of the majority to define the national identity according to history is still extremely strong in Orthodox countries, which is why, when human rights tend to promote a secular political model, they are met with a very negative reaction.

In the West, equality, laïcité, pluralism, and other secular values are much more widespread and deeply rooted in popular opinion, with the result that a strong tie between a specific religion and the state is perceived as unjustly discriminatory against adherents to other religions or nonbelievers. Pluralism, as a political doctrine, dictates that religion has to remain a private affair and that neither government nor the legislature should base its decisions on religious principles. By contrast, in popular opinion in Orthodox countries, the idea that pluralism should be imposed politically and judicially, with the intention of avoiding discrimination and to build a perfectly egalitarian balance between the diverse religions and worldviews, is rejected as a threat to national unity, which is grounded in a singular national history shaped by Orthodox faith.

Russia and the Symphonic Political Model

The political and religious history of each post-Communist Orthodox country is very different. The outline given above, which attempts to gather together the main features that explain the reaction of Orthodox countries during *Lautsi v. Italy*, only touches the surface of the various national contexts, and it is beyond the scope of this paper to investigate in more detail the differences between the individual countries. However, the exploration of at least one of them will give more weight to the whole argument.

Russia is a very interesting case. Russia is not a member of the European Union, but she is a member of the Council of Europe, and played a decisive role in *Lautsi v. Italy*. The demographic, economic, and political importance of Russia, as well as her independence from the European Union, gives her a unique position among post-Communist countries when it comes to issues related to Western secular policies and recent innovations in human rights. We must never forget that politics is always a *rapport de forces*. For example, in this regard, a country such as Romania, which depends economically on subventions from the European Union, cannot be expected to take a clear public stand against the dominant opinion of the European Union.

The evolution of Russia's dominant political philosophy since the fall of Communism is extremely interesting. Already in 1990, the Soviet authorities created a law on "Freedom of Conscience and Religious Belief," according to the Western liberal model, "which contains provisions against discrimination on religious grounds."[42] This was an important turn toward the Western model of freedom of religion. The dissolution of the USSR in December 1991 left Russia without any clear political trajectory. For a short period of time in the early 1990s, Russia sought political inspiration from the West, and so laws concerning religion were enacted during this period under Western influence: Freedom of religion was integrated in the new Russian Constitution of 1993, becoming a cornerstone principle of the Russian juridical system.[43] However, enthusiasm for the Western political model did not last long. Sergey Filatov writes:

Pro-Western democratic and market euphoria, and the expectations of the quick and painless achievement of the newly understood "bright future," were replaced by disillusionment and apathy. Numerous polls of those years showed that, prior to 1991, not less than two-thirds of the population thought that Russia should follow the Western example in everything, patterning Russia on its example. By 1992, the same overwhelming majority believed that Russia had its own way to follow. Russia was, in principle, a different civilization—and the West was no model for it.[44]

Since the mid-1990s, Russia has been seeking her own path, and recovering her own history, together with the role of Orthodoxy in her national identity. Russia resolutely turned to her pre-revolutionary past for inspiration, reviving the traditional Orthodox idea that the state and the church should collaborate.[45] The Moscow Patriarchate took an active role in this turn by promoting the idea of a particular bond between Orthodox religion and Russian identity. This resulted in the enforcement of a new series of laws, at the regional as well as at the national level, which introduced a distinction between different kinds of religions. The new Federal Law of 1997 demarcates established religions and "groups" which cannot obtain legal recognition.[46] The special role of Orthodoxy is mentioned in the preamble to the law.

On the one hand, it can be stated with Filatov that "the revival of religiosity in post-Soviet Russia is a unique phenomenon in the history of Christian civilization,"[47] and on the other hand, polls show that the population is still largely irreligious. The proportion of those who say they are believers in Russia is comparable with secular Western countries. The main difference, though, is that this proportion is increasing in Russia, whereas it is decreasing in Western Europe.[48] There is no doubt that Russia is being re-Christianized, even if the process has not yet deeply touched the population.

Davis states that, at the political level, post-Soviet Christianity in Russia may be characterized by two major movements: First, conservative patriots see Russian religion as a unique tradition to be defended against reforms; and second, democrats see religion as one element in a plurality of institutions contributing to the building of civil society. Both are represented in the post-Soviet development of Christianity and its representation in the media.[49] This tension and contradiction between these groups is noted by Marat Shterin:

> One basic tension stemmed from the perceived contradiction between the 1990 Law's thrust to treat all religions equally on the one hand, and the claims of historic faiths to recognition of their specific role for particular national or ethnic groups on the other. Undoubtedly, there was a revival of ethno-religious links after the decades of forcible disassociation between religion and ethnicity. As part of this process, past history became the most prominent reference point in what can [be] described as a struggle for legitimacy.[50]

This restoration of Russia's glorious past involves a specific idea about Russian identity as fundamentally different from Western Europe.[51] Patriarch Kirill introduced in the late 1990s the phrase "Russian civilization," understood as unique because it is grounded in the Orthodox faith, that sets Russia apart from Western Europe, which is essentially Protestant and Roman Catholic.[52]

This "turning to the past" in an attempt to find a political path distinct from those of Communism and Western liberal, secular, and individualistic democracy has even reached further than Russia's own past. In the media, as well as in political debates, the question as to whether the Christian Roman Empire must be used as a source of inspiration for political thinking has become significant. Over the course of more than a millennium, the Roman Empire developed a Christian political philosophy, which may be expressed by the Greek word *symphonia*, which means "harmony." It refers to a political philosophy that, according to the word of Christ, distinguishes the power of the state and the power of the church, and, at the same time, strongly affirms that the two powers must collaborate for the good of the people, each of them exercising its limited authority. *Symphonia* is the predominant traditional Orthodox model for Christian political philosophy. In the *Bases of the Social Concept of the Russian Orthodox Church*,[53] the Synod of the Russian Orthodox Church speaks highly of *symphonia* as a political model, quoting from the *Sixth Novella* of Emperor Saint Justinian I:

> The greatest blessings granted to human beings by God's ultimate grace are priesthood and kingdom, the former (priesthood, church authority) taking care of divine affairs, while the latter (kingdom,

government) guiding and taking care of human affairs, and both, come from the same source, embellishing human life. Therefore, nothing lies so heavy on the hearts of kings as the honour of priests, who on their part serve them, praying continuously for them to God. And if the priesthood is well ordered in everything and is pleasing to God, then there will be full harmony between them in every thing that serves the good and benefit of the human race. Therefore, we exert the greatest possible effort to guard the true dogmas of God and the honour of the priesthood, hoping to receive through it great blessings from God and to hold fast to the ones which we have.[54]

Orthodox tradition features several Christian Roman Emperors as models, having canonized them as saints.[55] Holy rulers of the Roman Empire are discussed in the media in Russia. There is no agreement about the *symphonia* model, but the very fact that it is seriously discussed shows how far Russia is from the model of Western liberal democracy: "The pattern of religious news coverage in broadcasting as a whole is therefore based on a strong inclination toward the Russian Orthodox Church and the expectation that Church policies will feature as a regular aspect of most major political, social, and cultural questions."[56]

Tsar Nicolas II, murdered by the Communists, was officially canonized in Russia in 2000 as a martyr for the faith, reconnecting political thinking to the traditional idea of "Holy Russia." Another prominent example of the collaboration of the state and the Church concerns the rebuilding of the monumental Cathedral of Christ the Savior in Moscow, which had been destroyed by Stalin. It was recently reconstructed essentially with state finances and was presented as a symbol of a new era in national life.[57]

To conclude this short exposition of some current political developments in Russia, the main fact that needs to be underscored is that there is a return of Christian tradition as a framework for political thinking in Russia.

Conclusions

This essay has explored the historical, political, and religious differences that set apart post-Communist Orthodox countries from other nations in Europe. The recent experience of radical secularization under Communism explains why Church and political authorities in formerly Communist states have begun to contest the secular interpretation of human rights that is so widespread in Western Europe. Their religious tradition is perceived by the majority of the local population as a self-evident foundation of national identity, and so the idea that the state should surrender its national identity (by promoting secularism) in order to respect individual human rights simply does not make sense. The creation of European unity around secular values (therefore excluding Christianity as of primary significance) has been challenged by several post-Communist Roman Catholic and Orthodox countries. They reject the idea that *laïcité* should be imposed on all European countries by an international court and they refuse to interpret pluralism as requiring strategies that disregard their own religious culture and traditional values.

The ECHR case of *Lautsi v. Italy* has brought to the fore the fact that Eastern Europe is not uncritical of Western European progress toward a fully secularized society. There are strong signs of a revival of Christianity in several countries in Eastern Europe including Russia, which is the most powerful actor in Eastern European politics. Russia seems willing to abandon altogether the idea of European unity in order to pursue the restoration of a glorious Russian civilization founded on Orthodoxy, and thus markedly differentiated from the Western political construction, which is based on individual human rights, prescriptive pluralism, and equality. Such an idea has been fully endorsed and outlined by the present patriarch of Moscow. If traditional Christianity continues to reinforce itself in Russia and other Orthodox and Roman Catholic post-Communist countries in the future, and at the same time Western Europe continues on its trajectory toward a more thoroughly secularized society, the fracture of Europe, brought to light by *Lautsi v. Italy*, will no doubt become a more forceful reality in European politics in the years to come.

Notes

1. *Laicità* in Italian. There is no exact equivalent for this term in English; it is perhaps best translated as "secularism." However, in Italian *laicità* and *secolarismo* have different nuances: *Laicità* refers specifically to the political and juridical principle of the separation of state and church, and is thus narrower in scope than *secolarismo*, which is a sociological and ideological term. In other words, *laicità* refers to a standing legal principle by which the state is bound,

whereas *secolarismo* is descriptive of an ideology and only theoretically prescriptive. In Europe, juridical literature in English uses the French *laïcité* (equivalent to the Italian *laicità*) to express the political and legal norm according to which the state should neither interfere in religious affairs nor be defined or influenced by religion. In this article, I will use the term *laïcité* in the English legal sense when speaking of the political norm apart from the social phenomenon of secularism. It is in fact the very term *laïcité* that stands at the center of the juridical debate pertaining to *Lautsi v. Italy*.

2. The principle of *laïcité* is not written into the Italian Constitution. However, it has received progressive recognition over a lengthy period as part of the Italian jurisprudence.

3. For a detailed review of the long and complex proceedings in Italy, see the reconstitution in the ruling of the European Court of Human Rights Grand Chamber, *Lautsi v. Italy*, 18 March 2011 (http://hudoc.echr.coe.int/sites/eng /pages/search.aspx, accessed 17 July 2014), §§10–16.

4. The European Court of Human Rights (ECHR) has its seat in Strasbourg and protects rights as set out in the European Convention on Human Rights. The ECHR is affiliated to the Council of Europe, which is constituted of forty-seven member states, representing approximately 800 million people. The Council of Europe must be distinguished from the European Union, a more recent and slightly different endeavor, which is constituted of only twenty-eight member states accounting for approximately 500 million people, and with its seat in Brussels. All member states of the European Union are also members of the Council of Europe.

5. A Chamber is a body of seven judges that represents the ECHR at a first hearing of a case. The ECHR is organized into different Sections, each having responsibility for different kinds of cases. The case *Lautsi v. Italy* was first heard by the Chamber of the Second Section. The Grand Chamber, composed of seventeen judges, gives final rulings on appeal cases. The Chamber and the Grand Chamber are often simply called "the court," since in both operations they represent the ECHR.

6. ECHR (Second Section), *Lautsi v. Italy*, 2009, §47e.

7. The core argumentation of the court can be found in ECHR (Second Section), *Lautsi v. Italy*, 2009, §§48–58.

8. ECHR (Second Section), *Lautsi v. Italy*, 3 November 2009, §47e.

9. See European Centre for Law and Justice, *Legal Memorandum: ECHR— Lautsi v. Italy*, April 2010. The Appendix to the *Memorandum* details the religious and constitutional specificities of all forty-seven member states of the Council of Europe. The full text is available at http://eclj.org/pdf/ECLJ -MEMO-LAUTSI-ITALY-ECHR-PUPPINCK.pdf (accessed 17 July 2014).

10. See, for example, the declaration of Kirill, patriarch of Moscow, available on Interfax: http://www.interfax-religion.com/?act=news&div=6675 (accessed 17 July 2014).

11. The Grand Chamber is the final court of appeal in the European Court of Human Rights, and its rulings cannot be overturned. See note 5 above for more details concerning the organization of the ECHR.

12. Repubblica Italiana, *Lautsi c. Italie, Saisine de la Grande Chambre*, 2010, §16 (my translation, from French). The full text can be found at http://eclj.org /pdf/mémoire_du_gouvernement_italien_pour_la_saisine_de_la_grande _chambre.pdf (accessed 17 July 2014).

13. The status of "third-party intervener" (*amicus curiae*) is usually used to allow NGOs, which are not directly involved in a case (either as plaintiff or as accused), to intervene officially in the written and oral proceedings.

14. Professor Weiler, an Orthodox Jew, was formerly the Joseph Straus Professor of Law and the European Union Jean Monnet Chaired Professor at New York University School of Law. Since 2013 he has been president of the European University Institute, Florence, Italy. A video of his defense in the *Lautsi and Others v. Italy* case can be viewed on YouTube at www.youtube.com /watch?v=ioyIyxM-gnM (accessed 17 July 2014).

15. "A Summary of the Submissions of the Intervening States," prepared by the European Center for Law and Justice, can be found at http://eclj.org/pdf /ECLJ-Summary-LAUTSI-20110315.pdf (accessed 17 July 2014). The full written submissions of the states are neither published in print nor available on the internet (as far as the author is aware); they are accessible in the archives of the ECHR.

16. "ECHR Crucifix Case: Ten Member States Join Italy in Support of the Crucifix," European Centre for Law and Justice press release (1 June 2010); available at www.eclj.org/Releases/Read.aspx?GUID=a77d9063–0475–408f -84a6-8a608be0077e (accessed 17 July 2014).

17. Armenia, Bulgaria, Romania, and Russia became third-party interveners in the *Lautsi and Others v. Italy* proceedings, so their involvement was more direct that that of Macedonia, Moldova, Serbia, and Ukraine, which made public declarations but did not take part in the juridical proceedings before the ECHR. A distinction between the two subcategories of official participants in the legal proceedings and unofficial commentators is present in each of the following groups also.

18. The exception is Belarus, which has not yet been accepted into the Council of Europe.

19. With the exception of Greece, which was the only Orthodox country in Europe that did not become Communist.

THE LAUTSI CASE AND THE FRACTURE OF EUROPE

20. The post-Communist countries that opposed the ruling of the Chamber of the Second Section represent 37 percent of the population of the countries that make up the Council of Europe (approximately 293 million people).

21. Russia is the clearest example (as will be elucidated below), but there are other countries that have recently taken political courses alien to Western secular politics—for example Hungary, which has just established a new constitution that gives an important place to traditional Christian principles.

22. European Court of Human Rights (Grand Chamber), *Affaire Lautsi et autres c. Italie*, with an official translation in English as *Lautsi and Others v. Italy*, 18 March 2011, available at http://hudoc.echr.coe.int/sites/eng/pages /search.aspx#{"dmdocnumber":["883170"], "itemid":["001–104042"]} (accessed 17 July 2014).

23. See § 61 and § 68–70 of the ruling of the Grand Chamber.

24. ECHR, *Lautsi and Others v. Italy*, § 78.

25. ECHR, *Lautsi and Others v. Italy*, § 57–81.

26. In fact, it has been argued with good reason that the very fact that twenty-one countries contested the first ruling had already diminished the authority of the ECHR.

27. ECHR, *Lautsi and Others v. Italy*, § 60: The court mentions the Folgerø Case, which is interpreted as imposing a "duty of neutrality and impartiality" on contracting states.

28. See Weiler's intervention, acting in the name of eight countries. Video available at: www.youtube.com/watch?v=ioyIyxM-gnM (accessed 17 July 2014). The written text of the intervention can be accessed at: http://www.ilsussidiario .net/News/Politics-Society/2010/7/1/EXCLUSIVE-Oral-Submission-by -Professor-Joseph-Weiler-before-the-Grand-Chamber-of-the-European-Court-of -Human-Rights/96909/ (accessed 17 July 2014).

29. G. Puppinck, "The Case of Lautsi v. Italy: A Synthesis," 873.

30. G. Puppinck, "The Case of Lautsi v. Italy: A Synthesis," 884.

31. See A. J. Menéndez, "A Christian or a *Laïc* Europe? Christian Values and European Identity," in *Ratio Juris*. 18, no. 2 (June 2005): 179–205. ("Laïc" should read "Laïque," since "Europe" requires the feminine adjectival form in French.) Secularists no longer consider the possibility of building European unity on Christian values, an idea that was still widespread in the 1950s.

32. This is clear in the argument of the Italian Republic found in *Lautsi c. Italie, Saisine de la Grande Chambre*.

33. See "ECHR Crucifix Case" (note 19 above).

34. With the exception of Albania, which became Communist at a time when Islam, Catholicism, and Orthodoxy were all well-established religions.

35. This process of privatization achieved momentum in the eighteenth century in Western Europe. It progressed very unevenly in different national contexts. Yet, there is now a clear movement toward secularization, which came to full fruition only in the late twentieth century, especially through the European Union and also, to a lesser extent, the influence of the ECHR.

36. Also known in Western scholarship by the pagan name of "Byzantium." This ancient name also gave itself to the expression "the Byzantine Empire," coined in the sixteenth century in French by Hieronymus Wolff. Both in Latin and Greek, the name of the Christian Empire was either "the Roman Empire" or "Romania." "Eastern Roman Empire" is also a modern historiographical term, used to distinguish the eastern Christian territories from the later western kingdoms.

37. Indeed, the word "Romans" was used to refer to "Christians," while "Greeks" was used to refer to the few remaining "pagans."

38. This Ottoman system gave the patriarch the highest political authority and responsibility over the Romans (i.e., those belonging to the Orthodox Church).

39. In Greece, the church also played a major role in the Roman Revolution of 1821 (the "Greek War of Independence"), which later was interpreted— under the influence of Great Britain and France, which took an active and decisive role in the revolution—as a *Greek* revolution against their Ottoman rulers.

40. This feeling was very strong in the nineteenth century, especially in the Slavophile movement (Khomiakov, Dostoevsky, etc.), which thought that Russia had a role to play as the redeemer of Europe, perceived as Western and profoundly alien. The feeling that the Russian Empire was the legitimate heir to the Christian Roman Empire led Moscow to proclaim herself as the "Third Rome" (a title still used today by traditional Orthodox).

41. There were, of course, violent and radical episodes. The most important was the French Revolution, which not only murdered, exiled, or imprisoned anti-Republican priests and annihilated whole populations in the monarchist and pro–Roman Catholic region of Vendée, but also abolished the Judeo-Christian week of seven days and changed the calendar in order to lay the foundation for a new society, free of the Judeo-Christian tradition.

42. H. Davis, "Mediating Religion in Post-Soviet Russia: Orthodoxy and National Identity in Broadcasting," in *Orthodoxy in Russia: Post-Atheist Faith*, ed. S. Filatov, Studies in World Christianity 14 (Project Muse, 2008): 65–86, here 71.

43. Davis, "Mediating Religion," 71: "The law was liberal and popular and the freedoms were endorsed in the 1993 Russian Constitution. Its guarantees of freedom of worship for all faiths, including foreign religious associations,

encouraged a boom in religious activity ranging form evangelism, pilgrimage, religious education, new religious movements and the resurgence of indigenous religious practices."

44. Sergey Filatov, "Orthodoxy in Russia: Post-Atheist Faith," in *Orthodoxy in Russia: Post-Atheist Faith*: 187–202, here 188.

45. This collaboration of the state and the church has progressively become more important since the first election of Vladimir Putin as president in 2000.

46. See Davis, "Mediating Religion," 72. Many, if not most, legal systems in Western Europe have similar distinctions even today. The striking aspect of this new law is that it moves away from equality between religions toward a system that grants privileges to only some religions on the basis of history, demographic importance, etc. This reversal in the prevailing trend is highly significant in reflection on the fate of secularism in Europe.

47. Filatov, "Orthodoxy in Russia," 188.

48. World Values Survey research in Russia, based on surveys at various intervals in the 1990s and 2000s, shows that:(1) a minority in Russia practice religion on a regular basis; (2) the proportion of Russians who believe in God and identify with Orthodoxy is growing. The data can be found on the official website at: http://www.worldvaluessurvey.org (accessed 17 July 2014).

49. Davis, "Mediating Religion," 71–72.

50. Marat Shterin. "Church-State Relationships and Religious Legislation in the 1990s," in *Religious Transition in Russia*, ed. M. Kotitanta (Helsinki, Kikimora Publications for Alexsanteri Institute), 218–50, here 231. Citation according to Davis, "Mediating Religion," 71.

51. Filatov, "Orthodoxy in Russia," 190: "The continuous strengthening of the Orthodox Church in Russia is first of all its strengthening as an ideological, cultural and political force expressing society's mood of restoration."

52. Filatov, "Orthodoxy in Russia," 191: "The term 'Russian civilization,' introduced into ecclesiastical vocabulary in the late 1990s by Metropolitan Cyrill (Gundyaev), has acquired a sacral, quasireligious meaning in church circles."

53. Department for External Church Relations of the Moscow Patriarchate, *Bases of the Social Concept of the Russian Orthodox Church*, 2000. The full text of the document is available in English at http://orthodoxeurope.org/page/3/14.aspx (accessed 17 July 2014).

54. The *Sixth Novella* of Saint Justinian is quoted here as found in the English translation in the *Bases of the Social Concept of the Church* (see note 53 above). The Synod of the Russian Orthodox Church endorses this *Novella* as a traditional reference, but noting that this ideal was never realized in its purity in the Christian Roman Empire. The whole presentation on the different

political models and their respective merits can be found in the *Bases of the Social Concept of the Church* § III.4.

55. Important examples of canonized Roman Emperors are Saint Constantine I the Great (272–337), Saint Theodosius I the Great (347–395), Saint Justinian I (482–565), and Saint Basil II (958–1025).

56. Davis, "Mediating Religion," 78.

57. See Davis "Mediating Religion," 76–78.

POLITICAL THEOLOGIES:
PROTESTANT-CATHOLIC-ORTHODOX CONVERSATIONS

POWER TO THE PEOPLE

ORTHODOXY, CONSOCIATIONAL DEMOCRACY, AND THE MOVE BEYOND *PHYLETISM*

Luke Bretherton

Introduction

I had the privilege a few summers ago of going on retreat to Vatopedi Monastery on Mount Athos, the ancient spiritual center of Orthodoxy.[1] Up some stairs from where the church and refectory were located, in a passageway the monks constantly traversed, were two clocks. One was marked "worldly"/cosmic time, keeping Greenwich Mean Time—a chronological order universalized as a result of contingent historical procedures developed mainly to serve the interests of industrial and imperial expansion and efficiency.[2] The other clock marked the time that determines the practices and life of the monastery and that was changed regularly according to a combination of the rhythms of nature (notably, the movement of the sun) and the liturgical calendar. This monastic, liturgical time is referred to on Athos as "Byzantine" time—revealing both its local and traditional character. To catch the ferry or arrange to meet someone, one has to operate on worldly time; to eat or worship (two dimensions of the same event at the monastery), one has to know the time set within your monastery, which, as St. Benedict tells us, is a school for the Lord's service. Such was my schooling that, for all the contingency and abstraction of worldly time, it still felt more "real" than the local time, despite the materiality, sociality, and concreteness of the latter.

As well as the problem of how to live faithfully at the intersection of two time zones—one eschatological and the other earthly—Vatopedi illustrates

61

the problem of how to live in overlapping and intersecting political spaces. Mount Athos is an anomaly that incorporates and disrupts key aspects of political order as it emerged in Europe since the tenth century. Each monastery is a self-governing polity, and governance of the mountain as a whole is overseen by a council of representatives of the twenty monasteries whose jurisdiction overlaps and must be negotiated with both its titular ecclesiastical ruler, the ecumenical patriarch of Constantinople, and the modern sovereign power responsible for Mount Athos within the post-Westphalian international order, the Greek nation state. In its national administrative structures, Greece locates responsibility for Mount Athos within the Foreign Ministry. The three different forms of monastic life practiced on the island (in the monasteries, the *scetes*, and the cells) add further differentiation and variation. Most of the monasteries are "Greek"— although they welcome monks and guests of all nationalities—but there are also the "foreign" monasteries of Russia, Serbia, and Bulgaria, at which, nevertheless, "Greek" monks may also reside (even if this is far less common today). Mount Athos can thus be said to represent an ongoing form of what John Milbank calls "complex space": That is, in contrast to the bounded nation state with a single law and indivisible source of rule, which at the same time is unbounded in the exercise of its sovereign will within its own borders, complex space entails overlapping jurisdictions in which the sovereign authorities of the pope, parliaments, kings, dukes, doges, and various forms of self-governing corporation are interwoven with each other and span disjunctive spaces.

In this essay I will reflect on the twin problematics Mount Athos presents us with—that is, how to live faithfully at the intersection of two time zones and how to live in overlapping and intersecting political spaces—in the context of thinking about the relationship between Christianity and democracy.[3] These reflections will serve as a prelude to some constructive suggestions for ways in which Orthodoxy might faithfully conceptualize its relationship to democratic politics in liberal states characterized by religious and moral plurality. But first let me say a word about democracy.

Defining Democracy

Democracy means collective self-rule by the people for the people, rather than rule by the one, the few, or the mob. This definition raises the question of who and what constitutes the people and thence what is the nature and form of this self-rule. Many accounts of democracy conceive of self-rule as an extension of individual autonomy. Popular sovereignty is derived from the sovereignty of the individual and is considered indivisible and singular. Legitimacy is premised on each individual having an equal say in the decisions that affect everyone. This "say" can be organized in a variety of ways; hence, there are debates about different ways of organizing collective self-rule. The adjectives "representative," "deliberative," and "direct" placed before the term "democracy" denote different forms of organizing collective self-rule and constituting individuals into a people. However, by conceiving of collective self-rule as an extension of individual autonomy, what is lost from view is the intrinsic relationship between collective self-rule and the forms of association in which the art of ruling and being ruled is learnt and performed. And thence the ways in which the people as a whole is constituted through different forms of association coming into relationship with each other and the negotiation of their different interests and visions of the good in the formation of a common life—this common life being what constitutes the people qua people.

We can begin to see that there is a paradox in the conceptualization of democracy in modern political thought: Democratic citizenship is seen as an expression of individual autonomy but its performance and defense are in great measure dependent on participation in a group. Without being embedded in some form of association, the individual citizen is naked before the power of either the market or the state and lacks *a*, if not *the*, vital means for his or her own self-cultivation. The relationship between Christianity and democracy encapsulates the triadic tension between market, state, and community within which the individual is located. State and market processes are seen to limit, challenge, and provide alternatives to those derived from religious obligations and identities, yet in an increasingly deinstitutionalized and atomized society religions provide one of the few corporate forms of life available for mobilizing and sustaining the ability of individuals to act together in defense of their common interests and in pursuit of their common objects of love.

An alternative approach to the relationship of democratic thought to individual autonomy—one that helps us address the paradox just outlined—begins with the relationships between individuals. If democracy is the rule of the people by the people, then at its most basic level it demands relationships between people. Without some kind of meaningful relationships between people there are just individuals, and an atomized and disaggregated crowd, whether at a local, national, or transnational level. If one is to begin with relationships, then one has to take seriously the arenas or forms of social life through which individuals develop and sustain relationships over time and in which they learn the arts of ruling and being ruled. This starting point for thinking about democracy is not in opposition to individual liberty but in recognition that individual liberty depends on and is mediated by multiple forms of association.[4] Much political theory has moved beyond the sterile dichotomies between "liberals" and "communitarians" to take seriously the symbiosis between individual freedom and communal formation in democratic politics.

The dark side of thinking about democracy by beginning with relationships, the side that rightly worries liberals, is the way in which such a beginning can lead to an emphasis on the collective taking precedence over and oppressing the individual. At a minimal level, the emphasis on relationships, and the necessary particularity of such a beginning point, is felt by some to threaten universalistic and egalitarian conceptions of citizenship.[5] Beyond this normative concern, and as Tocqueville and Montesquieu observed, there can be despotism of the people as well as that of a despot. Beyond even the problem of democratic despotism are those forms of political order that inherently subordinate the individual to a collective vision of peoplehood, as is the case with nationalist, fascist, state socialist, and state communist regimes. Polities characterized by one or another of these regimes may include democratic elements, but the constitution of the *demos* as a political community is substituted for some other, supposedly prepolitical species of peoplehood such as the *ethnos* or *Volk*. However, beginning with relationships between individuals can challenge collectivist, homogenous, and monistic conceptions of peoplehood and popular sovereignty. In these accounts a different set of adjectives come to the fore as ways of describing the organization of rule by the people for the people. The adjectives used foreground how relationships between individuals take multiple forms and the complex rather than simple nature of social and political space.

Sovereignty, Christianity, and Consociational Democracy

One conception that begins with relationships and allows us to make sense of the kind of complex space Vatopedi represents can be called "consociationalist." Consociation is a term derived from the work of the early seventeenth-century Dutch Protestant political thinker Johannes Althusius.[6] While literally meaning "the art of living together," the broader meaning of consociationalism denotes the mutual fellowship between distinct institutions or groups that are federated for a common purpose. In contrast to the likes of Hobbes, Rousseau, and Hegel, Althusius allows for the pluralization of political order so as to accommodate and coordinate the diversity of associational life, whether economic, familial, or religious. In his account, to be a political animal is not to be a citizen of a unitary, hierarchically determined political society. Nor is it to participate in a polity in which all authority is derived from a single point of sovereignty (whether of the general will or the Leviathan). Rather, it is to be a participant in a plurality of interdependent, self-organized associations that together constitute a consociational polity. Mount Athos is a clear example of such a polity. The singularity of each is constitutive of the commonwealth of all. In such a compound commonwealth, federalism is societal and political rather than simply administrative. In contrast to constitutional federalism as a way in which to limit sovereignty, as exemplified in the dominant interpretations of the US Constitution, which leaves undisturbed the indivisibility of political sovereignty, consociationalism envisages a full-orbed confederalism whereby sovereignty is distributed across distinct corporate entities. For Althusius, sovereignty is an assemblage that emerges through a process of mutual communication between consociations and their reciprocal pursuit of common ends. Unity is premised on the quality of cooperation and relationship building and is not secured through either legislative procedure, the singular nature of sovereign authority, or the formation of a unitary public sphere premised on a homogeneous rational discourse.

The consociational approach is not as alien as may first appear. The theories of Hobbes, Carl Schmitt, and Giorgio Agamben are one thing; historical practice is quite another. As Mount Athos illustrates, the medieval Gothic order did not wholly disappear with the advent of the "Westphalian" order of nation states. Rather, it was displaced and redescribed so that forms of political community became relocated and renamed as "economic" or "social." For example, the joint stock trading company—the early modern archetype of the contemporary capitalist firm—was an explicitly political community based on the concept of the *corpus politicum et corporatum* or *communitas perpetua* that went back to Roman law. The paradigmatic example of the early modern mercantile republic was the East India Trading Company, which, as a colonial proprietor, did what early modern governments did: erect and administer law; collect taxes; provide protection; inflict punishment; . . . regulate economic, religious, and civic life; conduct diplomacy and wage war; make claims to jurisdiction over land and sea; and cultivate authority over and obedience from those people subject to its command.[7]

This could be a description of Halliburton in Iraq, mining and oil companies in the Congo, or even any number of company towns in the US. Yet the nature of such companies as political and sovereign institutions is either viewed as anomalous or it is denied. Such entities are labeled as economic, not political. However, contrary to how it is presented in political and economic theory, legal and political pluralism is the norm rather than the exception in contemporary societies. As the political theorist James Tully argues, most nations are in fact "federations of more or less self-governing and overlapping political associations with somewhat dissimilar legal and political ways."[8] Sovereignty is an assemblage that opens up different conditions and possibilities for agency depending on where one is located.

In the realm of theory, it is as variations on a consociational conception of sovereignty that we can make sense of a theologically and philosophically diverse yet interlinked tradition of political reflection. If Althusius is its progenitor, a key mediator is the German legal historian Otto von Gierke and those he influenced, notably the English Pluralists (John Neville Figgis, and the early work of G. D. H. Cole and Harold Laski).[9] While there were substantive differences between them, the English Pluralists advocated a decentralized economy based on the noncapitalistic principles of cooperation and mutuality and proposed a radically confederalist and politically pluralist conception of the state.[10] Sovereignty was not something that could be appropriated by a single agency or institution. Rather it emanated from the complex and divided governing powers that compose the body politic.

A further strand of consociationalist thought can be identified in the sphere sovereignty of the Dutch Neo-Calvinists Abraham Kuyper and Herman Dooyeweerd.[11] For various complex reasons, Kuyper does not explicitly name Althusius as an antecedent. However, he was clearly aware of his Dutch Calvinist forebear, and the conceptual debt is striking.[12] Kuyper and Dooyeweerd envisaged the independence of distinct spheres—notably, family, education, and work—as expressions of the sovereign will of God.

Each sphere was said to have a relative autonomy and specific character that needed to be respected by other authorities. Derivatively, specific consociations (such as a university or school) within each sphere had their own integrity and autonomy that was not to be usurped by a higher authority. Government had a role in ordering and protecting the general good but it did not have the authority to interfere with or determine the character or telos of each sphere. In turn, the state was bounded by the sovereignty of other spheres.

It was in the Netherlands that notions of sphere sovereignty overlapped with and found a parallel expression in the emergence of Catholic Christian Democratic thinking. Central to this current were the philosopher Jacques Maritain and the development, from *Rerum Novarum* (1891) onwards, of Catholic Social Teaching (CST). Bryan Hehir gives a full outline of CST and its development in this volume, but the consociational aspects of CST are worth sketching in further detail. Maritain argues for a genuine plurality and a consociationalist conception of civil society as a way of limiting the power of the state and the market. Maritain describes the plurality of civil society as "an organic heterogeneity" and envisages it as being constituted by multiple yet overlapping "political fraternities" that are independent of the state.[13] Maritain distinguishes his account of a consociationalist political society and economic life both from fascist and communist ones that collapse market, state, and civil society into a single entity and from collectivist and individualistic conceptions of economic relations.[14] Crucially, civil society constitutes a sphere of social or "fraternal" relations that has its own integrity and telos but that nevertheless serves the defensive function of preventing either the market or the state from establishing a monopoly of power and thereby either instrumentalizing social relations for the sake of the political order or commodifying social relations for the sake of the economy. Within this sphere there can exist multiple and overlapping and, on the basis of subsidiarity, semiautonomous forms of institutional life and association—forms that are not reducible to either a private or voluntary association. Indeed, in contrast to his overall theological framework, Maritain's account of a consociationalist body politic overturns the kind of divisions between public and private at work in, for example, the thought of John Rawls and late-modern liberalism more generally. The consociational approach exemplified in Maritain's work was a rival to and eventually displaced the "throne and altar" authoritarianism that informed a figure such as Carl Schmitt. In a very different context we could speculate about a parallel development in Russian political thought that drew on Orthodox theology. I am thinking here of the work of Vladimir Soloviev and Nicholas Berdyaev.

Animating the Christian consociationalist tradition, of which the Pluralists and Neo-Calvinists and Catholic Social Teaching are a part, is the sense that we participate in a cosmic order that can disclose to us some measure of meaning and purpose. It is this cosmic social imagination that distinguishes the Christian consociationalism of Figgis, Kuyper, and Maritain, amongst others, from their secularist confrères, notably Emile Durkheim and the political theorist Paul Hirst.[15] It is my contention that one way Orthodoxy might think about its relationship to democracy is via some account of consociational democracy—an account that takes the church qua church seriously. A consociational conception of democracy prioritizes the relationship between distinct but reciprocally related consociations (or communities or forms of life together) as the best way to generate the collective self-rule of a people conceptualized as a non-natural political community.[16]

Such a conception chimes with a central aspect of modern Orthodox theology: An emphasis on the centrality of the Trinity. With a renewed emphasis on the Trinity in contemporary Western theology, good order comes to be seen not as the result of the exercise of sovereign will. Instead, good order is constituted through participation in right relationships as encountered and empowered through participation in the perichoretic communion of Father, Son, and Holy Spirit. In place of images of political rulers (emperors, kings, or lords), music, drama, and dance become more common analogies for the nature of God. In such accounts God is no distant sovereign but both loving Creator and intimately and vulnerably involved in creation through the ongoing work of the Son and the Spirit. In the light of this kind of God, monarchical, absolute, and indivisible claims to political sovereignty that override the freedom and dignity of the one, the few, or the many are revealed as in opposition to the divine nature and the true order of being, which is one of harmonious difference in relation. Likewise, humans are not monadic individuals but persons in relation with a status above and beyond any immanent social, economic, or political claims upon them. But before simplistically (and naïvely) turning the Trinity into a social program, an eschatological note of caution must be sounded. And for this I turn to a theologian not often cited in contemporary Orthodox theology: Augustine of Hippo.

Augustine's eschatology can be read as a response to both Constantinian triumphalism (marked by an expectation of progress until the Church would overcome the world and universally display heaven's glory in history) and Donatist separatism from the world (wherein history is orientated toward regress or a movement away from God).[17] In place of both these polarities, Augustine reestablishes a Pauline eschatological perspective through his conception of the two cities.[18] For Augustine, the city of God is an alternative, yet coterminal society to the earthly city. These two cities are two political entities coexistent in time and space and thus part of this noneternal age or *saeculum*. Within this framework human history is secular (rather than neutral): That is, it neither promises nor sets at risk the Kingdom of God. The Kingdom of God is established, if not fully manifest, and the "end" of history is already achieved and fulfilled in Christ. On this account, political authority is not neutral (it is either directed toward or away from God) and the *saeculum* (the time between Christ's ascension and his return) is open, ambivalent, and undetermined.[19] Thus the Church can reside in this age in its structures and patterns of life as relativized by what is to come, and therefore see them as contingent and provisional.

R. A. Markus argues that Augustine's eschatology warrants positing an autonomous secular sphere that is neither wholly demonic, sinful, or profane, nor wholly sacred, either for the pagan or the Christian.[20] However, this seems an overstatement that does not keep in play the dynamic relationship between the earthly city and the city of God within the *saeculum*. Markus is right insofar as the *saeculum* is an ambiguous time, a field of wheat and tares, neither wholly profane nor sacred. However, it is not autonomous—Christ's sovereignty holds sway over all that happens in this age. The *saeculum* constitutes a single reality or realm, ruled by Christ, and this reality is the mutual ground on which the city of God and the earthly city coexist. Eric Gregory helpfully summarizes this conception of the secular as follows:

> The drama of the secular lies precisely in the human capacity for good or evil, rather than in some autonomous *tertium quid* that is delivered from moral or religious significance. The "secular" refers simply to that mixed time when no single religious vision can presume to command comprehensive, confessional, and visible authority. Secularity . . . is interdefined by its relation to eschatology. This definition does not deny the Christian claim that the state remains under the Lordship

of Christ, providentially secured in its identity "in Christ." But it does claim that the secular is the "not yet" dimension of an eschatological point of view.[21]

Citizenship is the currency that the city of God and the earthly city share within the mutual ground of the *saeculum*. Citizens of both cities seek peace; however, in the earthly city peace is achieved through the imposition of one's own will by the exercise of force. For Augustine, the only true society and true peace exists in the city of God. With Aristotle, Augustine can say that humans are naturally social animals who find fulfillment in a polity of some kind. But against Aristotle and much other political thought, he argues that the political societies we see around us, and thus the form citizenship takes in them, are neither natural nor fulfilling, because they are fallen and oriented away from the true end of human being—communion with God—and toward their own prideful, self-destructive ends. So Christians would be fools to try and unfold a "Trinitarian" blueprint for society. Rather, for Augustine, politics in the *saeculum* is about enabling a limited peace that is on the one hand shorn of messianic pretensions and on the other not given over to demonic despair. A democratic and consociational political space is, I contend, a necessary condition for keeping in check messianic forms of political program (whether by the church or any other "party") and dystopian underinvestments in the good of political order.

Building on Augustine, we should be deeply suspicious of any project of salvation or human fulfillment through politics, and alert to the temptation of rendering the prevailing hegemony as "natural" or ontologically foundational.[22] All political and economic formations and structures of governance are provisional and tend toward oppression, while at the same time, whether it be a democracy or a monarchy, any political formation may display just judgments and enable the limited good of an earthly peace through the pursuit of common objects of love. Moreover, "the better the objects of this agreement, the better the people; and the worse the objects, the worse the people."[23] Thus, while existing on a spectrum, there is a difference between the Roman Empire and a band of brigands.[24] No political formation is neutral, but one can be better or worse, rather than simply good or bad. As Markus puts it: "Being imperfectly just is not the same thing as being unjust."[25]

A consociational conception of democracy makes possible the affirmation of: (1) an eschatological vision of the *saeculum* (not collapsing pursuit of the Kingdom of God into pursuit of penultimate goods in common); (2) the Church as a distinct community of belief and practice; (3) the possibility of a common life between different communities within a specific earthly polity; and (4) the need for a genuinely pluralistic or complex space in order to hold in check the formation of anti-Christic and idolatrous monopolies of power. How so?

First, nonviolent, participatory, and grassroots democratic politics is a vital means through which to ensure that the state and market recognize that humans have ends and vocations beyond political and economic life, and that the role of the market and the state is to serve humans, not vice versa. It thereby helps prevent democracy from becoming a "thinly disguised totalitarianism."[26]

Second, a consociational, pluralistic body politic provides a context in which the Church learns to listen to others and put people before program. For the Church, listening is *the* constitutive political act. Through listening and responding to the Word of God, the Church is assembled as a public body—the *ekklesia*—out of the world. This initiatory act of listening forms the body of Christ. In being called out, this body is then enabled to participate in God's hearing of the world, and so it can both discern the truth of the world and know itself truthfully. Listening to others through involvement in democratic politics both presumes a common life (no listening takes place in contexts of violence or social atomization) and is an act that intends and embodies such a life. Thus listening not only constitutes the Church but is itself a primary form of faithful witness within political life as it embodies and points to the reality that in Christ all things were made and all things are reconciled and therefore a common realm of meaning and action is now possible. Involvement in a consociational and participatory democratic politics is one way of listening to the world and thereby becoming the people of God and being a faithful witness.

Third, as well as being a way of bearing witness, of listening to and encountering the other in political and economic life, democratic politics is a vital way in which the Church learns to tell the truth about itself as such practices foster the humility and penitence necessary to hear God and neighbor. Listening is a therapy for the self-love or pride that is the attempt to secure oneself outside of relationship with God and pursue illusions of self-sufficiency in relation to both God and neighbor. By contrast, listening inoculates the Church against developing false securities, because in listening one has to deal with the world as it is. In listening, one must take seriously who is before one and attend to the situation rather than predetermine what to do in accord with some prior agenda, ideology, or strategy of control. When I listen to someone I encounter them neither as a statistic nor a stereotype but as a human being, as one who bears the image of God with all the density and complexity being human entails. In sum, listening is vital to deepening one's moral conversion in relation to God and others, and thus one's ability to reason rightly about what is the just and truthful judgment to be made with these people, at this time, in this place. In order to know what is true, we must first listen. In certain configurations, democratic politics is one such way of listening well.

Ecclesiology and National Identity

A consociational account of democracy contests perhaps the most fundamental theological challenge modern democratic thought poses: the immanent attempt to ground a moral political life. This constitutes the refusal of eschatology or rather the historicization of eschatology and thence the absolutization and divinization of the finite. If this time is all there is, then politics has no limits as it has to bear the full weight of human meaning and possibilities. The problem is not totalitarianism but the totalization of politics as such, which leads either to an overinvestment in political projects as programs of salvation or an underinvestment that despairs of any meaningful political activity being possible. In contrast, when politics is understood to be an activity in the *saeculum*—that time between Christ's ascension and his return—it is freed to bring about a limited but nevertheless meaningful peaceableness. Vatopedi Monastery, with its daily and yearly round of worship, embodies the great gift of Christianity to politics, which is time, and in particular the relativization of historical time.[27]

Christians have time to hope and live in a time when change is possible and in which past and present are connected in the communion of saints.[28] At the same time, as Stanley Hauerwas has forcefully argued, Christians do not have to establish regimes to control the time so as to determine the outcome of history; rather, they can live out of control because the fulfillment of history is already inaugurated in the resurrection of Jesus Christ. A Christian vision of time as history, as open to redemption and as fulfilled in the *eschaton*, undergirds a theological apologetic for democratic politics understood as a finite and contingent activity that has limits but also significance beyond the immediate needs and vicissitudes of the moment. The kind of Augustinian eschatology sketched above disqualifies any absolute claims of a political sovereign to shape human life and reasserts the need for the pluralization of political space as reflective of the complex nature of this time between Christ's ascension and *parousia*. The complexification of political space is theologically necessary so as to hold open the existence of times and spaces that are not subject to political control. On this account, the status of the Church as a *res publica* is based on its vocation to bear witness within the political order to an order and rule that is over and beyond this or that spatiotemporal order.

On this account, any idea that there can be a Christian society or nation needs to be treated with suspicion, like any project of salvation or human fulfillment through politics. Here the witness of Mount Athos points both to a profound problem within Orthodoxy and, paradoxically, to what faithful witness might entail in relation to this problem. Here I am talking about *phyletism*—that is, the move beyond ecclesial autocephaly to national churches whereby national and religious identity become synonymous, such that to be Greek is to be Orthodox and, conversely, for a Greek to attend a Russian or Romanian Orthodox church is to participate in a foreign or alien entity. *Phyletism* was condemned as a heresy at the Synod of Constantinople in 1872. Yet it was the failure to address it through the proper upholding of an eschatological tension and something like a consociational vision of political authority that prepared the way for the emergence of ethnoreligious nationalism throughout much of the Orthodox world in the twentieth century. Having spent time in Russia, Armenia, Romania, and Kosovo, I've encountered the phenomenon of ethnoreligious nationalism first hand. We see the ongoing legacy of ethnoreligious nationalism on Mount Athos where, since 1989, certain monasteries have been converted into nationalist enclaves. At the same time, I've met the antidote. Men like Fr. Sava and the other monks of Decani Monastery in Kosovo who protected Albanians from racist Serbs and then, in turn, protected fearful Serbs from vengeful Albanian militias. And some monasteries on Mount Athos are polyglot *entrepôts* drawing together the faithful from all over the Orthodox world in common worship—albeit only of men. What these faithful monasteries witness to in a fragile and often broken way is that, after Christ, the Church should be *the* paradigmatic people:

That is, it is to be that body—the people of God—which is to be the training ground for that time when creation is fulfilled and when people from every nation shall be reconciled in Christ. That it is so often not should be a source of lament and a goad to pursue deeper faithfulness.

Notes

1. I am grateful to Father Demetrios Bathrellos for comments on an earlier draft, and in particular for helping me unravel some of the complexity of Mount Athos.

2. The actual word used was *kosmic*. I have translated this as "worldly" in keeping with certain New Testament usages. The term "world" (*kosmos*) in the New Testament can denote either the unified order of created things, understood as a neutral description (John 17:5, 24; Rom. 1:20; 1 Cor. 4:9), or the worldly system that is hostile to God's good order (John 15:18–19; 17:14–16; 1 Cor. 1:20, 5.10). In New Testament Greek a number of variations on these two basic connotations can be discerned. For example, Paul Ellingworth identifies six variations: (1) the universe; (2) the earth; (3) human beings and angels; (4) humanity as a whole; (5) humanity as organized in opposition to God; and (6) particular groups of human beings. See Paul Ellingworth, "Translating Kosmos 'World' in Paul," *The Bible Translator* 53, no. 4 (2002): 414–24. See also David J. Clark, "The Word Kosmos 'World' in John 17," *The Bible Translator* 50, no. 4 (1999): 401–6.

3. It should be noted that in reflecting on Mount Athos I am not thereby holding it up as necessarily the normative form of Christian life. There are many aspects of Athonite monasticism as an ongoing, all-encompassing form of life that are theologically problematic: most notably, the exclusion of women. Rather, like any other "real existing" embodiment of Christianity, its very existence deserves and may provoke theological reflection.

4. The term "association" is used here in a generic way and encompasses both voluntary and nonvoluntary (rather than involuntary) forms of association. For a discussion of the distinction between voluntary, nonvoluntary, and involuntary, see Mark Warren, *Democracy and Association* (Princeton: Princeton University Press, 2001), 96–103. There are, of course, extensive debates about: (1) how to distinguish various forms of associative relationship such as contractual, covenantal, and corporate; (2) the corporate personality of groups as these relate to the state; and (3) what happens to different forms of social relations within processes of modernization stemming from Tönnies's distinction between *Gemeinschaft* (community) and *Gesellschaft* (society/association). These sociological distinctions echo a distinction in Roman law between *societas* (partnership/voluntary association) and *universitas* (a corporation with a

common identity and that is capable of common action) brought to prominence in political theory by Michael Oakeshott. Important as these debates and
distinctions are, for the purposes of this essay, a generic use of the term
association suffices.

5. For a discussion of such concerns, see Michael Walzer, *Politics and Passion:
Toward a More Egalitarian Liberalism* (New Haven: Yale University Press,
2005).

6. Althusius, *Politica* I.1. It is probable that Althusius derived his use of the
term from Cicero (*De Re Publica* 1.25–27), although in Cicero's usage its
meaning is restricted to the legal bond for the organized conduct of public life
rather than an all-encompassing term for social and political relations. See
Thomas Hueglin, *Early Modern Concepts for a Late Modern World: Althusius on
Community and Federalism* (Waterloo, Ont.: Wilfrid Laurier University Press,
1999), 79.

7. Philip Stern, *The Company-State: Corporate Sovereignty and the Early
Modern Foundations of the British Empire in India* (Oxford: Oxford University
Press, 2012), 4–6.

8. James Tully, *Strange Multiplicity: Constitutionalism in an Age of Diversity*
(Cambridge: Cambridge University Press, 1995), 164.

9. Otto von Gierke, *Community in Historical Perspective*, ed. Antony Black,
trans. Mary Fischer (Cambridge: Cambridge University Press, 1990); and for
the English Pluralists, see Paul Hirst, ed., *The Pluralist Theory of the State:
Selected Writings of G.D.H. Cole, J.N. Figgis, and H. J. Laski* (London:
Routledge, 1993).

10. For an account of the conceptual differences between the English
Pluralists, see Cécile Laborde, *Pluralist Thought and the State in Britain and
France, 1900–25* (Basingstoke: MacMillan Press, 2000), 45–100; and Marc
Stears, "Guild Socialism," in *Modern Pluralism: Anglo-American Debates Since
1880*, ed., Mark Bevir (Cambridge: Cambridge University Press, 2012), 40–59.
Stears uses the term "guild socialist" rather than "English Pluralist" but this
alternative designation more directly relates to the work of Cole and Laski
rather than Figgis. For the differences between the English Pluralists and
American traditions of political pluralism, notably that of Robert Dahl, see
Avigail Eisenberg, *Reconstructing Political Pluralism* (New York: SUNY Press,
1995). Eisenberg conflates forms of American political pluralism with an
aligned but distinct tradition of consociational thought to which the English
Pluralists are more directly related.

11. See Jonathan Chaplin, *Herman Dooyeweerd: Christian Philosopher of State
and Civil Society* (Notre Dame, Ind.: University of Notre Dame Press, 2011).

12. See James Bratt, *Abraham Kuyper: Modern Calvinist, Christian Democrat*
(Grand Rapids, Mich.: Eerdmans, 2013), 133–35.

13. Jacques Maritain, *Integral Humanism: Temporal and Spiritual Problems of the New Christendom*, trans., Joseph Evans (New York: Charles Scribner's Sons, 1968), 163, 171.

14. Jacques Maritain, *Integral Humanism*, 169–71, 186–95. A parallel distinction is made by Pius XI in *Quadragesimo Anno* (1931), §§ 94–96, as a way of distinguishing a Christian corporatist vision of politics from fascist ones. On the Christian account, corporatist and personalist forms of civic association and economic organization are precisely a means of preventing the subsuming of all social relations to the political order.

15. See, for example, Paul Hirst, *Associative Democracy: New Forms of Economic and Social Governance* (Cambridge: Polity, 1994).

16. It could be suggested that a consociational vision of democracy has, within the context of Orthodoxy, unfortunate echoes of the *millet* system used in the Ottoman Empire. However, against such a connection, consociational democracy is precisely an anti-imperial measure as it normatively refuses any single hegemonic group or discourse as able to determine the public sphere and is precisely a means to ensure a meaningful plurality of associations is maintained so as to prevent any single group from monopolizing control of political authority.

17. This is to summarize what I take to be Oliver O'Donovan's reading of Augustine in *The Desire of the Nations: Rediscovering the Roots of Political Theology* (Cambridge: Cambridge University Press, 1999).

18. For how Augustine's eschatology directly draws on Paul's eschatology, especially the Pauline account of the "principalities and powers," see Robert Markus, *Christianity and the Secular* (Notre Dame, Ind.: University of Notre Dame Press, 2006), 14–17, 55–56.

19. Markus, *Christianity and the Secular*, 28–30, 51.

20. Markus, *Christianity and the Secular*, 37.

21. Eric Gregory, *Politics and the Order of Love: An Augustinian Ethic of Democratic Citizenship* (Chicago: University of Chicago Press, 2008), 79.

22. From the writing of Genesis as an alternative creation *mythos* to the Enuma Elish, to the refusal to bow the knee to the Roman emperor as the Pantocrator, to the Barmen Declaration, it is a foundational political insight of Christianity to deconstruct and offer an alternative to any instance of *cosmopolis*: that is, the writing of the political order into the cosmic order so that a historically contingent form of political rule is inscribed with an immutable character and posited as inevitable and "natural."

23. Augustine, *City of God* XIX.24.

24. Augustine, *City of God* IV.4.

25. Markus, *Christianity and the Secular*, 44. It is important to note that defining Augustine's conception of justice in the earthly city as "imperfectly

just" is itself problematic. Augustine argues in *City of God* XIX.23–27 that true justice does not exist without true piety. The implication of this is that knowledge of justice is not possible outside of knowledge and worship of God through and in Christ. Thus the order found in Rome, or any other instance of the earthly city, is not just. However, this does not mean its order is wholly evil—it is an earthly peace. But this earthly peace should not be viewed as on a continuum with the just order of the city of God. For a detailed examination of Augustine's conception of the relationship between justice and the "justice" of the order found in the earthly city, see Robert Dodaro, *Christ and the Just Society in the Thought of Augustine* (Cambridge: Cambridge University Press, 2004), 27–114.

26. *Centesimus annus* §46.

27. Sheldon Wolin, *Politics and Vision: Continuity and Innovation in Western Political Thought* (Princeton: Princeton University Press, 2004), 111–15.

28. Stanley Hauerwas, "Democratic Time: Lessons Learned from Yoder and Wolin," in *The State of the University: Academic Knowledges and the Knowledge of God* (Oxford: Blackwell, 2007), 147–64.

POWER, PROTEST, AND *PERICHORESIS*

ON BEING CHURCH IN A TROUBLED WORLD

Mary Doak

W e have entered the twenty-first century with global systems of communication and trade binding the world's population together more thoroughly than perhaps at any other time in history. Unfortunately, this globalization is also presenting unprecedented challenges to human survival and flourishing. Our increasingly global economy holds out the hope that all might participate in the benefits of economic development; yet thus far this economic system is evidently more inclined to increase inequality, resulting in a small group of super-rich and massive populations of deeply impoverished people. And many of these poor today find that the local resources that at one time provided at least subsistence levels of food and shelter for their families and communities have now been appropriated for the global economy. Perhaps even more alarmingly, our economic system is dependent on practices of production and consumption that are unsustainable in their current form, and that are effecting a global change in climate, threatening the conditions of life on this planet. Together, climate change and a globalized economy are increasing rates of human migration, destabilizing established communities through large-scale shifts in populations.

Given these urgent problems, the task of developing an appropriately Christian theology of democracy may not seem compelling. After all, these global problems exceed the control of the nation state and will not be solved by tinkering with forms of national government. Besides, democracy often appears to be broadly accepted as the most legitimate form of government today, even to the point that dictators at times feel compelled to hold elections that mimic the procedures of democracy. Isn't providing a theology of democracy *at best* a case of theology showing up—yet again—a little breathless and a little late to provide a Christian defense of what everyone has already accepted anyway?[1] At worst, as some argue, efforts to provide a theological defense of political democracy risk prolonging the failed project of liberal Christianity, continuing the misguided effort to baptize the ethos of secular society at the cost of a distinctively Christian perspective.[2] Rather than further defending what the world (especially the secular world) has already embraced, some argue that theological energies should be focused on the distinctively Christian perspectives and practices that offer hope for a real alternative to the suffering and oppression of this world.

Before deciding too quickly that attitudes toward democracy are irrelevant to the grave problems the human community faces today, it might be worth noting that current processes of globalization involve a system of power analogous to the imperialism that Christianity has too often embraced in the past: The world is being united in an economic system that is directed by, and for the benefit of, a very small group of human beings. Further, the ethos of our current form of globalization and the effects of total global climate change are thoroughly undemocratic: What affects all is most definitely not being decided by all! In fact, democratic practices of working together for the common good are seriously undermined by the magnitude of global systems that far exceed local control, while at the same time electronic media foster interactions that are definitely atomizing (and often narcissistic). Texting, Facebook, and whatever other electronic network is briefly the rage, take time and attention away from face-to-face encounters with the real, embodied, and diverse people with whom we share the structures and conditions of our lives. To overcome the imperialist globalization that imposes uniformity and undermines collective agency, humanity today needs renewed commitment to diverse, participatory communities and to practices of inclusive decision-making that value the distinctness of each person. To the extent that democracy involves people coming together to order their common life, we need more, not less, democracy![3]

Empire, it is now clear, has not disappeared but rather has mutated into new yet no less virulent forms. Faithful Christian resistance thus requires that we continue to reexamine critically "the shadow of Constantine" and the often unacknowledged dream of harnessing imperial power to create a world order that serves the interests of elite Western Christians.[4] To be sure, democracy is no guarantee of justice, and tyrants can be elected. Yet as Bruce Bueno de Mesquita and Alastair Smith have argued (conclusively, in my judgment), the best guarantee that policies will serve the general welfare is a structure that ensures that the broadest possible number of people are involved in determining who will govern.[5] Further, and no less significant from a theological perspective, inclusive communities that foster recognition of human dignity and a person's right to contribute to society are valuable ends-in-themselves. Democratic forms of community are not only *the means* through which people can join together to combat poverty, inequality, and environmental destruction, then; participatory, democratic communities are also in themselves *a countercultural alternative* to atomization, uniformity, and the global disregard by the powerful of the value of ordinary people.

Christianity, with its concept of the person fulfilled in community, has the resources to contribute to movements in opposition to imperialist globalization and social atomization. As many have argued, Christian eschatological hope for ultimate harmony calls us to develop increasingly democratic structures that foster (however imperfectly) participatory communities in civil and political society.[6] However, as I will further argue, this Christian ideal of reconciled, harmonious communities must be understood in a way that does not preclude responsible engagement with the realities of power, conflict, coercion, and domination. The same theological resources that challenge Christians to seek more inclusive forms of community can too easily prevent effective Christian opposition to injustice, especially if the hope for ultimate reconciliation is understood as an immediate possibility that delegitimizes Christian engagement with conflict. In brief, we need a theology of democracy that will enable Christians to resist the ongoing temptation to be "court chaplain to the pride of nations,"[7] without becoming so afraid of power that Christians refuse the opportunities—and the responsibilities—to oppose the destruction of human beings, their communities, and their environment.[8]

My discussion here proceeds in three steps. First, I begin with a brief assessment of the growing theological consensus that the mission of the Church is to witness to, and to work toward, the goal of divine-human communion. I argue that the Church's mission as thus understood calls Christians to oppose the antidemocratic forces of imperialist globalization and societal atomization that divide and oppress rather than unite humanity. More explicit engagement with this widespread and ecumenical understanding of the Church's unifying mission would enable political and liberationist theologies to defend inclusive, participatory political structures with the resources of Trinitarian theology, contemporary ecclesiology, and the sacramental practices of the Church.

I then turn to the main focus of this essay, which relates power, conflict, and even coercion, to the ecclesial goal of ultimate harmony. As Marcella Maria Althaus-Reid has aptly noted, theologies that emphasize inclusion risk reinforcing current power structures by neglecting the role of conflict and confrontation in the pursuit of liberation.[9] While Christians cannot and should not give up the eschatological hope that exclusion and marginalization will be overcome in God's reign, a political or liberationist theology that seeks a more humane and liberating society will need to pay particular attention to theologizing the relation of power and conflict to this hope for ultimate unity. A clearer articulation of how conflict can serve the goal of harmony might overcome the resistance to liberation theologies of some of the privileged, though well-meaning, theologians and church authorities who currently reject as divisive liberationist (and especially feminist) theologies.

Finally, I will conclude with a brief reflection on the importance of forming Christians to deploy power responsibly and gracefully in this world.

Communion and Democracy

As a Catholic theologian committed to a strongly ecclesial, nonindividualistic form of Christianity, my approach to political theology is based on the mission of the Church as proclaimed by the Second Vatican Council: The Church is to be the sign and instrument (that is, a sacrament) of union with God and unity among humanity.[10] This is stated early in *Lumen Gentium* and provides the theological basis for that document's account of the nature and internal structures of the Church. More important for our purposes, this sacramental understanding of the Church is also proclaimed in *Gaudium et Spes* as the basis for the Church's mission to the world and the principle of Christian activity in all spheres of culture and society.[11] We should note that the Church, as described in these ecclesial documents, is called to be *both* sign *and* instrument: The Church is to witness to divine-human communion in its ecclesial life; at the same time, the Church is to work extra-ecclesially, to serve as "an instrument" cooperating with God's intention of increasing harmony throughout the world.

This emphasis on the Church's mission to foster divine-human communion in the world is by no means unique to Catholic Christianity. Divine-human communion, or *theosis*, has been and continues to be central to Orthodox theology, and indeed Orthodox thought has been identified as the source for the renewed emphasis on communion at the Second Vatican Council.[12] Further, the mission of the Church to be a sign and instrument of the union of all in God has been recently affirmed in the World Council of Churches' document *The Church: Towards a Common Vision*,[13] and is presupposed (for example) in the otherwise quite different theologies of John Milbank and Miroslav Volf.[14] Indeed, the centrality of the goal of divine-human communion to the mission of the Church has become the prevailing consensus in contemporary Christian ecclesiology in recent decades.

Orienting the mission of the Church as witness to and in service of communion helpfully integrates a commitment to this world with a hope that transcends history: The Church is called to further the unity of all in God that can be experienced in part now but will only be given in full beyond history. This is therefore an eschatological perspective as well as a thoroughly sacramental (indeed, Eucharistic) approach to the mission of the Church, acknowledging that the telos of harmony within the divine life gives value and orientation to, but cannot be identified with, historical projects. God's grace is at work in this world, but the final perfection of our life within the Triune God cannot be achieved in this world, as Reinhold Niebuhr consistently—and rightly—maintained.[15]

The theological significance of divine-human communion has been further clarified by the explosion of Trinitarian theology in Western Christianity in the late twentieth century. This renewed attention to the doctrine of the Trinity emphasizes that humans are made in the image of a God who is not an identity in stasis, but rather distinct persons in a perichoretic communion of self-giving love that is fundamentally other-directed, bringing new beings into existence and into the life of the Triune God. Humanity is thus made for, and only fulfilled in, inclusive communities of love in which distinctness is valued and diversity enriches the whole. As so many have argued, a Trinitarian perspective reminds us that each human person contributes uniquely to the human (and ultimately divine) community while, at the same time, finding his/her fulfillment in participating in that common life.[16]

Christianity thus has obvious implications for efforts to resist a global-ization that appropriates the benefits of the global economy (and wrecks the planet) for a small percentage of the human population, while treating the majority as disposable.[17] Where once hierarchy was defended by invok-ing a monarchical view of the one God over the universe and one absolute ruler over society, it is now more commonly—and appropriately—argued that Christianity calls for human communities that seek to model the divine community of nonhierarchical, other-directed, loving harmony that is the source and the goal of human life.[18] Instead of legitimizing an im-perialism (including the imperialism of global capitalism) that imposes uniformity for the benefit of a powerful elite, a consistent Trinitarian Christianity supports inclusive, diverse communities modeled on the mu-tual self-giving of the Trinity, communities in which people work together for the common good and are mutually enriched through each other's unique contributions.

This recovery of an emphasis on divine-human communion provides the basis for a political theology thoroughly rooted in the central beliefs and practices of Christianity: Belief in a Triune God, salvation through Jesus Christ, and the eschatological goal that is proleptically experienced in the Eucharist all inform the Christian view of the person as oriented to communities of mutuality.[19] Christians are thus equipped to engage issues of public life—and democracy—with the substance of Christianity, in-formed by essential Christian beliefs about what it means to live as people called to communion with God and with all else that God has created. Rather than being paralyzed by, for example, the false dilemma of either productive engagement with a secular public life or the formation of com-munities for a distinctly Christian witness, Christians must recognize that their mission, as Christians, is to image the Trinity in openness to others for the greater good of all.

Although it is beyond the scope of this essay to explore the matter in detail, it is worth noting here that Western Christians have much to learn from Orthodox Christianity about how to return the doctrine of *theosis*, or divine-human communion, to its proper place as central to the Christian account of creation, sin, and the redemption of humanity. It might then become clearer, for example, that Catholic social thought is not in fact an arbitrary list of rules derived from moral principles several steps removed from essential Christian doctrines. Instead, this body of thought strives to articulate what it means to live in society as persons oriented toward community and harmony with one another and with God.[20] When one considers how seldom Western Christians (including American Catholics) recognize the centrality of divine-human communion to Christian faith, or offer a faith-inspired resistance to the rampant individualism of US culture, the importance of current theological work—including theological dialogue with Orthodox Christianity—on the Trinitarian, ecclesiological, and sociopolitical implications of communion becomes especially evident.

The Ambiguity of Power

To further the project of developing a more adequate Christian political theology based on divine-human communion, I would like to explore here one particular challenge that should interrupt any too easy focus on harmonious community: the stubborn persistence and even prevalence of human conflict in this world. John Milbank is right to insist that Christians understand harmony, not conflict, to be the ultimate reality, but this does not absolve Christians from acknowledging the role of conflict in human relations this side of the *eschaton*.[21] I fear that, without sufficient attention to power dynamics and to the reality of human conflict and coercion, a theological emphasis on harmony may undermine Christian efforts to achieve more justly structured and diverse communities. After all, creating a more inclusive and participatory common life is never a simple, cooperative process in this world (whether in matters of statecraft or even on parish councils!). Rather, efforts to achieve the common good usually require that we struggle with and against those who oppose that good—or who have a very different idea of the common good—and such struggle involves the deployment of power. As Robin Lovin has recently stated, "Hope cannot overcome oppression without acquiring some countervailing power."[22] If a commitment to harmony inclines Christians to avoid conflict and eschew power, are we likely to proffer any significant resistance to the life-destroying oppression all around us?

Perhaps the difficulty will become clearer if we briefly return to the doctrine of the Trinity, particularly as the source of the Christian ideal of harmony. As argued above, the Trinity is the divine perichoretic communion of self-giving love and, as the source and goal of human life, the

Trinity is the model of mutual love that properly inspires our work for harmonious and diverse communities. But a Christian praxis intent on modeling the divine harmony would seem to leave little room for agonistic engagement; after all, there are no power struggles among the persons of the Trinity.

Must Christians then affirm that the use of coercive power, even to protect the vulnerable, is a cooperation with the logic of sin?[23] Should hope in God's reconciling grace lead Christians to refuse all conflictual politics, and respond to violence by simply refusing to recognize its existence, by persisting in a commitment to "act as if . . . sin is not there"?[24]

To be sure, violence is not the ultimate power, and a practice of breaking the cycle of sin with a forgiveness that refuses to retaliate is indispensable. Nevertheless, we must ask: If Christians refuse *in principle* to interrupt the violence and domination in human life and social structures, whose interests are served? Does such intentional blindness truly lead to the harmony Christians claim to seek, or is it more likely to support the false harmony of an oppressive status quo, which often asks only that we pretend that this deployment of violent power is not happening?

It may be that women are particularly attuned to the potential for tension between protesting injustice and seeking reconciliation through self-sacrificial love. The ideal of loving harmony is frequently invoked to argue that women should give up "selfish" demands for their rights and refrain from disruptive conflict and opposition, even when the intent of the conflict is to attain a more just world. Feminist political theories have for this reason not only emphasized relationality, but also dissensus, conflict, and self-assertion as essential to the achievement of more just communities.[25] Perhaps unsurprisingly, such feminist theories have been criticized by the Vatican for presuming that conflictual power dynamics exist between the sexes and even within intimate family relation.[26] I submit that this ecclesial critique lends further support to suspicions that the ideal of communion may be wielded to delegitimize struggles for justice and thus to support oppressive power structures.

To be sure, the points of coherence between the Christian ideal of divine-human communion and feminist theories of relationality (especially with a feminist focus on affirming difference in relation) give reason to hope in the ultimate coherence of a thoroughly feminist and communion-centered political theology. Yet an adequate feminist political theology cannot be achieved without further theological attention to the appropriate role for dissensus and conflict even (especially!) within a Christian praxis of modeling and working for more harmonious communities.

Some developments within communion ecclesiologies in the Catholic tradition provide further evidence that an emphasis on divine-human communion can be invoked in support of unjust power structures. Gerard Mannion has rightly described as "authoritarian" the communion ecclesiology that defends a hierarchical harmony in which the laity is united in unquestioning obedience to the magisterium, as implied in the "Petrine" and "Marian" structures advocated by communion ecclesiologies influenced by Hans Urs von Balthasar.[27] When the communion of the Church is understood as comprising a harmonious union between the initiatory leadership invested in the official (Petrine) hierarchy and the loving reception of this leadership by an obedient Marian laity, there is little room for the laity to engage in valid criticism of the hierarchy (even when the hierarchical abuse of power includes covering up the rape of children). Instead, and notwithstanding protestations that the Marian principle is of greater value, this model of communion suggests that when the laity question or challenge their leaders, they have failed to be appropriately receptive and are damaging the communion of the Church.[28] Imagine the implications if that approach were to be followed in public life!

This interpretation of communion becomes even more troubling when the Petrine-Marian division of roles is applied to the relations within the Trinity. Instead of presuming that Trinitarian nonsubordinationism entails a mutual equality-in-difference as the Trinitarian ideal of community, David Schindler, for example, builds on von Balthasar's work to defend a thoroughly gendered concept of initiation and reception proposed as a description of the inner relations of the Trinity as well as a theological rationale for the different roles of the clergy and laity, and of men and women, in church and in society.[29] For Schindler, obedient reception of hierarchical authority is not merely an ecclesiological principle but one that is inscribed within the Trinity and so is both fundamental to human relations (especially between men and women) and the basis for all harmony in society. As noted above, many communion theologies (rightly, in my judgment) refute this explicitly authoritarian concept of social harmony; nevertheless, Schindler's position reminds us of the importance of attending to how concepts and images of communion actually function politically in the world. Communion no doubt requires leadership and authority, but if there is no room to challenge abuses of power in the hope of a more perfect union, we are in deep trouble! Indeed, it would seem that we have come full circle here, having returned to the previously rejected idea that political domination reflects the dominion of God.[30]

In brief, a focus on communion with and within the Trinity *should* interrupt injustice and contribute to the development of diverse, participatory communities. Yet at times the goal of harmonious communion in the image of, and ultimately within, the divine is invoked instead to encourage acceptance of unjust structures and power in the name of harmony, whether by explicitly enjoining obedience to authority or simply by failing to make room for conflict within a Christian witness to unity. Given this very real danger of supporting an unjust status quo (from which educated theologians and church leaders often benefit), Christian political theologies cannot prescind from the task of determining the proper role of power and the place of conflict in the service of greater communion.

In considering this question of the use of power and conflict in an unjust, fallen world, it is important to avoid conflating power, which is the capacity to effect something, with violence (a physical attack on person or property) or coercion (the attempt to compel). As Reinhold Niebuhr knew well, power in itself is not evil since power can be positive or negative, defensive or offensive.[31] Indeed, power in feminist theories is usually a good that women desire, in opposition to the evils of violence and domination that have denied women their proper power.[32] The primary theological difficulty here is not, then, power per se, but rather the appropriate response to the reality of conflict and the use of coercion in Christian witness to the goal of harmonious community.

I intend to set aside here the more narrow (and difficult) question of the use of violence by Christians. Not all coercive power involves physical attacks or threats of such attacks, and I am convinced that that we must first come to terms with conflict and coercion in themselves, before dealing with the more thorny issue of the Christian use of violence. Even nonviolent coercive power can make Christians uneasy and, in fact, can be horrifyingly destructive (especially when it involves psychological coercion). Nevertheless, coercive power can also be deeply inspiring, as when the Rev. Dr. Martin Luther King Jr. famously refused violence and instead deployed not only rhetorical power and the power of suffering witness, but also the coercive power of boycotts and strikes that remained nonviolent in the face of terrifically violent opposition.[33]

One the one hand, we must ask whether a responsible commitment to the goal of a just and harmonious community is possible without engaging in political coercion and navigating what is rather redundantly called "power" politics (since all politics is concerned with power).[34] On the other hand, coercive power to attain the goal of one party against the goals of others, at least on the political level, seems antithetical to the ideal of reconciliation. The question still haunts: Are we perhaps denying our true vocation as Christians when we participate in the conflict due to sin, rather than exemplifying the eschatological harmony possible in part now? However much the world follows its own dictates, shouldn't the Church do otherwise?[35]

While I cannot fully answer these complex questions in the space of this essay, I would like to suggest that a sound basis for integrating the ambiguity of power into our understanding of divine-human communion can be found in Paul Tillich's classic work on love, power, and justice.[36] There is much still to be gained from Tillich's insightful account of the relation between love and justice—and of the role of power in each—particularly as his perspective is predicated on the goal of divine-human communion. As Tillich argues, the goal of love is union: Love seeks to unite what is in fact (but should not be) separated, while justice preserves what love intends to unite. Justice and love are thus integrally related, though not identical: Without the preserving work of justice, the unity that love seeks cannot be achieved. Tillich further contends that, in extending forgiveness, love fulfills the demands of justice, while ultimate justice will be found in the reunion of all in the reign of God.[37]

Tillich thus provides a theological basis for explaining that a harmony without justice is a perversion of—and not a witness to!—the communion we seek, because without the preservation of what is to be united, there is only a false peace that obliterates, rather than reconciles with, the other. A love without justice, as Tillich further warns, destroys the one who loves as well as the one who accepts such love.[38] Unfortunately, the destruction of the other is one of humanity's deepest temptations, since in finite existence we continually face the threat that the other will not make room for us, and, in turn, we fear making room for that other. Those who benefit from the status quo—including Christians—may thus be especially tempted by appeals to a false harmony that, without justice, destroys the other as well as the harmony Christians claim to serve. Insofar as Christianity calls us to live (in church and in society) in hope for true unity, the

Church's mission requires that Christians seek a justice that permits genuine diversity and allows for the harmony in which all find they are more fully themselves because of their relationships with all others.

If love thus requires justice, then love must be consistent with the exercise of power, insofar as justice requires that we deploy power, even coercive power, against the destructive power of injustice. In classic Tillichian language, power is integral to all that is because power is ultimately the power of being (particularly its ability to overcome nonbeing). It is a mistake then, as Tillich noted, to identify love with the refusal of power, on the one hand, and power with the denial of love, on the other hand.[39] To the contrary, he argues, love inherently acts with power to destroy whatever is against love, which is anything that would deny justice and thus annihilate what should instead be gathered into unity. Nevertheless, as Tillich further insists, love extends forgiveness, seeking always to preserve rather than to destroy the person who is acting against love.[40]

In Tillich's ontological analysis, power—as the power of being—is inherently good and comes ultimately from God, who is the creative source of all being and to whom power is properly attributed. Although love, power, and justice are ambiguous, separated, and at times in conflict in this world, they are, as Tillich maintains, united in the divine ground of being.[41]

Tillich's analysis thus reminds us that the divine, reconciling love is present in the world not only as a force of forgiveness but also as a power that destroys the injustice that opposes love and impedes the ultimate harmony of all. Perhaps, then, more theological attention should be given to the canonical stories of divine judgment that disturb any simplistic account of God's love manifest directly in peace and harmony. Is not the story in Genesis 3 of the exile from the garden, now guarded with a flaming sword, a description of God acting with power to prevent human sin from becoming everlasting? Certainly the Jewish canon has insisted on remembering a history in which God repeatedly threatens destruction when injustice becomes ensconced in the life of the people. And, of course, there is no denying the role of coercive power in the New Testament imagination of Jesus's return as judge to establish the full reign of God: There is much coercion and even violence in the Book of Revelation. Indeed, even while we rightly insist that the divine love suffers—and Christian love must also suffer—with *all* under our current conditions of unjust separation, it should also be remembered that Jesus is described as confronting unjust authority

and acting with power to restore to the community what society had ab-
jected in the name of harmony.[42] Had Jesus not been a real threat to the
authorities of his day, it is hard to imagine why they would have bothered
to crucify him.

A Trinitarian, communion-centered political theology might do well to
remain rooted in the canonical stories of God's power (and of humans
called to use power) to right injustice, even while this theology focuses on
the ultimate reconciliation of all in God. As John de Gruchy has similarly
argued, a Trinitarian theology of God as a perichoretic communion of love
must be complemented by the prophetic tradition of protest against injustice in hopes of a more perfect harmony.[43]

Resisting any account of divine-human communion that stifles the demands of justice or denies the exercise of power necessary to achieve this
justice will, I believe, be further aided by keeping in mind two key points.
First, divine-human communion must be understood as an eschatological
goal that is only partially achievable in this life, so that Christians grapple
honestly with the fact that what is ultimately integrated in the divine remains separated and ambiguous in the world. An adequate political theology
will not proceed as though ultimate harmony is irrelevant to this world,
but neither will such a theology presume that this harmony is completely
available here. The second point to keep in mind is that the Trinity is, and
invites us to, a unity-in-diversity. Focusing on the fact that the goal is not
a uniformity that obliterates otherness, but rather a unity enriched by diversity, Christians may yet be inspired to greater consistency in their rejec-
tions of false harmony and their oppositions to the injustices that are
diminishing the human community—and thus all of us—today.

A Christian Ascetics for the Use of Power

In closing, I would like to mention briefly the importance of Christian formation for a discipleship that seeks harmony with justice. After all, a Christian witness to reconciliation that accepts responsibility for the use of coercive
power in a fallen world requires growth in wisdom, prudence, and mature
judgment, along with a willingness to risk oneself in love. However much
people may yearn for a clear list of "dos" and "don'ts" to follow, there is no
simple prescription for an adequate public praxis. But, then, most of us
have learned that love seldom is simple. We don't always know what is the
best thing to do and, in any case, our motives are often not as selfless and

loving as we believe them to be. The use of coercive power in the service of
love is especially fraught because we are all (including Christians) inclined
to hide our self-serving intentions even from ourselves, and this is true
whether our interests are served by using or by refusing power. Considerable spiritual wisdom is needed to negotiate the complexities of one's own
self-deception as well as the deceptions of the world.

The recent work of Aristotle Papanikolaou is especially helpful here in
pointing to the need for disciplinary practices as formation of the capacity
to love, particularly as Christians struggle to learn to love the stranger—
and the enemy—inevitably encountered in public life.[44] Indeed, it is rather
surprising how little attention has been given to the need for such lay
formation in the Catholic Church, even though the difficulty of resisting the
individualism of our culture and the global economic injustice from which
we in the United States often benefit is quite apparent.[45] Papanikolaou's
insightful analysis reminds us that truth telling and forgiveness (both highlighted in sacramental confession) are essential to communion. Indeed, as
he argues, "Free speech as truthful expression . . . can lead to relationships
of difference that involve respect, mutuality, and friendship not previously
imaginable."[46] At the same time, without the willingness to risk the conflict that so often results from telling an unpleasant truth, relationships (in
society and in personal life) become distorted. Similarly, the ongoing need
for forgiveness for ourselves, as well as for others, is essential given human
failures, limitations, and the reality of continued conflict even in the struggle
for deeper communion.[47]

Given this significance of practices of truth telling and forgiveness
for the development of loving relationships, including the development
of deeper and more honest bonds in public life, Christian communities
would do well to expand these practices beyond the confines of sacramental confession. Our churches might then better prepare us for the
continual giving and receiving of forgiveness and for publicly speaking
and hearing the truth as we seek an ever-greater harmony with God and
each other.

Consideration should also be given to fostering occasions of attentive
engagement with one another in Christian communities and families. If
Christians are to grow in our commitment to inclusive, participatory communities, they need to have deep experiences of the unique contribution
of each to the whole. This may be as simple as returning to such enduring
church practices as potlucks and coffee hours (with electronic devices

turned off!) where Christians grow in relationships and learn to appreciate one another.

The broader Christian community might also want to consider the Quakers' discipline of consensus seeking, rooted in a belief in that of God in everyone. While I wouldn't recommend this process as an efficient decision-making practice for large groups, it deserves attention as a spiritual practice that springs from and reinforces a deep commitment to the idea that each person matters and has a unique perspective to contribute to the good of the whole.[48] Such a practice might increase awareness of the ways this world's political processes lead to the silencing or dismissal of many voices. This discipline of ecclesial consensus seeking might also strengthen resistance to the domineering political discourse so inconsistent with the ideal of an inclusive divine-human communion in which all are valued in their uniqueness.

Conclusion

Our highly interactive yet deeply divided—even atomized—world desperately needs people to come together to resist the increasing inequality and environmental abuse threatening the planet today. Even while democracy is widely touted, at least as a form of secular government, a very undemocratic economic imperialism dominates our planet and imposes conditions of suffering and dehumanization on many for the benefit of a privileged few. It is generally acknowledged (at least theologically) that these destructive conditions are contrary to Christian beliefs about the good of human beings and indeed of creation, yet the Church as a whole has not yet offered the sustained and powerful witness of resistance that Christian faith calls for. Recovering the centrality of the eschatological goal of divine-human communion may prove to be an invaluable resource for forming Christians to resist the new forces of imperialism, provided that we have the wisdom to imagine power in the service of justice and love, and the discipline to accept and use such power appropriately.

Notes

1. The critique of theology as "showing up a little breathless and a little late" is especially familiar to students of David Tracy, who has used the expression in public lectures. See also the use by Matthew L. Lamb, "Liberation Theology and Social Justice," *Process Studies* 14, no. 2 (1985): 102–22.

2. For insightful analyses of various theological arguments against liberal democracy, see Aristotle Papanikolaou, *The Mystical as Political: Democracy and Non-Radical Orthodoxy* (Notre Dame, Ind.: University of Notre Dame Press, 2012), especially 55–86 and 131–46. See also Eric Gregory, *Politics and the Order of Love: An Augustinian Ethic of Democratic Citizenship* (Chicago: University of Chicago Press, 2008), 125–48.

3. As Richard Harries argues, "There is another aspect of democracy, and that is the natural coming together of human beings to order their common life." Richard Harries, "What Makes Us Think that God Wants Democracy?" in *Reinhold Niebuhr and Contemporary Politics,* ed. Richard Harries and Stephen Platten (Oxford: Oxford University Press, 2010), 154–68, here 159.

4. The immediate source for my use of the phrase "the shadow of Constantine" is the apt title of the 3rd Patterson Triennial Conference, "Christianity, Democracy, and the Shadow of Constantine," hosted by Fordham University's Orthodox Christian Studies Center. I am grateful to have had the opportunity to take part in this conference and this essay is enriched by the feedback received from the conference participants.

5. Bruce Bueno de Mesquita and Alastair Smith, *The Dictator's Handbook: Why Bad Behavior Is Almost Always Good Politics* (New York: PublicAffairs, 2011), especially 102–25.

6. In addition to Papanikolaou, *Mystical*; Gregory, *Politics*; and Harries, "What Makes Us Think," see Charles Mathewes, *A Theology of Public Life* (Cambridge: Cambridge University Press, 2007); John W. De Gruchy, "Democracy," in *The Blackwell Companion to Political Theology*, ed. Peter Scott and William Cavanaugh (Oxford: Blackwell Publishing, 2004), 439–54; and, for an authoritative Catholic position, *The Pastoral Constitution on the Church in the Modern World "Gaudium et Spes,"* especially §73–76, http://www.vatican.va /archive/hist_councils/ii_vatican_council/documents/vat-ii_cons_19651207 _gaudium-et-spes_en.html (accessed Sept. 16, 2013).

7. Reinhold Niebuhr, *The Nature and Destiny of Man: A Christian Interpretation.* Vol. 2, *Human Destiny* (New York: Charles Scribner's Sons, 1943), 216.

8. Due to the limited nature of this essay and its focus on democracy, the perspective developed here is more anthropomorphic than Christianity ought to be. What is presented here is by no means intended to be a fully adequate treatment of Christian hope, which would require more attention to the inherent dignity and value of nonhuman life.

9. See especially Marcella Maria Althaus-Reid, "Demythologizing Liberation Theology: Reflections on Power, Poverty, and Sexuality," in *The Cambridge Companion to Liberation Theology,* ed. Christopher Rowland (Cambridge; New York: Cambridge University Press, 2007), 123–36.

10. *The Dogmatic Constitution on the Church "Lumen Gentium,"* §1, http://
www.vatican.va/archive/hist_councils/ii_vatican_council/documents/vat-ii
_const_19641121_lumen-gentium_en.html (accessed Sept. 16, 2013).

11. "The Church recognizes that worthy elements are found in today's social
movements, especially an evolution toward unity, a process of wholesome
socialization and of association in civic and economic realms. The promotion
of unity belongs to the innermost nature of the Church, for she is, 'thanks to
her relationship with Christ, a sacramental sign and an instrument of intimate
union with God, and of the unity of the whole human race'" *(Gaudium
et Spes,* §42).

12. On the centrality of *theosis* in Orthodox theology, in addition to
Papanikolaou, *Mystical,* see also his *Being with God: Trinity, Apophaticism, and
Divine-Human Communion* (Notre Dame, Ind.: University of Notre Dame
Press, 2006). For a discussion of the influence of Orthodox though on the
Second Vatican Council, see Marie-Dominique Chenu, "The New Awareness of
the Trinitarian Basis of the Church," in *Where Does the Church Stand?* Con-
cilium 146, ed. Giuseppe Alberigo and Gustavo Gutierrez (New York: Seabury,
1981), 14–21.

13. World Council of Churches, *The Church: Towards a Common Vision,*
Faith and Order Paper no. 214 (Geneva, Switzerland: World Council of
Churches Publications, 2013), esp. 5. See also the earlier "The Nature and
Mission of the Church: A Stage on the Way to a Common Statement," Faith
and Order Paper no. 198, 15 December 2005, http://www.oikoumene.org/en
/resources/documents/wcc-commissions/faith-and-order-commission/i-unity
-the-church-and-its-mission/the-nature-and-mission-of-the-church-a-stage-on
-the-way-to-a-common-statement (accessed 16 September 2013).

14. See especially John Milbank, *Theology and Social Theory: Beyond Secular
Reason* (Cambridge, Mass.: Blackwell, 1990) and Miroslav Volf, *After Our
Likeness: The Church as the Image of the Trinity* (Grand Rapids, Mich.:
Eerdmans, 1998).

15. See especially Niebuhr, *Nature,* vol. 2, 68–97.

16. For a few of the most notable contributions to this theological conversation, see Leonardo Boff, *Trinity and Society* (Maryknoll, N.Y.: Orbis Books,
1988); Elizabeth A. Johnson, *She Who Is: The Mystery of God in Feminist
Theological Discourse* (New York: Crossroad, 1992); and Catherine Mowry
LaCugna, *God for Us: The Trinity and Christian Life* (San Francisco: Harper,
1993); as well as Papanikolaou, *Being.*

17. See especially Orlando O. Espín, *Idol and Grace: On Traditioning and
Subversive Hope* (Maryknoll, N.Y.: Orbis Books, 2014).

18. See Pantelis Kalaïtzidis, *Orthodoxy and Political Theology* (Geneva: World
Council of Churches, 2012), esp. 15–44; and Papanikolaou, *Mystical,* 15–54.

See also the discussion in Gerard Mannion, *Ecclesiology and Postmodernity: Questions for the Church in Our Time* (Collegeville, Minn.: Liturgical Press, 2007), especially 175–91.

19. While the emphasis on divine-human communion has been recently recovered in Western Christianity, it has remained a central concept in Orthodox Christianity. However, both Western and Orthodox Christianity for different reasons are currently exploring the political implications of a communion-centered Christianity. See Papanikolaou, *Mystical,* especially 9–12; Radovan Bionic, *The Orthodox Church in the 21st Century* (Belgrade: EKOPRESS, 2009); and Mathewes, *Theology.*

20. Of course, Catholic Social Thought can also be interpreted as a development of general moral principles available to all. Insofar as Christians believe that God made humans for communion, the principles that guide human flourishing will reflect this human orientation toward mutual relations.

21. Anthony Paul Smith, "The Judgment of God and the Immeasurable: Political Theology and Organization of Power," *Political Theology* 12, no. 1 (2011): 689–86; and Ben Quash, "Radical Orthodoxy's Critique of Niebuhr," in *Reinhold Niebuhr,* ed. Harries and Platten, 58–70, for perceptive discussions of the priority of peace in Milbank.

22. Robin W. Lovin, "Reinhold Niebuhr in Historical Perspective," in *Reinhold Niebuhr,* ed. Harries and Platten, 6–17, here 11.

23. Among his many writings espousing pacifism, see especially Stanley Hauerwas, *The Peaceable Kingdom: A Primer in Christian Ethics* (London: SCM, 1984); see also John Milbank, "The Poverty of Niebuhrianism," in his *The Word Made Strange: Theology, Language, Culture* (Oxford: Blackwell Publishers, 1997), 233–54.

24. Milbank, *Theology,* 411. To be sure, there is much to be said for the forgiveness Milbank advocates, even as a public alternative to cycles of violence.

25. See especially Ewa Płonowska Ziarek, *An Ethics of Dissensus: Postmodernity, Feminism, and the Politics of Radical Democracy* (Stanford: Stanford University Press, 2001); Iris Marion Young, *Justice and the Politics of Difference* (Princeton: Princeton University Press, 1990); and Bonnie Honig, ed., *Feminist Interpretations of Hannah Arendt* (University Park: Pennsylvania State University, 1995).

26. See, for example, the Congregation for the Doctrine of the Faith's 2004 "Letter to the Bishops of the Catholic Church on the Collaboration of Men and Women in the Church and in the World," http://www.vatican.va/roman_curia/congregations/cfaith/documents/rc_con_cfaith_doc_20040731_collaboration_en.html (accessed Sept. 16, 2013).

27. Mannion, *Ecclesiology,* 43–71.

28. It should be noted that the failure to confront the Catholic hierarchy over persistent patterns of sex abuse did the Church no good and caused great harm to countless children.

29. See, for example, the discussion in David L. Schindler, *Heart of the World, Center of the Church: Communio Ecclesiology, Liberalism, and Liberation* (Grand Rapids, Mich.: Eerdmans, 1996), 237–74.

30. See especially the thoughtful discussion of Carl Schmitt's monarchical and authoritarian political theology in Kalaïtzidis, *Orthodoxy*, 15–44.

31. See especially Niebuhr, *Nature* vol. 2, 265–69 and the discussion in Tony Lee Richie, "Pragmatism, Power, and Politics: A Pentecostal Conversation with President Obama's Favorite Theologian, Reinhold Niebuhr," in *Pneuma* 32 (2010): 241–60.

32. See, for example, the discussion in Debra Dean Murphy, "Power Politics, and Difference: A Feminist Response to John Milbank," *Modern Theology* 10, no. 2 (April 1994): 131–42, as well as the discussion of Hannah Arendt's concept of power in Honig, ed., *Feminist Interpretations.*

33. Surely coercion is inevitable in the raising of children, since any limits (or "natural" consequences) that parents set involve the use of power to coerce behavior. A similar reality is evident in teaching: How many students would find the time to do all their assignments carefully if there were no penalty compelling them?

34. As Anthony Paul Smith astutely observes, "Politics is largely concerned with the organization of power" (Smith, "Judgment," 69).

35. Among his many arguments for a distinctively countercultural church witness to the world, see especially Stanley Hauerwas, *With the Grain of the Universe: The Church's Witness and Natural Theology* (Grand Rapids, Mich.: Brazos Press, 2001), 205–41.

36. Paul Tillich, *Love, Power and Justice: Ontological Analyses and Ethical Applications* (Oxford: Oxford University Press, 1954).

37. Tillich, *Love*, 62, 67–71.

38. Tillich acknowledges that self-sacrifice may be necessary, but this self-sacrifice must be in accord with the demands of a justice that ultimately fulfills the self—even if beyond the limits of this mortal life—rather than a self-surrender that destroys the self and its development. See especially *Love*, 69, 83.

39. Tillich, *Love*, 11.

40. Tillich, *Love*, 114.

41. Tillich, *Love*, 108.

42. See, for example, John Dominic Crossan's analysis of the meaning of Jesus's healings in his *Jesus: A Revolutionary Biography* (San Francisco: Harper-Collins, 1994), especially 85–114.

43. De Gruchy, "Democracy," 449–50.

44. Papanikolaou, *Mystical,* 163–94.

45. My own Catholic tradition has developed extensive formation programs for clergy and vowed religious, but has largely neglected the formation needs of the laity who are theoretically most responsible for the public witness of the church. The recent increase in availability and popularity of lay spiritual direction may prove especially significant in filling this gap, particularly if this direction provides disciplined guidance that avoids an individualistic and therapeutic approach alone, and instead truly challenges Christians to grow in political wisdom and humility.

46. Papanikolaou, *Mystical,* 194.

47. At times, forgiveness may be especially necessary for a truth telling that is unduly harsh or, as Papanikolaou observes, demonic, in that it is wielded to destroy rather than to restore right relationship. See *Mystical,* 198.

48. A good descriptive analysis of Quaker consensus can be found in Michael J. Sheeran, *Beyond Majority Rule: Voteless Decisions in the Society of Friends* (Philadelphia: Philadelphia Yearly Meeting of Religious Society of Friends, 1983).

STRANGE FRUIT

AUGUSTINE, LIBERALISM, AND THE GOOD SAMARITAN

Eric Gregory

Anotable feature of contemporary Anglo-American theology is the welcome revival of engagement with Orthodoxy. But it is a less prominent feature of the resurgent interest in "political theology." This neglect is unfortunate. There are historical and historiographical reasons for a preoccupation with the Latin West, especially given the vexed relation of Augustinianism to democratic constitutional traditions mediated by followers of Augustine and his critics. When Orthodoxy does appear, familiar charges of caesaropapism or otherworldliness are seldom far behind. Augustinians sometimes sponsor such readings, painting Constantinianism with a Eusebian face in order to relieve themselves of theocratic misunderstanding or to contrast their concern for the dynamism of history with the ahistorical speculations of Greek metaphysics. Like many in the Orthodox tradition, modern Augustinians have worked hard to reject the caricature of "the individual striving for a mystical, nonhistorical, world-denying union with God."[1] Both traditions remain subject to similar challenges in a secular age.

For example, the sometimes-cramped alternatives in political theory marginalize their shared concern with relating the incarnational and eschatological dimensions of the church's witness to a cosmic redemption of history. Such redemption must take account of the dramatic ruptures that follow any Christian understanding of sin and the conditions of politics. But, as one recent Orthodox theologian has argued, a redemptive vision "cannot be dissociated from the dialectic between the present and future, between affirmation and denial of the world, between participation in politics (the life of the city) and the transcendence of politics."[2] That basic, shared concern is what I want to pursue in order to think about the theological significance of democratic political *action in time*, though not in any explicit comparative fashion.

In the background, recall familiar tensions between supposedly world-affirming incarnational Constantinians and world-denying cruciform sectarians. These tensions, which frame much of contemporary political theology, map onto what Luke Bretherton helpfully describes as "Constantinian triumphalism" and "Donatist separatism."[3] Often constructed as ideal types for broader polemical purposes, these temptations nonetheless give rise to temporal forgetfulness in thinking about political life. Liberal realists tend to emphasize eschatological deferral in ways that separate civic life from ethical and spiritual value. Antiliberals tend to emphasize an apocalyptic ecclesiology that imagines the Church as the only site of formation in virtue and participation in eternity. To speak theologically, both neglect the porous fluidity of one world and one history groaning toward fulfillment in Christ. This fulfillment imagines an immanent teleology that draws together creation and redemption without conflating the two.

The topic of this essay is not Augustine as such. Our topic is time, or less ambitiously, an invitation to think about time, a venerable Augustinian and Platonic theme. It is one that has received less theological attention than we might expect, particularly given the "strange fruit" of the *spatial* separation of church and state that Augustine's modern interpreters have supposedly found in his pregnant biblical imagery of "two loves" and "two cities" in this time between the times. Oliver O'Donovan has complicated this post-Hobbesian separation of religion and politics by rediscovering a vision of "politics not as a self-enclosed field of human endeavour but as the theatre of the divine self-disclosure."[4] On these terms, the emergence of democracy can be linked to divine purposes in history. O'Donovan's own juridical conception of government does constrain our expectations of political institutions. Such institutions are taken to be indirect witnesses to divine providence in humble recognition of their distinctive temporal purposes. The state, on O'Donovan's view, is not an end in itself. It exists in the service of the historical mission of the Church. Nonetheless, for O'Donovan, the state "remains under the direction of the First Person of the Trinity; it is not filled with the Holy Spirit at Pentecost."[5] The state, under the authority of God, has its historical role in preserving the common good and securing conditions for the preaching of the gospel.

Its political prominence—and its representative claim on our identity—
fades in the face of the gathered Christian community. And yet, even
O'Donovan's distinction and emphasis on the ambiguities of history open
"an account of secular authority which presumes neither that the Christ-
event never occurred nor that the sovereignty of Christ is now transparent
and uncontested."[6]

Analogizing political history and salvation history offers a more direct
theological route for evaluating democratic action than more familiar terms
like realism and idealism or optimism and pessimism. These latter categories can be helpful for heuristic purposes. But they are not native to Christian theology and risk abstraction. No politics can save us, Augustinians
consistently remind us, but can politics teach us anything about the nature
of salvation in time? Will meaning in history always only be a retrospec-
tive? Is politics always only remedial beating back of sinful desire? I am
here provoked by what my colleague Jeffrey Stout has called a pressing
question for modern Christian theology: "Is it not possible to discern the
workings of the Holy Spirit, and thus some reflection of God's redemptive
activity, in modern democratic aspirations?"[7] If all historical events are
marked by God's entry into time, might political history also bear witness
not only to the first person of the Trinity but also to Christ and the Spirit
that testifies to Christ? To put it more concretely, by way of example, might
we imagine the civil rights movement or the struggle against apartheid as
Christian events for both church and society, a partial embodiment of that
kingdom from "every nation, tribe, people, and language" (Revelation 7:9)?
Would this reading of history reflect a dangerous desire to baptize the
secular, a promiscuous sacramentalism confusing God's providence with
salvation? How can we distinguish pneumatological enthusiasm from
authentic Christian faith in the wondrous yet fugitive mixing of time with
eternity? My remarks have three parts, tracking roughly from Augustine's
piety to its modern appropriations and moral sentiment in a democratic
culture anxious about politics itself.

Piety and Augustinian Politics

James O'Donnell tells us that "Augustine was lucky that he never had to
read anything like Augustine."[8] We should respect the distance of this
Berber from the margins of empire, famous for his own difficulties with
time. I want to think about what his strangeness might mean for us,

whether you adore or despise Augustine, in part because he gave Christianity a voice that echoes with us today. Augustine's enchantment not only declared things in this world to be sacred. He experienced the world as sacred, participating in the goodness of his crucified deity. For Augustine, unlike fallen angels, those pure intellects without bodies that fall completely, we embodied and historical creatures ascend and descend with restless desire for wholeness that he thought was part of human nature. Such wholeness will always be incomplete, groaning in the "not yet" of history. Yet there is no neutrality. All of life, and so all of time and all of politics, are bound up with our fellowship in God.

Augustine was neither a democrat nor what we might call an ardent political activist. Democratic participation, for the most part, is a distinctively modern phenomenon made possible by cultural developments unknown to the ancients. Indeed, Augustine is not the first name on a list for those known for democratic virtues of self-restraint, respect for diversity, concern for social justice, and openness to deliberation. He was a culture warrior, preoccupied with psychic distortions wrought by what he took to be counterfeit mythologies of glory and false claims to achieved justice. His polemics left him vulnerable to caricature and his own rhetorical excess. For Augustine, however, it was pagan culture that did not have the resources to adequately name its own self-deception, its desire to revel only in its own glory, to worship itself.

His *City of God* responds to the anxieties of pagans and Christians made distraught by the fall of Rome. There are few analogies in modern history to this distress and moral panic. I tell my students to picture 9/11 multiplied by ten thousand. Augustine's great work is his reflection on this shattered world. As with 9/11, many sought scapegoats to blame. Pagans blamed the Christians for worshipping the wrong gods (namely, the one God that they were too uptight about) and failing to keep up the proper civic practices because of their meek religion of the Sermon on the Mount. In response, Augustine claimed that the pagans had turned imperial ambition into a religion. Christians could make the same mistake after Rome's apparent conversion to God's purposes. This mistake reflects the great temptation of politics identified by Augustine as idolatry. It is a profound biblical theme, taken up by Israel's prophets, and powerfully echoed in democratic culture by Abraham Lincoln's second inaugural address. Yet, despite his suspicion of Rome's pretension, Augustine could still see that its imperfect peace revealed a natural law in the order of nature. Robbers themselves maintain "some shadow of peace."[9] And, by God's providence, "even the heavenly city . . . while in its state of pilgrimage, avails itself of the peace of earth."[10] History has its ironies, as Reinhold Niebuhr tells us. But it is not tragic. Temporal peace is known both by comparison and contrast with this eternal peace.

In diagnosing this exilic yearning, Augustine is thought to "secularize" politics, stretching history with eschatological tension, hoping for a far-off country and the resurrection of the dead. Here we find something like an apophatic political theology, veiled in the ambiguity of pilgrimage and sin-stained temporality. Politics, like our experience of grace, operates more in the modality of healing than elevation. It tempers imperfection rather than tutors perfection. This is the realist's persistent wisdom. But political activity also speaks to some end, albeit chastened by the future rather than the present dimensions of salvation.

A common distinction among Augustinians finds a sociality that is natural and a politics that is sinful. In fact, this is sometimes thought to distinguish Augustinians from other Christian political traditions, notably heirs of Thomas Aquinas. For Augustinians, politics is that part of providential history divided by time after Babel. According to Romans 13, and given our misdirected loves, the purpose of politics is to restrain the wicked with a measure of "earthly" justice and peace for the time being. Redemption waits for the fullness of time. It is historical, but it is not dependent upon the process of time.

So Augustinians wait for the kingdom. They do not build the kingdom. Augustine, however, did not sit quietly with a clenched fist watching his clock with despair. This reputation risks banality. His unmasking of Rome's idolatry suggests a powerful historical consciousness that human forms change. Nothing is permanent. He was a busy leader, judging and governing a community through political controversy and economic hard times. In fact, we find him writing letters to public officials encouraging them to use their offices, with humility and lamenting necessity, for the promotion of Christian reconciliation. This suggests that not all earthly politics is prodigal. To be sure, Augustine's premodern experience with law and economics placed severe constraints on his political imagination, confirming the darker moments of his theology. It would be left to later Christian thought to develop notions of structural reform that might make possible goods we otherwise could not enjoy. Such reformers would seek to modify our political situation, even if we cannot radically change the structures of human desire. I happen to think Augustine could distinguish the failing empire from the republic, Theodosius from Nero, and Regulus from other pagans. He knew the slave trade and torture were wicked practices. In a different age, he might have launched efforts to abolish them. He did not.

Modern Appropriations

Later reformers did take inspiration from Augustine, mining the anthropology and eschatology of Book 19 of the *City of God* for democratic purposes of a low-flying variety. They took their counsel from Augustine's vision of the limits of politics and the fragile possibilities of just action. In the twentieth century, figures like Reinhold Niebuhr and Robert Markus found Augustinian resources that might aid democrats facing the crises of totalitarianism and fascism. But demands for a truly just politics were channeled by a release valve that either funded compensation in another world or took comfort in the value of an ethical personality protected from the flux of this world. These versions of Augustinian politics typically equated a moralized politics with sentimentalism. In particular, invocations of love in conceptions of political life were met with suspicion. While Niebuhr's Augustinianism, which can degenerate into vulgar pragmatism, has returned to public discussions via President Barack Obama and his defenders, things have changed in the academy.

Different varieties of Augustinian liberalism remain, including a republicanism committed to principle exemplified in a figure like Martin Luther King Jr. By my lights, he is America's greatest (and most radical) Augustinian, tapping into Augustine's notions of both love and sin. His analysis of America's loves was able to historicize rather than simply psychologize injustice, offering a vision of a "beloved community" that joined the structural and the personal by diagnosing failures of will as much as flaws of will. Many of today's Augustinians, however, adopt Augustine's critique of empire in order to expose democratic action as a repressed work of violence. For some, democratic action is itself idolatrous.

Augustine's language of *using* the world and *enjoying* God can drain activity in time from theological significance, dreaming only of reconciliation beyond history. Politics is just one example of misplaced faith. But supposed Neoplatonic oppositional contrasts betray Augustine's effort to refuse a tournament of competitive loves between God and the world, especially one predicated on strong distinctions between "natural" and "supernatural." A competition between time and eternity, between the inner and the outer, is what his Christology actually rejects. Here, I think, is a powerful resource for what Pantelis Kalaïtzidis calls "the hidden Christological dimension of social and political action on behalf of our neighbor."[11] Political action, which promotes just relations among persons, becomes a means by which one loves God and neighbor.

Such hiddenness, however, risks virtual denial by many political Augustinians. They are confident in their rejection of any political confidence. Augustine admittedly confessed a hope familiar to both Eastern and Western traditions: We only find happiness and redemption in the afterlife. His restless heart yearned for something more than the fairer distribution of scarce resources, the hope of modern democratic politics. He longed for a shared redemption of the world and its common objects of love. Such freedom could only be found after death. This Augustine, it might be thought, could sing the blues only as a lament for the mediocrity of the fallen human condition in exile. Unlike Billie Holiday's singing of the song "Strange Fruit" in which the "strange fruit" is "hanging from the poplar trees"[12]—which like Augustine's critique of Rome, unmasked the innocence of American democracy—Augustine's meditations on eating forbidden fruit and a Christ nailed to a tree tend not to inspire protest or reform, let alone revolutionary ambition in a world incapable of moral redress. They provide occasions for mourning, possibly the consolation of spontaneous compassion as symbolic gesture.

For critics of dour Augustinianism, this is the world of merciful slave owners, compassionate doomsayers, or perhaps, bourgeois consumers of fair-trade goods who write checks to Oxfam from time to time. Those more hopeful about democratic action worry about this Augustinian legacy, one that can make Christians comfortable with injustice or lethargic in despairing fatalism. Highlighting the limits of politics can promote a charity complicit with injustice, a benevolence that supports domination and exploitation just as much as innocent hopes in the prospects of liberalism.

Humanitarians and Good Samaritans

This theme, launched by many Enlightenment figures disappointed with Christian politics of charity, has been powerfully examined in recent critical discussions of the rise of humanitarianism and the ideology of "humani-tarian space."[13] While scholars raise questions about the exclusionary politics of humanitarian practices (now predicated on the "empire" of neo-liberalism), many of my Princeton students, disillusioned by modern poli-tics and hungering for moral clarity, see such direct action as the last best hope to make bearable an unbearable world. Hearing their voices has led me to that curious and fraught last figure in my title. The story of the Good Samaritan is often heralded as a defining moment in the universalism of Christian charity, an exemplar of humanitarian concern for the suffering of strangers. Augustine's influential reading of the parable helped to de-velop its reception in this egalitarian direction.

But much of modern politics (and theology) subsumes benevolence under the rubric of justice, or considers it only a second-best response to injustice. Justice is seen as the primary virtue of politics lest we fall prey to libertarian or conservative attacks on the welfare state. After Kant and Nietzsche, moreover, charity is seen by many as a semblance of political virtue that obscures the demands of justice. It is hard to read about the sociology of compassion without tripping over references to "the will to power," "class control," and "disciplining technologies." If you google "hu-manitarianism," for example, you immediately find titles like *The Dark Sides of Virtue* or *Humanitarianism in Question*.[14] Tracing links between humanitarianism and colonialism has been a major preoccupation of his-torians, yielding a consensus that movements like the abolition of slavery were motivated by far more than the morality of compassion.[15] Charles Tay-lor has argued that the moral demandingness of modern politics can itself be traced to secular transformations of the parable. In his long story about our new moral order and the pressures of time, Taylor expresses a Webe-rian lament about the nature and character of these demands that form their own guilty political subjects and missionary agendas. He argues that modern ethics and politics have distorted the message of the Good Samari-tan by reducing its prescriptions to a rigorous code in an immanent frame. For him, the parable must be understood as an event, a fleshly act of love in time that participates in the life of God.

Augustinians have their own resources to support each of these suspi-cions. Christian charity, funded by Augustine's emphasis on love as the form of worshipping God, has fostered compelling commitments to the equal dignity of persons and the creation of democratic institutions that manifest this commitment in ways that do not rely solely on a good will.

It also has a shadow side, rendering victims of injustice merely as objects of suffering. Far from an expression of cosmopolitan solidarity, humanitarianism can become the mask worn by the powerful, the supposed virtue confessed by the paternalist and the realist.[16]

So humanitarianism is as contested as democracy and Augustinianism. Some humanitarians link their actions to broader political commitments to development; others resist such linkage in the name of charity and the distinct identity of victims. These debates, however, reveal more than they sometimes admit in their discussions of moral obligation and the legacy of Christian charity. They raise fundamental questions about how to interpret the character of life in our world as such (including judgments about history). For example, anthropologist Peter Redfield's work in comparing Albert Schweitzer's medical mission, the Red Cross, and Médecins Sans Frontières highlights the subtle yet profound religious difference in modern humanitarianism that finds "moral certainty in alleviating anguish and protecting life" and a "distinctly material project of salvation."[17] Redfield prefers to characterize this project as a reoccupation of the religious rather than its transposition, though others argue that humanitarian practices are best understood as a secular theodicy, accenting terms of "spiritual awakening" and "vocation" now in the face of constant emergency.[18]

Conclusion

Henry Kissinger once quipped that the secret of success in life is low expectations, something psychologists have labeled "defensive pessimism," a strategy of damage control to manage anxiety and despair. Things can always get worse, but they are always better than we deserve. In politics, as in the rest of life, there are no good choices, only lesser evils, full of sacrifice: not just in places like Syria and Afghanistan, but everywhere, anytime. Such bleakness is taken to be Augustine's tonic for a world that hopes too much from politics.

Peter Kaufman recently has reminded us of the political implications of how bad Augustine thought the bad news of Genesis and the tumult of North Africa really was. For all the apparent success we might have in struggling against the darkness, political action "amounts to little more than damage control in dystopia."[19] The *City of God*, Kaufman tells us, is Augustine's "disorienting device for those who [grow] too comfortable with time."[20] Augustine was "convinced that Christianity could not redeem terrestrial cities. Life in time was a Gulag or—in current coin—a Gitmo, a detention camp."[21] Time is anything but comfortable.

All politics involves loss, even the most liberal thinkers admit to us, either because the goods of life are themselves in conflict, or as Augustine might have it, because the most fundamental battles are problems internal to the will. Augustine's moderation does offer a cautious wisdom about politics, perhaps not too dissimilar from Rawlsian meditations on realistic utopia. But Augustine's metaphors for politics are pastoral and medicinal, rather than technocratic or economic, requiring delicate and discerning practical skills, calling into question the confident psychologies that support many of today's moral and political theories, including both humanitarians *and* their critics. Kaufman's challenge to Augustinian liberals is formidable, posing the most difficult questions for those trying to imagine a different Augustine for our time. Differences may arise not simply from interpreting the historical Augustine, but from assessing the needs of our age. We might need to transcend some Augustinian lessons we have learned too well, including the fear of demanding too much from our politics and ourselves. Augustine's allegorical, even parabolic, reading of history resists closure and resignation. Even-tempered aspirations should not be trapped in a God-forsaken time that is only a race to death, loitering on the stage of a Samuel Beckett play.

Never demoralized, Augustine sought to provide for a confused, disillusioned, and anxious culture something to live for, rather than simply stand against. There is no certain knowledge, and constant recognition of limits, but can the exercise of political virtues—responsive to true human goods—be a part of the life of piety, even proleptically referred to those virtues perfected in heaven? Augustine's vision of participation in excellence complicates his received dualisms because being for the good involves being for particular goods, even if our virtues are fragmented, frail, and partial, always resisting our integrative efforts. Given a God who suffers time with us, the perfecting of virtue requires such time. On my reading, Augustine's heavenly city cannot erase time's virtues. They are consummated, but not consumed.

Salvation may not be internal to history, but it is also not thoroughly external: "Time stands as both the wound of existence and as the salve necessary for healing this wound."[22] I have not offered a theology of history, let alone prophecy, but I think more reflection in this direction might re-lieve possible tensions between anti-Pelagian doubts about politics and their hyper-Augustinian refusal. It might also allow for a deeper recognition of the plurality of moral excellences nurtured in the graced time that is po-litical history.

Theological interpretation of political history, in a world with real detention camps, is always in danger of self-deception and excess. Augus-tinians, at their best, remain critics of empires and nationalisms (especially ones that lay claim to democratic virtue). But I have suggested a political Augustinianism that wants to be more than a counsel against idolatry risks saying something about the mysterious and hidden ways of God, even in political action. Some still need to be reminded of Augustinian limits and the enigmas of temporal life. But in a world that has largely abandoned any hopes for redemption (in this life or the next), articulating the possi-bility of redemptive agency in the world strikes me as urgent. Such a po-litical theology might offer more than critique, even for those who long for another city after time.

Notes

1. Aristotle Papanikolaou, *The Mystical as Political: Democracy and Non-Radical Orthodoxy* (Notre Dame, Ind.: University of Notre Dame Press, 2012), 1.

2. Pantelis Kalaïtzidis, *Orthodoxy and Political Theology* (Geneva: World Council of Churches Publications, 2012), 138.

3. Luke Bretherton, *Christianity and Contemporary Politics* (Oxford: Black-well Publishers, 2010), 82. Bretherton argues that Augustinian (and Pauline) eschatology aims to avoid a triumphalism that is "marked by an expectation of progress until the church overcomes the world" and a separatism "wherein history is oriented by regress or movement away from God."

4. Oliver O'Donovan, *The Desire of the Nations: Rediscovering the Roots of Political Theology* (Cambridge: Cambridge University Press, 1996), 82.

5. Oliver O'Donovan, "Response to Gerrit de Kruijf," in *A Royal Priesthood? The Use of the Bible Ethically and Politically: A Dialogue with Oliver O'Donovan*, ed. Craig Bartholomew, Jonathan Chaplin, Robert Song, and Al Wolters (Grand Rapids, Mich.: Zondervan, 2002), 239.

6. O'Donovan, "Response," 146. For a more explicit discussion of O'Donovan on politics and salvation history, see Eric Gregory, "The Boldness of Analogy: Civic Virtues and Augustinian Eudaimonism," in *The Authority of*

the Gospel: Explorations in Moral and Political Theology in Honour of Oliver O'Donovan, ed. Brent Waters and Robert Song (Grand Rapids, Mich.: Eerdmans, forthcoming).

7. Jeffrey Stout, *Democracy and Tradition* (Princeton: Princeton University Press, 2004), 104.

8. James O'Donnell, *Augustine: A New Biography* (New York: HarperCollins, 2005), 125.

9. Augustine, *City of God*, trans. R.W. Dyson (Cambridge: Cambridge University Press, 1998), 19.12.

10. Augustine, *City of God* 19.17.

11. Kalaïtzidis, *Orthodoxy and Political Theology*, 122.

12. Billie Holiday. *Strange Fruit*, by Abel Meeropol. In *The Best of Billie Holiday: 20ᵗʰ Century Masters*. Hip-O 589995. CD. 2002. Recorded 1939.

13. See, for example, Didier Fassin, *Humanitarian Reason: A Moral History of the Present* (Berkeley: University of California Press, 2012).

14. David Kennedy, *The Dark Sides of Virtue: Reassessing International Humanitarianism* (Princeton: Princeton University Press, 2004) and *Humanitarianism in Question: Politics, Power, and Ethics*, ed. Michael Barnett and Thomas G. Weiss (Ithaca, N.Y.: Cornell University Press, 2008).

15. See, for example, David Brion Davis, *The Problem of Slavery in Western Culture* (Ithaca, N.Y.: Cornell University Press, 1966). According to Davis, "Antislavery was a highly selective response to labor exploitation. It provided an outlet for demonstrating Christian concern for human suffering and injustice, and yet thereby gave a certain moral insulation to economic activities less visibly dependent on human suffering and injustice" (251).

16. On welfare and pity, see Avishai Margalit, *The Decent Society* (Cambridge, Mass.: Harvard University Press, 1998). For an elegant, and exceptional, defense of state welfare provisions based on the parable of the Good Samaritan, see Jeremy Waldron, "Welfare and Images of Charity," *The Philosophical Quarterly* 36, no. 415 (October 1986): 463–82.

17. Peter Redfield, "Secular Humanitarianism and the Value of Life," in *What Matters? Ethnographies of Value in a Not So Secular Age*, ed. Courtney Bender and Ann Taves (New York: Columbia University Press, 2012), 144–78, here 148 and 169.

18. On the spirituality of secular humanitarianism, see Stephen Hopgood, *Keepers of the Flame: Understanding Amnesty International* (Ithaca, N.Y.: Cornell University Press, 2006).

19. Peter Iver Kaufman, "Augustine's Dystopia," in *Augustine's City of God: A Critical Guide*, ed. James Wetzel (Cambridge: Cambridge University Press, 2012), 55–74, here 57.

20. Peter Iver Kaufman, "Christian Realism and Augustinian (?) Liberalism," *Journal of Religious Ethics* 38, no. 4 (December 2010): 699–724, here 719.

21. Kaufman, "Augustine's Dystopia," 55–56.

22. Richard Avramenko, "The Wound and Salve of Time: Augustine's Politics of Human Happiness," *The Review of Metaphysics* 60, no .4 (June 2007): 779–811, here 784.

An Orthodox Encounter with Liberal Democracy

Emmanuel Clapsis

The majority of the Orthodox churches, living in liberal democratic societies, are free to worship God and live the fullness of the Orthodox tradition in its diverse ethnic and cultural expressions. However, the freedom that liberal democratic societies ascribe to their citizens generates an unprecedented pluralism of voluntary communities and lifestyles, which has challenged the central role that the Orthodox Church played in moral formation in traditional societies. The attitudes and sensibilities that the Orthodox churches are called to develop within the contextual realities of liberal democracies are highly contested issues among Orthodox theologians today. Some face the new contextual realities with an alarmist attitude, fearing the capitulation of the Orthodox Church to liberal sensibilities. They adopt an adversarial, activist posture against the modernizing liberal societies, proposing defensive demarcations of radical separation between Orthodoxy and other Christian churches, other religions, and liberal democracy in general. They seek to construct the identity of the Orthodox Church in opposition to all who are not Orthodox, espousing a stringent, hierarchical, authoritarian, and exclusivist vision of what the Orthodox Church should be, in order to maintain the purity of Orthodoxy. Others perceive the changing social realities of liberal societies as opportunities to reconfigure and communicate the Orthodox faith and tradition without compromising the Church's particularity. Still others, for the sake of relevance and ecumenical collaboration, may have unconsciously surrendered the particularity of the Orthodox tradition, reducing the Church to a cultural agency that legitimates for its members the prevailing social realities.

Generally, this debate expresses the fear and the anxiety of some about the possible loss of the unique Orthodox identity and its capitulation to the pluralistic culture of liberal democracy as well as the strong belief of others that the Orthodox ethos can be embodied in and through different socio-cultural delineations, aspirations, and achievements. Formally, it can be argued that the Orthodox churches, despite the objections of the tradition-alists, through their active participation in the ecumenical movement and interfaith collaboration have signaled the abandonment of attitudes of stringent and defensive demarcation, rejecting sectarianism and focusing their attention on the task of witnessing God's love for all.[1]

In this essay, I will focus on the challenges that liberal democracy poses to the traditional understanding of the Church's mission and witness in the world and how it has already affected the life of the Church and its structures of authority. Furthermore, I will explore the role of the Ortho-dox Church in public life once it has critically accepted the intrinsic plu-ralism that liberal democracy generates. Perhaps this paper is an exercise in theological and moral imagination reflecting not where the Orthodox churches actually stand in relation to liberal democracy, but how they should understand their place guided by the fullness of the Orthodox faith, its eschatological orientation, and the Eucharistic experience that decisively shapes the mind of Orthodoxy.

Freedom in Liberal Societies

In liberal societies, personal freedom has priority over social unity, regard-less of whether this unity is imposed by tradition or modernizing institu-tions and ideologies. The individual is free to act in ways that are impossible in traditional societies. He can collaborate with others to form freely chosen communities, without the constraints of ethnic, religious, or class identity, or choose life-goals that go beyond the boundaries of traditional expectations and norms. In that context, he can fashion and practice di-verse patterns of life that express individual creativity and aspiration. He may choose from a range of possibilities that may have been denied to him by a traditionally prescribed social order. Freedom in liberal societies is in-terpreted purely and exclusively as absence of constraint on the possibili-ties of seeking self-fulfillment and self-discovery. It might lead some to a rejection of all traditions, while others might be led to a free appreciation of tradition as a resource for the development of communal life based on mutual respect and affinity.

Citizens in liberal democratic societies are free to pursue their self-interests, and choose to relate to other persons only for the purpose of gratifying their own desires. The notion of *self* in such an attitude can be expanded to include a particular group of people, which acts like a selfish person in relation to other groups, defining and claiming the common good at the expense of others. In such relationships the others are reduced to objects of use, often expressed by economic exploitation and commodification, in acts of psychological and emotional manipulation, or in their reduction to objects of sexual gratification. These dominative and exploitative relationships tell the negative story of liberal societies, in which individual freedom becomes a license to exploit others. Freedom, however, provides another possibility to the citizens of a liberal democracy that leads to the recognition of discovering the importance of relationships as indispensable elements of human identity. It leads them to the recognition that it is only in life-sustaining and transforming relationships of love that human fulfillment can be experienced. Such relationships are not relations of domination and consumption, but relations formed primarily for the sake of a shared life. There is a sharp contrast between these two possible ways of exercising freedom: The one views the individual self as seeking its own goals, so that relationships have a purely instrumental character, and the other considers the self as willing to allow its own goals to be transformed through a commitment to a relationship distinct from those individual goals.

Is it possible to give a critical but positive interpretation of this shift of focus from the community to human autonomy, while simultaneously adhering to the importance of relations that lead to communion? The philosophical and sociological insights of Charles Taylor can be illuminating in developing a positive, but critical appreciation of the turn to the self in a culture that emphasizes relationships as constitutive of a healthy community. He argues that the culture of subjectivity is neither to be rejected nor to be uncritically endorsed as it is.[2] The way to address the culture of subjectivity is to enter sympathetically into the culture's animating ideal and to try to show what it really requires. This can be done by demarcating the higher and nobler ideals of subjectivism from its malignant practices and using these positive and motivating ideas to critique its negative expressions.

Such a posture presupposes an engagement in the work of persuasion, being in conversation with the prevailing cultural realities. He believes that people are not so locked in by the various social developments that condition them that they cannot change their ways, regardless of strong arguments concerning atomism and instrumental reasoning.[3]

Taylor acknowledges that in liberal democratic societies, subjectivity has become a unique source of significance, meaning, and authority. "Good life" human flourishing is identified with living one's life in full awareness of one's state of being; in enriching one's experiences and finding ways of handling negative emotions; and in becoming sensitive enough to find out where and how the quality of one's life—alone or in relation—may be improved. The goal is not to follow established paths, but to forge one's own inner-directed, subjective life; not to become what others want one to be, but to "become who I truly am." Thus the key value for the mode of subjective life is an authentic connection with the inner depth of one's unique life-in-relation. People have the potential to choose what they wish to be and with whom they want to associate.

Taylor proposes that in the cultural conflicts over subjectivity, instead of taking a position either for or against we need to persuade people that self-fulfillment, so far from excluding unconditional relationships and moral demands beyond the self, actually requires these in some form. It is in the nature of their increased freedom that people through their choices can sink morally lower, as well as rising higher. In liberal democratic societies, the higher forms of self-responsible moral initiatives and dedication will coexist with debased practices. Taylor argues that

> the best can never be definitively guaranteed, nor are the decline and triviality inevitable. The nature of the free society is that it will always be the locus of a struggle between higher and lower forms of freedom. Neither side can abolish the other, but the line can be moved, never definitively but, at least for some people for some time, one way, or another.[4]

Taylor advocates that, through winning hearts and minds, social action and political change, the better forms of collective life, can gain ground, at least for a while. This perspective, in his view, breaks quite definitively with the prevailing cultural pessimism. Taylor considers that cultural pessimism is not only mistaken; it is also counterproductive.

Some Orthodox theologians, because of the corrosive effects that the primacy of freedom has upon all forms of communal life, consider liberal democracy to be incompatible with the basic ethos of Orthodoxy, without meaning that that they do not recognize the contribution of liberal democracy in affirming the dignity and the freedom of all human beings against oppressive and alienating social structures.[5] Orthodox tradition is incompatible with the negative aspect of liberalism that threatens all forms of communal life, but it provides invaluable resources in forming moral habits that enable freedom to be expressed in ways oriented to community rather than domination or gratification.[6] In Orthodox theology, commitment to community is not about the stifling of individual freedom but the fulfillment of the self in interpersonal relationships.

The communal pattern of life that the Church espouses through the anthropological implications of the Trinitarian faith and the experience of the Eucharistic life is a distinct contribution of the Church to the world, a prophetic reality that challenges or inspires the world to be in the process of social transformation and openness to God and others.[7] Freedom by its very definition may lead either to a transcendence of the limitations and the necessities of nature as well as of history or to an unconditional subjection to them. The task of the Church is not to be the advocate of the eradication by secular force of those practices of freedom that lead to human alienation and abuse, but to be an authentic communion of people who actively participate in the ongoing dialogue in the civil society that aims to strengthen human solidarity, justice, and peace as well as openness to a future that transcends the oppressive realities of the present.[8] In the public space of civil society, the Orthodox Church may discover that other Christian churches, religious communities, and secular movements may operate with similar anthropological understandings through their commitment to society, or even humanity, at large. Such commitments in advancing human solidarity, compassion, human dignity, and rights enhance human welfare and generate a high degree of cooperation in pursuit of common goals. Such commitments and relationships, either explicitly or implicitly, are open to the love of God in their recognition that the fulfillment of human life lies beyond the self as self-referential goal.

The Church is called to communicate its theology of personhood that, in my judgment, can redress the harm caused by distorted theologies of self-abnegation and invite the citizens of liberal societies to allow personal relationships to flourish through commitment.[9] The Kingdom of God, as it has been disclosed by Christ and continuously lived in the Church, especially in the celebration of the Eucharist, must be communicated within liberal societies as the life of communion and communication that espouses relationships of respect and love marked by justice and peace.[10] The coming of God's Kingdom is embodied in the active involvement of Christ in the life of the world, in collaboration with God's Spirit, disclosing the love of God for all creation. God's goal of bringing life to the world through the advent of His Kingdom defines his mission; for the realization of this mission, Christ is subject to death, without abandoning or modifying His proclamation of the Kingdom, or avoiding confrontation with the powerful.

The Church, in the context of liberal societies, should contribute its own theological insights and witness on the nature of human freedom as the fundamental potential for community and creativity, rather than as a destructive self-assertion. The Christian faith's own understanding of freedom, as a response to God's gift of life and love, can serve and nourish all expressions of freedom in liberal societies that are oriented to mutual respect and just relationships. For Orthodoxy, the fullest expression of this free self-disposition is in the realization of personal existence through relationships of mutual commitment, relations with God as the source of human life and with other persons as the essential context for personal fulfillment. Freedom is understood as the possibility of fulfillment through relationship, rather than, as in the secular liberal conception, the absence of any warrantable and justified claims on the individual autonomy.

How does the primacy of the self over the community affect the inner life and structures of the Orthodox Church? Focusing now on how liberal society has affected the ethos of the Orthodox people in the United States, I want to argue that the Orthodox churches in this country have already opted to develop their identity by using their religious and cultural tradition as a resource rather than a constraint.[11] The profile of the Orthodox communities in this country has changed dramatically because of the social upward mobility of Orthodox people, their progress in education, and above all their daily encounters and interactions with people of different religions, races, cultures, and ethnicities. Most especially for Orthodox young people, neither ethnicity nor differences in religion or cultural background can be an obstacle to uniting their lives with those of their loved ones. Second- and third-generation Orthodox prefer the language of their birth country over that of their parents' home country, and they speak English better than Greek, Arabic, Russian, or Slavonic. They view their Orthodox identity in a very different way than either their parents or their peers did only two or three decades ago. They are decoupling the Orthodox faith from its cultural embodiments, and they are in the process of recasting it into what is seen by them as a "pure" religion, based on isolated religious markers and American sensibilities. The principal authority in crafting their identity is the sovereign self. They are distrusting or have already moved away from the organizations, institutions, and causes that used to anchor their religious and cultural identity and behavior. Each person performs the labor of fashioning his or her own self, pulling together elements from the various aspects of Orthodoxy, ethnic heritage, existential quests, and present cultural sensibilities, rather than stepping into an "inescapable framework" of identity. Community is a felt need, even a real hunger for some, but it is, in my judgment, subordinate to individualism.

The individualization of the Orthodox faith and its decoupling from its traditional ethnic, cultural embodiments lead to the development of multiple orthodoxies within the Orthodox Church. The pluralization of Orthodoxy is a threat to the Church's unity, since the institutional aspects of Church life have limited capacity to persuade those who have embraced or crafted an individualized version of Orthodoxy about the need to correct, enhance, or recraft their particular orthodoxy. Perhaps the Orthodox churches in liberal democratic societies must learn not only to accept the prevailing pluralism of the public realm that freedom generates, but also to live with an internally differentiated Orthodoxy—multiple orthodoxies— that maintain their unity in the Apostolic faith, the Eucharist, Scripture, and *diakonia*. Acceptance of the pluralistic nature of liberal democratic societies inescapably invites the Orthodox churches to come to terms with the nature and the limits of pluralism that tradition-as-resource generates within the life of the Church, most especially on issues of ethics and morality.

The Orthodox Church must recognize that while, in traditional, culturally and religiously homogeneous countries, it was inevitable that the personal search for human fulfillment led most of the people to the Church, in liberal societies people have a range of options for exploration of personal meaning. In traditional settings, the Church relied primarily on the process of socialization for the purpose of communicating and passing on the practice of faith, neglecting the question of personal religious conversion.

Once it is recognized that the process of socialization in the present contextual reality no longer necessarily leads to a faith commitment and that
the range of options for human fulfillment is multiplied, the social expressions of the Orthodox faith need to be recast with the aim of communicating, through dialogue and persuasion, a personal faith that fulfills the
perennial human existential quest for meaning.

The Orthodox Church in the Public Sphere

In reflecting on the presence and participation of the Orthodox churches
in the public life of liberal societies, it is important to avoid all forms of
reductionism that limit their role either to serving the poor or operating
only in the subjective and private realms of life. Generally, the role of
religion in the public life is much more than "faith-based boostering" of
efforts to contribute to material betterment of individual lives and mending
society's safety net. This kind of understanding misrepresents the capacity
of the religious communities to carry the burden of social welfare for dis-
advantaged people, families, and communities. And furthermore, it misrec-
ognizes the identity and priorities of the religious communities in the
public realm, such as increasing moral and spiritual capacities, inspiring citizens to serve neighbors, building relationships across barriers of race and
income, and providing a vision of what kind of community people are
called to be.[12]

For the same reasons, we must argue against "dogmatic secularism" that
devalues the effects of faith practices on the vibrancy of civil society and
democratic life by considering them to be simply subjective and private phenomena with no public significance. Dogmatic secularism dismisses the
beliefs and values of a significant number of people who have chosen to
shape their identity through the values and virtues embedded in the narratives of their religious communities. This prevents liberal societies from
responding adequately to the global surge of growing religious pluralism.
Most importantly, it deprives them of opportunities to give renewed
strength and vibrancy to the moral values, principles, and virtues needed
for democratic participation and civility.[13] Dogmatic secularism, however,
should not be confused with a functional secular ethos that allows all citizens
of liberal societies (secular, religious, agnostics, indifferent, or unbelievers)
to withhold the full range and depth of their convictions in order to maintain mutual respect, cooperation, and civility in public settings. Dogmatic

secularism wrongly equates a public ethos of tolerance and civility with the absence of religious commitments.

The Orthodox Church, based on her distinctive ethos, understands her public role in liberal societies as an agent of reconciliation that promotes human solidarity (communion), justice, and peace through the totality of her life and in collaboration with other Christian churches, religious communities, secular movements, and people of good will. Such collaboration, as we have already noted, is feared by some on the grounds that it might gradually render the distinctive stance of the faith secondary and inessential or conceive the ethical principles and values of Orthodoxy apart or independently from their theological basis. Others refute such arguments, advocating that not to be involved in such movements means that the Church would pay less attention to the ideals of human rights and dignity and focus on its own internal life. In essence, it is feared that these options may lead either to a dissolution of the Church's identity or a withdrawal from the moral challenges and potentials of the secular world.

The justification of the Church's participation in the public life of liberal society should not be guided by secular ideals and principles but based on the fullness of the Orthodox tradition and life. It must not be a matter of political expediency, but it should reflect the will and the love of God for the world. What God has granted to the world most especially through his incarnate Word and the sending of the Holy Spirit is what the Church offers to the world. The primary task of the Church is to be an icon of God's Kingdom, the new creation, in which all in their particularity are united with God. This is experientially lived in the celebration of the Eucharist that constitutes the Church. In the celebration of the Eucharist, the Church becomes the living presence of Christ by the grace of the Holy Spirit. An indispensable aspect of the Church's being in the world is to witness the coming reality of God's Kingdom beyond herself and to live in solidarity with all those who strive to realize, however imperfectly, the principles and the values of God's Kingdom in various ways and historical contexts.

Orthodox theology in its ecumenical dialogue has been criticized on the grounds that its Eucharistic ecclesiology is susceptible to the danger of leading to ecclesiolatry, limiting God's presence and operation only within the canonical boundaries of the Church and more specifically among the baptized faithful. In response to such criticism, Orthodox theologians have developed the notion of "liturgy after Liturgy,"[14] wishing to maintain the normative role that the liturgy plays in constituting the Church and at the same time to acknowledge that the experiential relationships of love that they have in the Eucharist with God, humanity, and creation must guide the life and the witness of the Church. The danger of escaping from the challenges and conflicts of history to an eschatology that justifies ethical indifference—although it need not be thus—is a real challenge that Orthodoxy continues to grapple with.

The recognition that the celebration of the Eucharist demands an ethical response from the human side does not mean that God's presence in the world through his Church somehow depends on fallible human responses and actions. The Eucharistic ethos excludes all forms of messianic ethics that imply that human efforts and actions can establish and advance the Kingdom of God in history. Human efforts independent of God's Spirit and apart from Christ cannot bring humanity and the world into God's Kingdom. Yet the Kingdom, by virtue of Christ's resurrection and the sending of the Holy Spirit, is already an active presence in history without being contained or absorbed by it.

The Church lives in and communicates to the world the eschatological gift of hope that God has bestowed to his beloved creation. This hope goes beyond history and cannot be satisfied or exhausted by anything in human history. Whatever the outcome of human history or the fate of particular historical communities, God's eschatological gift of hope cannot be destroyed. Human history cannot fulfill that hope, nor can it abolish it. Phenomenologically, it is in the nature of hope to be able to see the future, despite the possibility of horrors, disappointments, and failures, as an open possibility: a future in which human beings can persevere in their historical existence and pass on their hope to succeeding generations. A belief in the openness of the future to human striving implies a confidence that the future will, in some way, be hospitable to human aspirations. It expresses human confidence that human achievements will have some lasting value despite the risk of being corrupted and perishing because of their historical contingencies. At the same time, a detachment from these achievements, a sense that they are not the ultimate manifestations of what humans beings are capable of being, is essential to the human sense of independence from history. This is the sense that human beings can transcend past failures and begin anew, that their essence has not been exhaustively poured out in one fragile historical project. Such a vision is at home in the Orthodox conception of human existence in the sense that the future is in God's hands and that human worth will not be measured by the success of human projects but by the virtues that informed and motivated their efforts. In theological terms, the sense of the openness of the future has its ultimate source and meaning in the Kingdom of God, and the independence of human personal worth from historical vicissitude is given an eternal foundation in the proclamation of the resurrection of Christ from the dead. All that is good in human efforts prepared in some way for the Kingdom of God, yet human destiny is never determined by the success or failure of human efforts. Nevertheless, Christians are called to solidarity in history, to achieve a bond with their fellow human beings that is forged and strengthened within history. It is in the historical circumstances of their lives that they come to know God through his image in their neighbor and use their freedom to help make God's Kingdom visible in sign and anticipation.

In the history of the Christian tradition, we can identify three inseparable and equally important modes of unity with God that have shaped the identity of the Church and need to guide her life and mission: unity through the word of God as it is found in Scripture; unity through the celebration of the Eucharist; and unity in serving the poor, the needy, and the oppressed. While the word of God transforms the human sense of reality and the Eucharist unites all with God in the risen Christ through the power of the Holy Spirit, serving the poor is a sign of recognizing in them the suffering God, who awaits healing and comfort by our love and compassion. In the active love of the victims of history and empathy for the most vulnerable ones, the Church becomes a sign of witness of the in-breaking of God's Kingdom. Aspects of God's Kingdom can be found in the world and in all human beings through the prayers, the mission and the witness of the Church and the unceasing operation of God's Spirit who moves all in mysterious and still incomprehensible ways into unity in truth.

The recognition that the new creation is already an active reality in the world as a gift of God implies that Christians exercising discernment must identify and affirm what is of God that reflects in imperfect and multiple ways signs of his presence. Each of the noble quests and struggles for greater justice, peace, and advocacy of freedom, dignity, and human rights for all despite their inherent weakness and corruptibility is not alien in all respects to God's purpose and love. The Church discerns in them the human quest for God's Kingdom, which is the fruit of God's Spirit. Thus, in the functional secular public space of liberal society, all life-sustaining and life-transforming principles and values such as human dignity and rights along with freedom can constitute the common realm in which followers of different religious creeds and ideologies along with secular people can meet and dialogue, contributing dialogically to the common good.[15] Dialogue creates the necessary space in which citizens and communities can meet one another and deliberate about how the common good might be embodied in policies that regulate their political life. Dialogue in such a pluralistic setting aspires as much as possible to resolve conflicts discursively, not manipulatively, coercively, or violently. It transcends not only the skeptical view that there is no point in continuing to discuss the issues that divide us but also the realist position that assumes that conflicts and differences among people and communities can only be resolved through the use of power or coercion. Dialogue is neither futile nor conclusive, but it helps to sustain the unity of conflicting communities in the conversation process. If the interlocutors in a conversation do not achieve agreement, they may at least mediate their conflicts temporarily and consider the conflict from the perspective of what they already share. Provided that all are free to participate in the process of deliberation, dialogue advances the common good of society.[16]

The Orthodox Church can play a role in liberal societies that always retains—in fidelity to God's Kingdom—a critical distance from any particular political form, and yet never remains aloof from all those whose experience of evil inspires them to struggle for justice. The eschatological orientation of the Orthodox faith does not allow the Church to be an apologist of any national and racial ideology, political system, economic theory, and praxis since all of them are effected by the pervasive corrupting presence of evil and their anthropocentric operating conception of reality. What then is the function of the Church in the public realm if it cannot fully endorse any political and economic system and praxis, nor fully reject them, once it discerns traces of God's Spirit in them? The notion of being "connected critics," in the phrase of Michael Walzer, illuminates our vision of how the Church should operate in a democratic society.[17] Christians should be committed to the fundamental ideas of democracy and yet be able to see the shortcomings of any particular democratic regime and society. As connected critics, they deeply care about the values inherent in any particular political project, and their critique serves to call a commu-

nity back to its better nature. "Because people of faith share the fundamental values of democratic societies, they remain connected to public life
even as they engage in criticism; because their commitment to democracy
remains penultimate, however, they can appeal to transcendent ideals to
critique current practice and to elevate their understanding of democratic
values themselves."[18]

The Orthodox Church moving into the public realm as a theological
agency must operate in a space where the common good is built on affirmations of shared political values rather than of the sacred texts and teachings of any particular religious tradition. In such a context, the Church
must use her language of faith with an emphasis on its hermeneutical potential to illuminate and interpret shared meanings, rather than to witness to her sovereign truth. An insistence on particular religious doctrine
may be heard simply as an appeal to a particular group identity rather than
as an invitation to reflect on our common situation. The Church should
instead evoke the shareable human experience that allows the citizens of
democratic societies to reflect on their common human situation. In this
context, the promotion of human rights plays a key role in the Church's
relationship to the contemporary world and thereby in the process of shaping a renewed sociocultural identity. This form of identity does not have
demarcation from antagonistic ideological forces or other Christian communities as a constitutive feature, and for this reason it is capable of initiating
a wide range of alliances in promoting justice and peace for all. Refrain-
ing from religious language in circumstances where it may alienate other
citizens of good will is a form of respect, recognizing that Christian witness
must often take the form of anonymity precisely for the sake of respecting
the presence of Christ in our neighbor.

The Orthodox understanding of authentic human existence as the "being in communion" that Orthodox anthropology espouses is an important
contribution to the quest for building a human community woven through
personal relationships of freedom and love. Such theology needs to come,
however, in terms of the all-pervading and inescapable power of sin, corrupting all who are exposed to the temptations of wealth and power. Orthodox
anthropology, while acknowledging the pervasive presence of evil in every
human being and society, at the same time affirms the far greater power of
the presence of God in all human beings through the grace of God's Spirit
and of Christ's salvific life, death, and resurrection. The Christian vision
of the human person as sinful, redeemed, and capable of virtue should

inform democratic societies by helping people in their personal and communal life to develop ways to limit corruptibility and increase the range of opportunities for expressing the good present in them. The Church in her public presence is called to acknowledge both the human capacity for cooperation and solidarity and the human proneness to exclude and exploit others unless structures and sanctions are enshrined in law and in public institutions that promote human solidarity, justice, and peace, bringing all closer to each other and more especially closer to God's intention for the created world.

Notes

1. See "The 1986 Statement of the Third Preconciliar Pan-Orthodox Conference in Chambesy, October 28–November 6, 1986," in *For the Peace from Above: An Orthodox Resource Book on War, Peace, and Nationalism*, ed. Hildo Bos and Jim Forest (Rollinsford, N.H.: Orthodox Research Institute, 2011), 72–84.

2. Charles Taylor, *The Ethics of Authenticity* (Cambridge, Mass.: Harvard University Press, 1991), 23.

3. Taylor, *Ethics*, 72.

4. Taylor, *Ethics*, 78.

5. Christos Yannaras, *Η Απανθρωπία του δικαιώματος* (Athens: Domos, 1998), 171. "Οπωσδήποτε, σε σύγκριση με καθεστώτα αποκαλύπτου ολοκληρωτισμού, με αυταρχικά ή απολυταρχικά πολιτεύματα, ο πολιτικός φιλελευθερισμός συνιστά πρόοδο για την ανθρωπότητα."

6. Christos Yannaras, *Ορθός λόγος και Κοινωνική Πρακτική* (Athens: Domos, 1984), 119–39 and 277–320; and *Προτάσεις Κριτικής Οντολογίας* (Athens: Domos, 1985), 24–25, 77–78, 82–88; Kosta Delikonstanti, *Τό Ήθος της Ελευθερίας, Φιλοσοφικές απορίες και Θεολογικές αποκρίσεις* (Athens: Domos, 1990); Demetriou Tseleggidi, *Χάρη και Ελευθερία κατα την Πατερική Παράδοση του ΙΔ΄Αιώνα* (Thessaloniki: 1998).

7. John Zizioulas, *The Eucharistic Communion and the World* (New York: T & T Clark, 2011), 123–32.

8. Emmanuel Clapsis, "The Orthodox Church in a Pluralistic World," in *Orthodoxy in Conversation: Orthodox Ecumenical Engagements* (Geneva: World Council of Churches, 2000), 127–50.

9. John Zizioulas, *Being as Communion* (New York: St. Vladimir's Seminary Press, 1997), 27–65.

10. Emmanuel Clapsis, "The Eucharist as a Missionary Event in a Suffering World," in *Orthodoxy in Conversation*, 191–97.

11. The "Religious Landscape Survey" of the Pew Forum on Religion and Public Life in 2008 (http://religions.pewforum.org/reports; accessed 4 August

2014) provides illuminating findings about the Orthodox people in the United States that support my argument. The report estimates that the Orthodox people are approximately 1 percent of the American population. They are ranked according to their income in the middle and upper-middle class by either meeting or, in some instances, exceeding the national averages. 28 percent of them are college graduates and 18 percent hold a postgraduate degree while 22 percent have received some college education. 58 percent are married but only 30 percent have one to three children. As far as their faith is concerned, 71 percent percent have a strong faith in God but only 56 percent consider their religious faith important for their lives. 60 percent pray to God daily and the rest either weekly or seldom. Most of the Orthodox people go to Church once every month or a few times a year, while 26 percent attend services regularly once a week. Scripture is considered literally the Word of God only by 26 percent, while 33 percent believes that it is not the Word of God word by word and 29 percent that it has been written by men. In interpreting the Orthodox faith, 68 percent believe that there is more than one way to interpret it and only 28 percent believe that there is only one way to understand the teachings of the Church. Furthermore, 70 percent of Orthodox people believe that many religions can lead to eternal life and only 20 percent believe that only the Orthodox faith leads to salvation. 43 percent of the Orthodox people think that the government should do more to protect the moral fabric of American society, while 48 percent think that the government is too involved in legislating morality. On the issue of homosexuality, we have surprising numbers: 48 percent believe that it should be accepted by society while 30 percent believe that society should discourage its practices. On abortion, 24 percent (18 percent national) believe that it should be legal in all cases, 38 percent legal in most cases and only 20 percent illegal in most cases. These findings disclose that a substantial number of Orthodox people in this country have differentiated, to some degree, their religious and moral beliefs from the formal teachings of the Orthodox Church. They have done so not by denying the importance of their faith in God and even of their tradition, but mainly because of the contextual realities in which they live, their level of education, and their appropriation of God's love for all people.

12. Mary Jo Bane, Brent Coffin, and Richard Higgins, eds., *Taking Faith Seriously* (Cambridge, Mass.: Harvard University Press, 2005), 3.

13. Bane, Coffin, and Higgins, *Taking Faith Seriously*, 3.

14. Ion Bria, "The Liturgy after Liturgy," in *Orthodoxy Visions of Ecumenism*, ed. Gennadios Limouris (Geneva: World Council of Churches, 1994): 216–20.

15. Grace Y. Kao, *Grounding Human Rights in a Pluralist World* (Washington, D.C.: Georgetown University, 2011), 131–72.

16. Clapsis, "The Orthodox Church in a Pluralistic World."

17. Michael Walzer, *Interpretation and Social Criticism* (Cambridge, Mass.: Harvard University Press, 1987), 39.

18. Ronald F. Thiemann, "Public Religion: Bane or Blessing for Democracy?" in *Obligations of Citizenship and Demands of Faith*, ed. Nancy L. Rosenblum (Princeton: Princeton University Press, 2000), 85.

DEMOCRACY AND THE DYNAMICS OF DEATH

ORTHODOX REFLECTIONS ON THE ORIGIN, PURPOSE, AND LIMITS OF POLITICS

Perry T. Hamalis

The phrase "shadow of Constantine," which appears in this volume's title, can be interpreted as encompassing at least two reflective trajectories. The more common of the two is Constantine's legacy as the first emperor to self-identify as a Christian. Here, Constantine's "shadow" includes the sociopolitical repercussions of the coincidence of supreme political power and Christian faith. As other essays in this collection demonstrate, this trajectory raises historical questions—*what* really happened and *why?*—as well as normative questions—how *should* the "Constantine event" shape our beliefs and practices today regarding Christianity and politics? A second trajectory of reflection pertains to the Christian theological-ethical tradition, which developed extensively during the remarkably long (1,100+-year) existence of Byzantium and continued, especially in the East, in various Orthodox Christian communities. Again, there are historical and interpretive questions within this trajectory—*who* developed particular theological claims, *why* were they developed, and *what* did they mean?—as well as normative claims—how *should* Byzantine theology be appropriated, applied, and communicated in present-day contexts?

Today's Orthodox Christian leaders and thinkers unanimously affirm their commitment to preserving and sustaining the "second trajectory" of Constantine's shadow, Orthodoxy's theological tradition; however, their

attitudes toward the "first trajectory" lack consensus. Some argue enthusi-
astically for the compatibility of Orthodoxy with American-style liberal
democracy; others call for a neo-Byzantine *symphonia* model headed by an
Orthodox king or queen; and still others express ambivalence over whether
or not Orthodoxy can endorse any form of government without significant
caveats.[1] For those within or leaning toward the pro-*symphonia* view,
whether rooted in the legacy of Byzantium, Tsarist Russia, or another
Constantine-inspired regime, there are ample historical examples and
theological-political resources from which to draw, beginning in the early
fourth century with Eusebius of Caesarea (260–339 CE) and continuing
through the early twentieth century with various pro-imperial or pro-
monarchy voices in Russia and the Balkans. For those within or leaning
toward the pro–liberal democracy view, however, the case is more difficult to
make, since far fewer authoritative sources exist within the Orthodox tradition that explicitly defend—or even critique—democracy using theological arguments.[2] Elizabeth Prodromou refers to this as "the theory gap,"
which, she contends, contributes both to the ad hoc quality of Orthodox
communities' strategies for democratization and to the dismissal of Orthodoxy's tradition as not meriting the attention of scholars.[3] Yet, as Nikolas
Gvosdev states, "If democratic forms of government are to take root in
cultures that have been shaped by the values and practices of Orthodox
Christianity, there must be some [historical or spiritual] foundation upon
which such institutions can be constructed."[4] Put differently, Orthodox
thinkers must work to fill "the theory gap" if we hope to better understand
both the promises and the pitfalls of democracy for Orthodox Christian
communities.

Recent contributions toward this goal have tended to take two forms.
Some, like Gvosdev,[5] have started by identifying the defining characteristics
of a democracy (popular sovereignty, processes of deliberation/debate, open
and free elections, etc.) and have then mined both trajectories of Constantine's legacy for support. Notwithstanding this approach's contributions,
some general criticisms of it are that it can be anachronistic and, at times,
unconvincing in connecting elements of democracy with counterparts in
the Orthodox tradition.[6] Representatives of the second approach, like
Aristotle Papanikolaou, have argued that one or more core theological-
ethical teachings (*theosis*, the Holy Trinity, personhood, etc.) are expressed
well through democratic forms of government. For example, in *The Mystical as Political*, Papanikolaou constructively examines a core theological

theme—"divine-human communion"—with an eye toward its relevance for and compatibility with contemporary liberal democracy. He describes his project as "an attempt to draw out the implications for a political theology of the Christian claim that humans were created for communion with God."[7] Papanikolaou's strategy is to carry insights from the "second" reflective trajectory of Constantine's shadow (Eastern Christian theology) into the "first" realm of his shadow (Christian political thought), responding to the question: *On what theological basis, if any, can Orthodox Christians convincingly endorse modern democracy?* Again, while such efforts have yielded important insights, they have also been criticized for their tendency to sanctify democracy as a divine form of government, to advance a rationale for democracy that is wholly unconvincing to non-Christians (if not to non-Orthodox), or to extrapolate theological claims to the realm of politics in ways that are somewhat naïve, if not politically and theologically dangerous.[8]

In what follows, I aim to bridge and complement the two existing approaches by focusing on a theme that is basic to both: the dynamics of death. This term, "the dynamics of death," encompasses both the predicament of human death and the ways in which the reality and awareness of death shape human life in personal and political contexts. Given the massive scope of this theme and the space limitations of this essay, what follows is a necessarily suggestive argument for the value of "the dynamics of death" as an interpretive lens for examining democracy within contemporary Christian ethics and for building a fresh rationale for democracy from an Orthodox standpoint.[9]

Like Gvosdev, my argument takes seriously the characteristics, potential, and tendencies of real people and real governments. I start with observable human phenomena and historical data that political decision makers must address. Specifically, my points of departure are the drive of human selfishness, the fact of human violence, and the acknowledgment that governments have both prevented and inflicted death on a massive scale—truths pounded into our consciousness by the events of the past century, but nonetheless requiring frequent recollection . . . and prayerful lament. My approach, then, is characteristically modern; Machiavelli, Hobbes, Locke, Montesquieu, and Rousseau have taught me much, and they all began by "taking men as they are and laws as they might be."[10]

Yet my point of departure also encompasses a set of theological-ethical claims that frame Orthodoxy's normative vision: (1) Humanity's predicament is constituted primarily by the problem of physical and spiritual death; (2) the presence and awareness of this problem forms our lives in profound ways; and (3) the aim of Christian life is resurrection.[11] Thus, like Papanikolaou, I seek to employ a theological-ethical theme drawn from within the Orthodox tradition for reflection on contemporary political thought. Yet, whereas Papanikolaou starts with the telos, or *summum bonum*, of "divine-human communion," with the fulfilled potential of human persons, or with the "way things ought to be," I begin with the *summum malum* of human death, with the depths of humanity's brokenness, or with the "way things are." This difference carries some important implications. Most significantly, by grounding my account of democracy's legitimacy upon the given human condition instead of grounding it upon the aim of *theosis*, I am better able to avoid granting democracy an ultimate or sacred status—as the apotheosis of political life—and thus better able to critique some of democracy's dangers. In addition, the theme of "the dynamics of death" lies at the foundation of modern politics, and of human experience more broadly, in a way that "divine-human communion" does not. This shared ground not only bridges the two general approaches to democracy among recent Orthodox thinkers; it also gives Orthodox theology a political relevance, realism, and appeal to those outside the tradition that is lacking in themes like "divine-human communion" and "communion in otherness."

My argument in what follows is simultaneously interpretive and constructive. I both demonstrate the value of "the dynamics of death" as a lens for studying Christian political philosophy and defend democracy by utilizing the resources of modern social contract theory, social scientific data, and selected resources of the early Christian, Byzantine, and post-Byzantine tradition. To start on a realistic note, I begin in Part 1 with a discussion of the dynamics of death theme in the writings of Thomas Hobbes (1588–1679). While later social contract thinkers like Locke and Montesquieu influence present-day democracies more directly than Hobbes, Hobbes develops the "dynamics of death" theme with an unparalleled incisiveness and lucidity. In addition, some of Hobbes's most "undemocratic" and dangerous claims become clear through the lens of the dynamics of death, providing an important basis for my critique of his proposal. In Part 2, my focus shifts to several Orthodox sources, examining them against the Hobbesian backdrop. My hope is that the constructive analysis I offer will help identify lineaments of an alternative Orthodox case for democracy and spur additional exploration in this area of inquiry.

The Dynamics of Death: Lessons from Thomas Hobbes

The Predicament of Death and the Origin of the State

At least one major trajectory in modern political philosophy, the social contract tradition, begins in Hobbes's work with a mythic "state of nature,"
characterized by violent death, from which the state/commonwealth is
born as a therapeutic response.[12] "During the time men live without a
common Power to keep them all in awe," Hobbes writes, "they are in
that condition which is called Warre; and such a warre, as is of every man,
against every man."[13] For Hobbes, the pre- or postcivil state of nature is a
state of total war, a *bellum omnium contra omnes*, which allows for no exceptions. It is a most miserable state of affairs, a true "predicament," which
he famously depicts as follows:

> In such condition, there is no place for Industry; because the fruit
> thereof is uncertain: and consequently no Culture of the Earth; no
> Navigation, nor use of the commodities that may be imported by
> Sea; no commodious Building; no Instruments of moving, and re-
> moving such things as require much force; no Knowledge of the face
> of the Earth; no account of Time; no Arts; no Letters; no Society;
> and which is worst of all, continuall feare, and danger of violent
> death; And the life of man, solitary, poore, nasty, brutish, and short.[14]

At its core, the Hobbesian state of nature is an ontological predicament,
a state of all-inclusive war and violent physical death. Life is "nasty," "brut-
ish," and—most importantly—"short." Elsewhere in *Leviathan* Hobbes
observes that human beings will risk their lives defending themselves rather
than suffer the "greater evil" of a certain and present death.[15] *A fortiori*,
Hobbes, in another work, identifies violent death as "the supreme evil
[*summum malum*] in nature."[16] While violent death is Hobbes's principal
concern, other passages suggest that Hobbes views not merely violent death
but death per se as the fundamental human problem.[17] He describes death
itself as "the greatest of all evils"[18] and "that terrible enemy of nature."[19]
For him, humanity's predicament is constituted most fundamentally by
the ontological problem of mortality and violence. Second, the state of nature for Hobbes is a predicament not merely on the physical level, but also
on the psychological level. It is a state of unceasing danger and "continuall
feare." As such, Hobbes contends, it is a condition of *perpetual* war: "For
Warre, consisteth not in Battell onely, or the act of fighting; but in a tract

of time, wherein the Will to contend by Battell is sufficiently *known*."[20]
Thus, on top of actual physical violence, the Hobbesian account of humanity's state of nature encompasses knowledge that death threatens perpetually, and the continual fear of death that this knowledge fuels. The presence of this intense fear severely limits the ability of human beings to trust one another, to collaborate, or to develop toward any higher possibilities. The Hobbesian view of humanity's prepolitical condition can be characterized by the "dynamics of death," wherein death, violence, and continuous fear together comprise a state of misery from which deliverance is urgently needed.

In light of this realistic—if not excessively pessimistic—account of the "way things are" in the state of nature, Hobbes goes on to articulate both the purpose of politics and the primary means through which this purpose is achieved. In doing so, he inaugurates the modern social contract tradition, which is subsequently developed by Locke, Rousseau, the American founders, and many others. With respect to the purpose of politics, Hobbes unambiguously contends that government exists—first and foremost—to protect the lives of citizens.[21] The significance of this point cannot be overstated. Death is what drives humanity's political impulse; it is the problem that spurs human beings to construct a commonwealth. The legitimacy of the sovereign authority thus stands or falls with its ability to protect the physical lives of its contracting members. "The office of the Soveraign (be it a Monarch, or an Assembly)," Hobbes writes, "consisteth in the end, for which he was trusted with the Soveraign Power, namely the procuration of the *safety of the people*."[22] For Hobbes, the state arises as a man-made therapeutic response to the ontological dimension of humankind's predicament. In light of this, the legitimacy of the state's sovereign authority depends upon its effectiveness in delivering a life-saving cure. So long as a sovereign authority ensures citizens' protection, citizens are obligated to recognize its legitimacy and obey its laws. Political legitimacy, for Hobbes, hinges not on the procedural integrity of political institutions but on the sovereign's effectiveness in providing protection and maintaining peace.[23]

Protecting citizens and maintaining peace might strike us as a truncated political telos—shouldn't a government do more than this? For Hobbes, a government should establish the conditions of peaceful coexistence where, within limits, human beings can pursue their private happiness and collaborate on endeavors of mutual interest.[24] Like other moderns, he rejects the view that a universal and comprehensive account of humanity's *summum bonum* can be known. Hobbes simply expects the civil sovereign to stop the perpetual war and terror that defines the state of nature. Although clearly not a supporter of democracy, Hobbes refuses to articulate a single, substantive account of human felicity, leading some even to identify him as a "proto-liberal."[25]

Since death lies at the core of Hobbes's account of evil, the protection of life effectuated by a government carries tremendous normative value. As others have noted and as Hobbes himself writes,[26] the state assumes the role of an artificially constructed "savior" in his proposal. "This great Leviathan, which is called a Commonwealth, or State, is a work of art; it is an artificial man made for *the protection and salvation* of the natural man, to whom it is superior in grandeur and power."[27] We will return to this striking claim below, but first we should consider how another Hobbesian teaching intertwines with the dynamics of death.

The Fears of Death and the Social Contract

In Hobbes's teaching on the means through which a government originates, two elements, popular sovereignty and the mechanism of the "social contract," are vital. He writes:

> Before the institution of Common-wealth, every man had a right to every thing, and to do whatsoever he thought necessary to his own preservation; subduing, hurting, or killing any man in order thereunto. . . . In the making of a Common-wealth, every man giveth away the right of defending another; but not of defending himself. Also he obligeth himselfe, to assist him that hath the Soveraignty, in the Punishing of another, but of himselfe not.[28]

Through the mechanism of the social contract, each natural individual, motivated by self-preservation, becomes an author and member of the commonwealth by entering a covenant with the other members to transfer her or his *natural right* to a single sovereign authority. Thus the Hobbesian commonwealth, which is composed of either a single individual or a small assembly, is erected by the combined power of all the covenanting citizens. Here Hobbes breaks decisively from the Divine Right of Kings theory, which dominated political philosophy in both Western and Eastern Christian contexts. Not God, but the governed people's consent now grounds the commonwealth's sovereign authority. Yet Hobbes also rejects democracy, seeing it as too diffuse, destabilizing, and cumbersome in attaining political aims.[29] In his proposal, the civil sovereign receives from its people *all* rights to judge *all* means and take *all* necessary measures to preserve citizens' lives and maintain common peace, a teaching that has generated much criticism in the wake of subsequent authoritarian and totalitarian states.[30]

Entering the social contract seems to be a rational and easy choice for any person whose only alternative is the state of nature; yet Hobbes acknowledges that there is still a major obstacle to participation in this saving covenant: pride. The problem with pride, according to Hobbes, is that it prevents natural human beings from seeing their need for the commonwealth. Pride blocks individuals from discerning the fragility of their existence in the state of nature. Michael Oakeshott writes:

> The precondition of the deliverance is the recognition of the predicament. Just as, in Christian theory, the repentance of the sinner is the first indispensable step towards forgiveness and salvation, so [in Hobbes], mankind must first purge itself of the illusion called pride. . . . The purging emotion (for it is to emotion that we go to find the beginning of deliverance) is fear of death. This fear illuminates prudence; man is a creature civilized by fear of death.[31]

The dynamics of death, specifically a sobering or humbling type of mindfulness of physical death's imminence, seems to be a cornerstone of Hobbes's proposal. The remembrance of physical death cuts through human pride and intensifies natural human beings' fear of physical death. For Hobbes, it is this fear that drives people to enter the social contract and create the commonwealth.

A second role for the fear of death emerges once the commonwealth has been created. Recall Hobbes's description of the state of nature: "During the time men live without a common Power *to keep them all in awe.*" A commonwealth achieves its purpose most basically by "over-awing" citizens into civil obedience. By constructing the commonwealth, citizens express their confidence that this governing body will severely punish or kill anyone who transgresses the law—anyone who dares to attack the life, property, or liberty of a citizen. So long as citizens fear the commonwealth as the enforcer of the law, they no longer need to fear each other; and so long as the commonwealth has sufficient power to inspire awe, both those inside and those outside its borders will fear the consequences of acting against any of its contracting members. The dynamics of death lie at the foundation of the social contract's effectiveness.

Finally, in Parts 3 and 4 of *Leviathan*, Hobbes's proposal includes an extensive series of laws and theological teachings, enforced by the commonwealth, that strive to minimize—if not eliminate—citizens' fears of the afterlife, of divine judgment, or of eternal punishment. Such fears, he contends, are susceptible to terrible abuses by religious leaders and fuel religious conflict among citizens, since they are based on doctrines that can never be convincingly adjudicated.[32] Most importantly, religious fears undermine the ability of the commonwealth to awe people into obedience. In a telling passage, Hobbes writes:

> It is impossible a Common-wealth should stand, where any other than the Sovereign, hath a power of giving greater rewards than Life; and of inflicting greater punishments, than Death. Now seeing Eternall life is a greater reward, than life present; and Eternall torment a greater punishment than the death of Nature; It is a thing worthy to be well considered, of all men that desire (by obeying Authority) to avoid the calamities of Confusion, and Civill war, what is meant in holy Scripture, by Life Eternall, and Torment Eternall; and for what offences, and against whom committed, men are to be Eternally tormented; and for what actions, they are to obtain Eternall life.[33]

The commonwealth's ability to "protect and save" human beings—and hence its legitimacy—hinges on its ability to shape the actions of both insiders and outsiders, deterring illegal activity through a supreme fear of retribution. The social contract is strengthened and the power of the state is enhanced when citizens remain *mindful* of the real possibility of physical death/punishment (should they transgress the commonwealth's laws) and *forgetful* of the real possibility of anything worse, like eternal suffering in the afterlife.[34] Hobbes therefore makes sure that the Christian doctrines and practices that his civil sovereign endorses minimize fear of eternal death, thus buttressing the civil sovereign's ability to command ultimate obedience.

Within a Hobbesian framework, then, the state originates through the dynamics of death: It arises as a cure to the natural predicament of death and terror; it is constructed through a social contract that is motivated and sustained by the desire for self-preservation; its legitimacy rests on its effectiveness in protecting citizens' lives; and it achieves its aim by employing the fear of violent physical death and minimizing the fear of eternal death in order to promote law-abidingness internally and deter outsiders from acting against its citizens.[35]

Death and the Limits of Politics

The lens of death's dynamics reveals two raw truths related to the limits of government. The first is the simple but crucial acknowledgment that, although the state is born out of its contracting members' mutual desire for self-preservation and its primary purpose is to protect citizens' lives, no state can ultimately protect those in its care against violent physical death. Human beings are too complicated, or too corrupted; no matter how massive and awesome the commonwealth's power is, human passions—anger, jealously, wrath—will, occasionally, trump the fear of retribution, and citizens will be killed. Furthermore, even in a hypothetical (or real) totalitarian regime where violent crime between citizens has been eliminated, no government can protect its citizens from physical death *per se*. Mortality sets a necessary limit on politics. As Epicurus said eloquently, "Against all else it is possible to provide security, but as against death all of us mortals alike dwell in an unfortified city."[36]

Hobbes knew this, of course, as we all do. Yet what is striking is the extent to which these uncontroversial truth claims could rock the very foundation of government within a social-contractarian framework. Recall Hobbes's teaching on political legitimacy, which many subsequent (and democratically oriented) political theorists share: *A government's legitimacy rests on its ability to protect citizens' lives*. Within this framework, every violent death of a citizen undermines, to some extent, the legitimacy of a government. Whether it comes at the hands of a fellow citizen (a jealous lover, a drive-by shooter, etc.) or at the hands of an outsider (an attacking enemy soldier, a foreign terrorist, etc.), the civil sovereign's legitimacy erodes each time a citizen dies violently.[37] Yet, notwithstanding this undeniable limit on a government's ability to fulfill its purpose, people are eager to forfeit a significant portion of their freedom and to enter the social contract. Some security, it seems, is better than no security, even if it comes at the expense of liberty.[38] We turn easily to the state, the Leviathan, seeking a cure for our predicament. Yet even if Hobbes's prescription for civil peace and salvation were to be followed completely—from the forfeiture of all rights (except the right to self-defense, which is inalienable), to the concentration of absolute power in a single ruler, to the reinterpretation of religious claims about the afterlife, martyrs, and the real possibility of eternal suffering in hell—it would not provide salvation from what he himself calls "the greatest of all evils"[39] and "that terrible enemy of nature,"[40] human death. In light of this, one wonders whether any civil sovereign within such a framework can claim full and unequivocal legitimacy.

A second raw truth that emerges pertains to the horrifying capacity of governments themselves to engage in killing, especially when their authority is absolute. While each major form of government has entered wars that have led to millions of violent deaths, social scientists have demonstrated that very rarely—if ever—does a stable democratic state go to war against another stable democratic state. The "democratic peace thesis," as it is called, has been described by one political scientist as "the closest thing we have to an empirical law in international relations."[41] While the democratic peace thesis does not contend that democracies have resisted wars in general (i.e., against nondemocracies) at a higher rate than other forms of government, the near nonexistence in the historical record of wars between stable democracies provides strong support for cultivating democracy as a way to reduce violent death.

Another empirical finding that strongly supports democratic forms of government concerns the phenomenon of violent death being inflicted by a state upon its own people. In his masterful studies, *Death by Government* and *Power Kills*,[42] R. J. Rummel provides a detailed analysis of "democide," defined as "the murder of any person or people by a government, including genocide, politicide, or mass murder."[43] The data Rummel reports are jaw-dropping. In the twentieth century (1900–99), an estimated 262 million people were murdered by their own governments.[44] Perhaps even more shocking is that this number is six times larger than the estimated total of battle dead from all of last century's interstate and civil wars. Democides, in other words, are much more deadly than wars. Heading up Rummel's list are four "decamegamurderer" regimes: China (PRC) 1949–87 (77 million democide victims), USSR 1917–87 (62 million victims), Germany 1933–45 (21 million victims), and China (KMT) 1928–49 (10 million victims). There is much that could be said about these shocking statistics, and much that is beyond words, yet one dimension of Rummel's analysis should be repeated and underscored: Of all forms of governance, totalitarian regimes are most likely and democracies are least likely to engage in democide.

While many factors distinguish totalitarian regimes from democracies, and many forms of governance dot the spectrum between these two extremes, history indicates that the closer a government moves toward absolute power, the more likely it is to murder those within its borders. Embellishing Lord Acton's famous words, Rummel writes:

> Power kills; absolute Power kills absolutely. . . . The more power a government has, the more it can act arbitrarily according to the whims and desires of the elite, and the more it will make war on others and murder its foreign and domestic subjects. The more constrained the power of governments, the more power is diffused, checked, and balanced, the less it will aggress on others and commit democide. At the extremes of Power, totalitarian communist governments slaughter their people by the tens of *millions*; in contrast, many democracies can barely bring themselves to execute even serial murderers.[45]

While Hobbes identifies violent death as the greatest evil and his political proposal aims—first and foremost—at protecting citizens against violent death, history has taught us that the nondemocratic form of governance he proposes is much more likely to exacerbate the problem than to solve it. Those committed to preventing democide should favor democracy.

The Dynamics of Death: Lessons from the Shadows of Constantine

The Predicament of Death and the Aim of Resurrection

In another work, I examine the phenomena of death, fear of death, and remembrance of death as a lens for assessing and comparing ethical visions.[46] I also argue that many voices from the Byzantine theological-ethical tradition advance ethical visions that are *thanatomorphic*, "formed by death." *Thanatomorphicity*, as I define it, carries three distinct but interrelated levels of meaning, which can be identified in a wide range of worldviews. The first level is ontological, the second is agential, and the third is noetic. According to the concept's first level of meaning, an ethical vision is *thanatomorphic* when it is framed by the problem of human death.[47] This applies to many representative voices from the "second trajectory" of Constantine's shadow because they posit that spiritual death and physical death together comprise the core of humanity's predicament, our *summum malum*, and that salvation consists in both spiritual and physical resurrection from the dead.[48] For them, humanity's broken-ness is an *ontological* brokenness, a brokenness that, in turn, requires an ontological cure, the live-giving action of the Holy Trinity.

Some may find it curious that many Eastern Orthodox theologians describe not only spiritual death but physical death—mortality itself—in a sharply negative manner. Georges Florovsky calls human mortality "a deep tragedy," a "painful metaphysical catastrophe," and a "mysterious failure of human destiny."[49] Kallistos Ware contends that physical death is "pro-foundly abnormal" and even "monstrous," reflecting a world that is "dis-torted and out of joint, crazy, *écrasé.*"[50] And Archimandrite Sophrony Sakharov writes, "All of us have a single enemy—our mortality. If man is [merely] mortal, if there is no resurrection, then the whole of world his-tory is nothing but senseless creature suffering."[51] In defending this view, Orthodox theologians sometimes appeal to the biblical accounts of Christ weeping for his friend Lazarus and agonizing in the Garden of Geth-semane.[52] Humanity's predicament, from an Orthodox perspective, is formed by the problem of spiritual and physical death. Correspondingly, salvation entails deliverance from both spiritual and physical death; it en-tails holistic resurrection. As Florovsky summarizes, "The death of our Lord was victory over death and mortality, not just remission of sins, nor merely a justification of man, nor again a satisfaction of an abstract justice."[53]

I emphasized above that Hobbes's account of humanity's predicament is ontological and that the *summum malum* in his vision is violent death. Within the Orthodox tradition, the core problem from which human beings seek deliverance is, similarly, ontological; for it is constituted by spiritual and physical death. Thus, notwithstanding some important differ-ences, both Hobbes and Orthodox Christianity frame their ethical visions by starting with the conviction that the reality and the possibility of death constitutes humanity's most basic problem. Furthermore, both Hobbes and Orthodox Christianity articulate normative proposals that aim to save humans from the death that torments us. Given the wars, democides, and other death-related horrors of the past century, one is hard-pressed to find fault with this shared basic concern.

The Dynamics of Death and the Purpose of Politics

In Hobbes's work, a description of the state of nature and the problem of death leads to his proposal for deliverance by a saving Leviathan. Does the

Orthodox tradition share Hobbes's view on the purpose of politics? I believe that the debate between "pro-monarchy" and "pro-democracy" camps
within the Orthodox community stems in part from different accounts of
government's purpose; in addition, different rationales for government may
be found within each of these two broad camps. As I noted earlier, many
more resources within the Christian East are available that reflect normatively upon politics within an imperial or monarchical framework than
within a democratic one. Yet using the "dynamics of death" lens reveals
resources for understanding the purpose of government from an Orthodox perspective that might otherwise be overlooked.

Well before Constantine, St. Irenaeus of Lyons (130–202 CE) writes the
following in his major work, *Against Heresies*:

> For since man, by departing from God, reached such a pit of bestiality
> as even to look upon his kinsmen as his enemy, and engaged without
> fear in every kind of disordered conduct, murder, and avarice, God
> imposed upon mankind the fear of man, as they did not acknowl-
> edge the fear of God; in order that, being subjected to the authority
> of men, and under the custody of their laws, they might attain to
> some degree of justice, and exercise mutual forbearance through
> dread of the sword suspended full in their view [see Romans 13:4]. . . .
> Earthly rule, therefore, has been appointed by God for the benefit of
> the nations . . . so that under fear of it men may not eat each other
> up like fishes.[54]

Notice, first, that Irenaeus begins with a reference to humanity's Fall ("by
departing from God"), and his description of the postlapsarian and prepolitical condition paints a dark picture of human tendencies and capacities. Selfishness and the fear of one's own physical death are dominant forces
in human agency and root causes of an array of "disordered conduct."
Irenaeus begins, in other words, with "the way things really are." Second,
government, in Irenaeus's judgment, is a postlapsarian institution provided
by God. Human beings are not political in our prelapsarian condition (although he believes we are social), and will not have structures of human
government in our postmortem condition. This teaching is significant for
many reasons, not the least of which is that it reminds Christians that government is an accommodation, an institution of penultimate and temporary value; it is not a component of humanity's original condition or of
our hoped-for eternity. Third, while government's necessity stems from hu-

manity's brokenness, Irenaeus points more directly to humanity's lack of "fear of God" as being a main reason why God's provision is required. Since corrupted humans have a deficient fear of God, the compulsion of human laws and the "dread of the sword" are necessary. The dynamics of death theme thus emerges vividly in Irenaeus's social thought: (1) The reality of death in the fallen condition drives selfishness and self-preservation; (2) a severely diminished fear of God, which is another characteristic of the fallen condition, is not capable of "awing" people into peaceful coexistence; and (3) the government is ordained by God to provide the "awe" that is necessary to prevent continuous violence. Thus while Irenaeus undoubtedly teaches that government has a divine origin, he also teaches that government is born as a response by God to the predicament of death, violence, and the real behavior of fallen humanity. Finally, we should note that Irenaeus's hope regarding government's effectiveness is refreshingly modest. He suggests that *some* degree of justice is possible when human beings are under the "authority of men" and "under the custody of their laws." For him, this is not an embarrassing revelation—an exposé of the state's limits; instead, it is a simple acknowledgment that full deliverance from humanity's predicament is only possible through God. The government cannot ultimately save its citizens or deliver fully on its protectionist purpose. Yet, while Irenaeus here suggests that the state can neither fully protect its citizens nor administer full justice, he also suggests that it can contribute toward these aims. Government cannot offer a cure to the predicament, but it can mitigate some of the predicament's effects.

The subsequent Byzantine period generated a plethora of writings praising Christian emperors and articulating a more comprehensive vision of the purpose of government, lending support to a pro-*symphonia* stance. Yet this period also includes thinkers like St. John Chrysostom who, like Irenaeus, articulate a more modest rationale for political power. Consider Chrysostom's homilies "On the Statues," wherein he responds to riots within Antioch that had erupted in 387 CE when Emperor Theodosius imposed a steep new tax. He writes:

> For if, whilst there are magistrates and soldiers living under arms, the madness of a few individuals, a motley crew of adventurers, hath kindled such a fire among us, in so short a moment . . . suppose the fear of magistrates to be wholly taken away? To what length would they not have gone in their madness? Would they not have overthrown

the city from its foundations, turning all things upside down and
have taken our very lives? . . . [S]o were you to deprive the world of
magistrates, and of the fear that comes of them, houses at once, and
cities, and nations, would fall on one another in unrestrained confusion, there being no one to repress, or repel, or persuade them to
be peaceful, by the fear of punishment![55]

Like Irenaeus before him, Chrysostom begins with fallen humanity's pro-
clivity for lawlessness, exploitation, and mutual destruction—even before
a total breakdown of governmental power. Chrysostom then highlights the
role that instilling fear in citizens plays, providing a rationale for politics
that centers on the government's ability to protect citizens and maintain
order. Government's purpose, he suggests, is compatible with the Church's
thanatomorphic aim of fighting against death; but it is also a purpose that
is focused, restrained, and limited to protecting human life and promoting peace amid a deeply broken humanity. Irenaeus and John Chrysostom
are not "prodemocracy" thinkers, and reading them as such would be
anachronistic; yet their affirmation of a limited protectionist telos for politics provides, I believe, a more modest and promising alternative grounding for an Orthodox defense of democracy.

The above discussion of Irenaeus and John Chrysostom reaffirms the
illuminative potential of the "dynamics of death" lens. In addition, considering these teachings against the backdrop of Hobbes brings out valuable
points of consonance and dissonance regarding the purpose of politics, the
basis of political legitimacy, and the methods by which a government fulfills its purpose. First, both the Hobbesian tradition and selected representatives from early Christianity share a dark account of prepolitical
human nature, one that highlights the problem of death and the selfish
and violent tendencies that our mortality fuels. For Irenaeus, Chrysostom,
and other Eastern Christian voices, humanity's Fall grounds this reality,
suggesting that humanity's predicament is contra-natural and providing a
basis from which to critique such tendencies and to hope for a restoration
of natural peacefulness and community. For Hobbes, humanity's predicament is the "state of nature," making critiques more difficult to defend
(since no pristine natural condition preceded it) and shifting the historical
narrative in ways that would distort the Christian gospel.

Employing the lens of "the dynamics of death" also helps to demonstrate that, like Hobbes, some historical Orthodox voices teach that a pri-

mary purpose—if not *the* primary purpose—of government is to protect human life. This shared claim grounds Orthodoxy in political realism and opens a path for understanding political legitimacy in a way that is less dependent upon explicitly theological claims, but also not contrary to Orthodox theology. In addition, whereas both Chrysostom and Irenaeus state that government is "ordained by God" as a response to the fallen condition (see Romans 13.1), Hobbes does not. For him, government is constructed by and draws its authority wholly from individuals transferring their natural rights to the commonwealth via the social contract. Yet, while Irenaeus and Chrysostom attribute a divine origin to human government, they resist the temptation to give the state or the emperor a sacred status that might easily go too far.[56] Irenaeus and Chrysostom do not regard the attainment of political power as an expression of God's favor on a specific person or people; nor do they regard a specific form of governance (monarchy, democracy, etc.) as the fulfillment of divine providence or the apotheosis of Orthodox theology;[57] in doing so, they provide a much-needed space for critiques of political leaders and political systems that have failed to fulfill their primary responsibility.

The dynamics of death lens also reveals that Hobbes, Irenaeus, and Chrysostom all emphasize the basic role that the fear of punishment and death play in effective governance. Government achieves its purpose because it is capable of deterring violence and disorder through the awe-inspiring power it wields. Chrysostom's claim, "Were you to deprive the world of magistrates, and of the fear that comes of them, houses at once, and cities, and nations, would fall on one another in unrestrained confusion," could just as easily have come from Hobbes's pen. Yet attention to the fear of death also reveals a core difference between the Orthodox thinkers and Hobbes. For Hobbes, the fear of God and the fear of eternal death are part of the problem; thus his proposal strives to undermine any fears that might trump a citizen's fear of death by the state and systematically reinterprets traditional Christian teachings on death, afterlife, hell, and martyrdom in order to maximize the power and effectiveness of the civil sovereign. In sharp contrast, Irenaeus teaches that too little—not too much—fear of God and of eternal death is the problem. For him, a deficient fear of God fuels the human predicament and moves God to ordain human governments. Thus Irenaeus and other Eastern Christian voices teach that the fear of God and the fear of eternal death (rightly understood) are not part of the problem; they are part of the cure.

The points of continuity and difference noted above, I believe, can contribute substantially to an alternative rationale for democracy within Orthodoxy. However, a crucial step must still be made in the argument, one that draws from the preceding discussion of Orthodox sources and returns to the issue of limits discussed in my analysis of Hobbes.

Death and the Limits of Politics

I have used the lens of the "dynamics of death" to argue that representative voices from the Eastern Orthodox tradition and the Hobbesian social contract tradition share at least three basic convictions: (1) Human death constitutes the core of humanity's predicament; (2) government is born as a response to humanity's predicament and its primary purpose is to protect the lives of those in its care; and (3) the principal means by which government achieves its purpose, and thus establishes its legitimacy, is fear—the fear of suffering severe punishment or physical death for breaking the laws that protect citizens and promote peace. Among these three convictions only the second is understood in nearly identical ways by Hobbes and the Orthodox thinkers here in focus. The first conviction is understood differently because, for Hobbes, humanity's predicament is constituted by physical death alone, with violent physical death being the *summum malum*. For the Orthodox sources, humanity's predicament is constituted by both physical death and spiritual death. Yet, while both types of death are "the enemy," the *summum malum* is eternal spiritual death, not physical death, a point to which the Church's martyrs bear witness. And the third conviction, related to the political role of the fear of death, is understood differently because, for Hobbes, minimizing—if not eliminating—the fear of eternal death is a cornerstone of his proposal. He sees traditional Christian teachings on the afterlife as a threat to the absolute authority of the civil sovereign and believes that such absolute authority is necessary if the civil sovereign is to fulfill its purpose and maintain its legitimacy. The Orthodox sources here considered agree with Hobbes on the importance of the government's use of the fear of physical death, but oppose him on the impact of the fear of God and eternal death, regarding the lack of these fears among citizens as a root cause of the predicament, not a prescription for its cure. What can these points of consonance and dissonance teach us about the limits of government?

Recall that Hobbes's teachings led to two raw truths that evoke serious doubts about his proposal. The first is that even if we were to grant Hobbes everything he asks for, the Hobbesian Leviathan cannot ultimately fulfill its purpose—it cannot prevent all violence, and it certainly cannot prevent all death. Yet, in order to attain this imperfect solution, Hobbes asks for nearly everything from citizens. The only inalienable right is the right to self-preservation; all other liberty, including religious liberty, is forfeited to the state. It seems undeniable that the Hobbesian state demands citizens' ultimate allegiance in exchange for a cure that never fully heals. While Hobbes may call the Leviathan "an artificial man made for the protection and salvation of the natural man," it is not capable of saving human beings from the fullness of our predicament. In the Orthodox sources here considered, the state's capability and effectiveness are expressed more modestly. Yes, the state's aim is principally citizens' protection, but its limited ability to fulfill this purpose is acknowledged. Furthermore, there is an important thread within the Orthodox tradition that reminds the civil sovereign of its inability to ultimately save human beings from death—either physical death or spiritual death—the most significant strand of which is its communal worship. Yet, in addition to the liturgical tradition, there are several more explicitly political sources. From the ritual use of the *akakia*, a small silk sack of dirt held by emperors to remind them of their mortality and need for God's salvation,[58] to the "mirror of princes" genre exemplified in the work of Agapetus the Deacon,[59] to the striking icon of St. Sisoes standing before of the tomb of Alexander the Great and acknowledging the transience of all earthly power,[60] there are several Orthodox sources whose purpose was to communicate a message about the limits of government—even within the context of Byzantium. While a full discussion of these fascinating "remembrances of death" lies beyond our present scope, their existence alone within the shadow of Constantine is salient. Taken together, and regardless of the actual impact they may have made on political leaders, these resources communicate a sharp critique of the absolute claims and expectation of allegiance found in the Hobbesian state and many others. They bear witness to the limits that death places upon politics, and point to the need for a true Savior—lessons that are just as important today as they were in Byzantium. For, as Stanley Hauerwas has written, "Our task [as Christians] is not to make these nations the church, but rather to remind them that they are but nations. From the world's perspective, that may not seem like much, but the perspective of the people formed by the story of God's redemption shows us how important a task it is. For the idolatry most convenient to us all remains the presumed primacy of the nation-state."[61] While I would not recommend sending our president—or each member of Congress—either an *akakia* or a copy of the icon of St. Sisoes, especially given the Leviathan's surveillance capacities, there is a lesson vital to healthy governance that these works of Christian art teach: Know and remember your limits.

The second raw truth pertains to the political lessons we have learned since the time of Hobbes. Historically, the kind of concentrated power for which Hobbes's proposal calls has made possible the most massive and horrific crimes against humanity ever known. Governments wielding such power are much more likely to generate violent death among those under their care than a government in which power is limited and separated, as it is in contemporary democracies. While there is no doubt that Byzantine emperors wielded near-absolute power in the civic realm, Irenaeus and John Chrysostom have reminded us that it is not the form of a government that gives it legitimacy, but rather its ability to fulfill its entrusted role. In other words, there is no singular "Orthodox" political system; neither a monarchy, nor a democracy, nor a specific church-state relationship is, in itself, sacred, pure, or always best.[62] Instead there are governments that are better and worse, or more compatible with and less compatible with Orthodox Christianity's normative vision. If my argument thus far holds, and a case can be made that (1) from an Orthodox perspective, the primary purpose of government is to protect the physical lives of citizens; (2) democracies are, overall, much better at protecting citizens against threats to their lives (especially against democides); and (3) the Orthodox tradition does not identify a specific form of government as "sacred," then it follows that democracy can and should be supported from an Orthodox perspective. Winston Churchill's famous words resonate with this conclusion:

> Many forms of Government have been tried, and will be tried in this world of sin and woe. No one pretends that democracy is perfect or all-wise. Indeed, it has been said that democracy is the worst form of government except all those other forms that have been tried from time to time.[63]

There is, however, a major objection to democracy from an Orthodox perspective that we have not yet considered. If one grants the Orthodox teachings that (1) the human predicament is constituted by both physical death and spiritual death, and (2) while both forms of death are "the enemy," spiritual death is the *summum malum*, then what if democracy, while minimizing violent physical death simultaneously promotes spiritual death—the greater evil? What if there is a form of government that may not be as effective as democracy is at protecting citizens' physical lives (especially against democide), but that is significantly more effective at protecting citizens' spiritual lives? Should this form of government be preferred from an Orthodox perspective? With these questions, I have arrived back to this study's starting point—the pro-monarchy/*symphonia* Orthodox and the pro-democracy Orthodox; yet, I have arrived here having identified an alternative grounding for each, one that has emerged by considering the origin, purpose, and limits of Christian politics through the lens of the dynamics of death. I conclude now with a summary and synthesis of why, in my judgment, democracy is the best option for Orthodox today.

Conclusion

My aim has been to draw out lineaments of Orthodox Christian political philosophy by utilizing the theme of "the dynamics of death" as an interpretive lens and Thomas Hobbes as a conversation partner. The "dynamics of death" theme focuses our attention on the telos of politics and the telos of Christian life. It also helps us to understand the methods through which governments are constructed and sustained, for good or for ill. Finally, the dynamics of death theme helps us to see, and remember, the limits of politics. Yet I have also argued that the "dynamics of death" are basic to a normative Christian vision of political life and, therefore, hold promise for constructing an approach that complements and critiques existing arguments for and against democracy. I return, now, to the question with which I began: *On what theological basis, if any, can Orthodox Christians convincingly endorse modern democracy?*

The most significant finding that the "dynamics of death" lens has revealed, I believe, is that the Orthodox tradition's *thanatomorphicity*, its identification of the human predicament with the problem of physical and spiritual death and its identification of the telos of human existence with spiritual and physical resurrection, provides a theological basis for cautiously supporting modern democracy, unless it can be shown that democracy is significantly more likely than its alternatives to promote spiritual death among its citizens. To be sure, the Church does not need the state's cooperation or support in order to fulfill its sacred and sanctifying mission. Neither an Orthodox monarchy nor democracy is a requisite condition for the possibility of living a fully Christian life. Saints have emerged out of every political context. However, the Church should not hesitate to express a strong preference for a government that protects human life over one that does not. The Byzantine *symphonia* model grew, in part, out of the conviction that it is better to have a government that is not hostile to Christians and to a Christian moral vision than to have a government that persecutes Christians and advances a moral vision that Christians regard as evil. I agree. But on this side of modernity there is a third option: modern democracy.

Orthodoxy should support modern democracy because it has proven to be more effective at protecting human life than nondemocratic forms of government. Given the extreme violence and terror that people have suffered at the hands of nondemocratic regimes in countries that, historically, have had large Orthodox populations (Russia, Ukraine, Romania, Armenia, Bulgaria, Greece, Turkey, Syria, Lebanon, Palestine, etc.), the Orthodox community has a strong experiential basis for critiquing authoritarian and absolutist regimes. Especially in light of the fact that the second most murderous regime in history—the Soviet Union—emerged in a region with the largest population of people self-identifying as Orthodox in history, Orthodox would do well to underscore the responsibility of government to protect human life and to prevent violence against its citizens.

Orthodoxy should support democracy because democracy, especially through its affirmation and protection of religious freedom, acknowledges its limits and its penultimate status. Governments cannot ultimately save people from death; they cannot offer the fullness of resurrected life. Thus a legitimate government must give space for people to freely pursue full salvation. While Orthodox Christians affirm wholeheartedly that the Church accomplishes this desired salvation by being the body of Christ and the dwelling place of the Holy Spirit, there is nothing un-Christian about resisting the opportunity to establish Orthodox Christianity and affirming religious freedom as a civil right. Again, my reason for this stems from Orthodoxy's acknowledgment of the depths of human corruption and the potential for abuse when power is concentrated. Better to have a Church that is separated from the government, and that can both critique political power and be critiqued by citizens, than to have a Church established and supported by the state.

Finally, Orthodoxy should support democratic governance not because democracy is the fulfillment of an Orthodox theological-ethical vision but because is it not inherently opposed to an Orthodox theological-ethical vision, so long as it stays within its limits. To elevate democracy as the apotheosis of Orthodoxy is neither consistent with Orthodox tradition nor spiritually wise. Democracy is our best available option; however, it is an option still wrought with spiritual dangers that must be continuously identified and sharply critiqued in our communities and our hearts. The "dynamics of death" lens has provided lineaments of a fresh argument for democracy, even as it reminds us that, without Christ, "all of us mortals alike dwell in an unfortified city."[64]

Notes

1. For helpful accounts of Balkan nations' use of "*symphonia*," see Lucian N. Leustean, "Orthodoxy and Political Myths in Balkan National Identities," *National Identities* 10, no. 4 (2008): 421–32, as well as Felicia Alexandru, "Church-State Relations in Post-Communist Romania: Real Deprivatization or the Way Back to Byzantine Symphonia," *Romanian Journal of Political Science* 6, no. 2 (Winter 2006): 57–69.

2. Aristotle Papanikolaou surveys Orthodox Christian perspectives on democracy in "Orthodox Political Theology through the Centuries," Chapter 1, in *The Mystical as Political: Democracy and Non-Radical Orthodoxy* (Notre Dame, Ind.: University of Notre Dame Press, 2012).

3. Elizabeth Prodromou, "The Ambivalent Orthodox," in *World Religions and Democracy*, ed. Larry Diamond, Marc Plattner, and Philip Costopoulos (Baltimore: Johns Hopkins University Press, 2005), 134.

4. Nikolas K. Gvosdev, "St. John Chrysostom and John Locke: An Orthodox Basis for the Social Contract?" *Philotheos* 3 (2003): 150.

5. See the appeals to patristic writings in Nikolas K. Gvosdev, *Emperors and Elections: Reconciling the Orthodox Tradition with Modern Politics* (Huntington, N.Y.: Troitsa Books, 2000).

6. One example is the attempt by Gvosdev to connect democratic election processes with Orthodoxy's emphasis on a conciliar form of ecclesiastical governance and with the Orthodox Church's use of local assemblies in identifying candidates for the episcopacy. See his "Rendering Unto Caesar . . . an Orthodox Perspective on Democratic Transitions in Eastern Europe," *St. Vladimir's Theological Quarterly* 37, no. 1 (1993): 79–89.

7. Papanikolaou, *The Mystical as Political*, 4.

8. For extended critiques of using the Holy Trinity as a model for political theory, see Ted Peters, *God as Trinity: Relationality and Temporality in the Divine Life* (Louisville, Ky.: Westminster/John Knox Press, 1993) and Miroslav Volf, "'The Trinity Is Our Social Program': The Doctrine of the Trinity and the Shape of Social Engagement," *Modern Theology* 14, no. 3 (July 1998): 403–23.

9. This essay builds on my extended study of the concept of *"thanatomorphicity"*—of being "formed by death"—and it serves as a précis of planned follow-up work on Orthodox political philosophy. See Perry T. Hamalis, "The Meaning and Place of Death in an Orthodox Ethical Frame-work," in *Thinking through Faith: Perspectives from Orthodox Christian Scholars*, ed. A. Papanikolaou and E. Prodromou (Crestwood, N.Y.: St. Vladimir's Seminary Press, 2008), 183–217. See also my forthcoming monograph, *Formed by Death: Insights for Ethics from Eastern Orthodox Christianity* (Notre Dame, Ind.: University of Notre Dame Press, 2016).

10. This expression comes from the opening sentence of Rousseau's *Social Contract*.

11. For a defense and discussion of this claim, see Hamalis, "The Meaning and Place of Death."

12. On reading Hobbes's political proposal as a therapeutic response to the predicament of violent death and fear, see Michael Oakeshott, *Hobbes on Civil Association* (Indianapolis, Ind.: Liberty Fund, 1975).

13. Thomas Hobbes, *Leviathan*, ed. Richard Tuck (Cambridge: Cambridge University Press, 1996), 88.

14. Hobbes, *Leviathan*, 89.

15. Hobbes, *Leviathan*, 98.

16. Thomas Hobbes, *On the Citizen* [*De Cive*], ed. and trans. Richard Tuck and Michael Silverthorne (Cambridge: Cambridge University Press, 1998), Epistle dedicatory [10], 6.

17. My own view on Hobbes's identification of physical death as the worst evil confronting human beings comports with the predominant interpretation among scholars, which was defended recently by Mark Murphy against challenges by A. Lloyd and Gregory S. Kavka. See A. Lloyd, *Ideals as Interests in Hobbes's Leviathan: The Power of Mind over Matter* (Cambridge: Cambridge University Press, 1992), especially 36ff.; Gregory S. Kavka, *Hobbesian Moral and Political Theory* (Princeton: Princeton University Press, 1986), 80–122; and Mark C. Murphy, "Hobbes on the Evil of Death," *Archiv für Geschichte der Philosophie* 82 (2000): 36–61.

18. Thomas Hobbes, "De Homine," xi.6, in *Man and Citizen* (= *De Homine* and *De Cive*), ed. Bernard Gert (Indianapolis: Hackett, 1991), 48.

19. Thomas Hobbes, *The Elements of Law, Natural and Politic: Part 1, Human Nature, Part II, De Corpore Politico with Three Lives*, ed. J.C.A. Gaskin (Oxford: Oxford University Press, 1994), I.14.6, 79.

20. Hobbes, *Leviathan*, 88.

21. In the opening line of *Leviathan*, Part 2, *Of Commonwealth*, Hobbes writes, "The final Cause, End, or Designe of men (who naturally love Liberty, and Dominion over others,) in the introduction of that restraint upon themselves, (in which we see them live in Commonwealths,) is the foresight of their own preservation, and of a more contented life thereby; that is to say, of getting themselves out from that miserable condition of Warre" (Hobbes, *Leviathan*, 117).

22. Hobbes, *Leviathan*, 231.

23. A full discussion of political legitimacy in Hobbes lies beyond our present scope; however, this is one of the concepts that Orthodox thinkers have not yet sufficiently examined.

24. Hobbes states that the objects of passions, the private good, will likely differ from individual to individual (see Hobbes, *Leviathan*, Introduction, 10).

25. See J. Judd Owen, "The Tolerant Leviathan: Hobbes and the Paradox of Liberalism," *Polity* 37, no. 1 (January 2005): 130–48.

26. For a good example, see the writings of William Cavenaugh, especially his *Theopolitical Imagination: Discovering the Liturgy as a Political Act in an Age of Global Consumerism* (London: T&T Clark, 2002), Chapter 1.

27. Hobbes, *Leviathan*, Preface to the Latin edition; cited in Michael Oakeshott, *Hobbes on Civil Association* (Berkeley: University of California Press, 1975), 77. Italics added.

28. Hobbes, *Leviathan*, 214.

29. See Hobbes, *Leviathan*, Chapter 19.

30. See Hobbes, *Leviathan*, 120. I will return to the dangers of such a concentration of absolute power below.

31. Oakeshott, *Hobbes on Civil Association*, 38–39.

32. For a further discussion of Hobbes's view on reason and revelation, see Paul D. Cooke, *Hobbes and Christianity: Reassessing the Bible in Leviathan* (Lanham, MD: Rowman & Littlefield, 1996), and A.P. Martinich, *The Two Gods of Leviathan* (Cambridge: Cambridge University Press, 1992), especially 185–219.

33. Hobbes, *Leviathan*, 306–7.

34. For present purposes, I am stipulating that "eternal death" refers to an unending state of spiritual death, and that "spiritual death" refers to a state of affairs in which the nonphysical dimension of a human person is in a condition of radical separation, rupture, or alienation from God, either prior to or after the person's physical death.

35. In the writings of subsequent social contractarians who are more supportive of democracy, such as John Locke, one nonetheless finds a very similar account of the dynamics of death in the functioning of the social contract and in defining the origin and purpose of government. See especially Locke's *Two Treatises of Government* (1690).

36. Epicurus, *Fragments*, Vatican Collection 31.

37. An exception to this, of course, is when the government takes the life of a citizen who broke the social contract by threatening to kill (or killing) another citizen, or by committing some other serious crime. In such a case, legitimacy is strengthened, not weakened, by the state's successful fulfillment of its responsibility to protect.

38. Recent examples of this within the American context are abundant. Consider the PATRIOT Act of 2001 and, more recently, the US surveillance program controversy, both of which clearly express the state's need to deliver safety in order to remain legitimate and the state's insistence that citizens forfeit more of their rights in order to enable the state to do so.

39. Hobbes, *De Homine* xi.6.

40. Hobbes, *Elements of Law* I.14.6.

41. Jack S. Levy, "The Causes of War: A Review of Theories and Evidence," in *Behavior, Society, and Nuclear War*, ed. P. Tetlock, J. Husbands, R. Jervis, P. Stern, and C. Tilly (New York: Oxford University Press, 1989), 270.

42. R. J. Rummel, *Death by Government* (New Brunswick, N.J.: Transaction Publishers, 1994) and R. J. Rummel, *Power Kills: Democracy as a Method of Nonviolence* (New Brunswick, N.J.: Transaction Publishers, 1997).

43. Rummel, *Death by Government*, 31.

44. In *Death by Government*, Rummel provides the data for 169,198,000 victims of democide between 1900 and 1987. In his subsequent work and on his website he revised this number upward by ~92 million to include Mao's famine in China (~40 million), colonial democide (~50 million), and the totals for 1988–99 (1.34 million). See http://www.hawaii.edu/powerkills/20TH.HTM (accessed: 22 July 2014).

45. Rummel, *Death by Government*, 2.

46. See Hamalis, *Formed by Death*.

47. Given this essay's limited scope, I will save detailing the second and third meanings of *thanatomorphicity* for a future study.

48. See note 34 above for stipulated definitions of "eternal death" and "spiritual death."

49. Georges Florovsky, *Creation and Redemption: Collected Works, Vol. 3* (Belmont, Mass.: Nordland, 1976), 105.

50. Kallistos Ware, *The Inner Kingdom: Volume I of the Collected Works* (Crestwood, N.Y.: St. Vladimir's Seminary Press, 2000), 30.

51. Archimandrite Sophrony Sakharov, *On Prayer*, trans. Rosemary Edmonds (Essex: Stavropegic Monastery of St. John the Baptist, 1996), 66.

52. See, for example, Boris Bobrinskoy, "Old Age and Death: Tragedy or Blessing?" *St. Vladimir's Theological Quarterly* 28, no. 4 (1984): 237–44.

53. Florovsky, *Creation and Redemption*, 104.

54. Irenaeus of Lyons, *Against Heresies*, Book 5, in *From Irenaeus to Grotius: A Sourcebook in Christian Political Thought*, ed. Oliver O'Donovan and Joan Lockwood O'Donovan (Grand Rapids, Mich.: Eerdmans, 1999), 17.

55. John Chrysostom, *On the Statues*, Homily VI, Chapter 2, in *Nicene and Post-Nicene Fathers of the Christian Church*, Series I, volume 9, ed. Philip Schaff (Grand Rapids, Mich.: Eerdmans, 1886), 421–22.

56. Gvosdev elaborates on this point in Chrysostom's work, arguing that Chrysostom teaches that government is ordained by God, but that he also suggests a type of "popular sovereignty." See Gvosdev, "St. John Chrysostom and John Locke," 152.

57. As I noted earlier, these are temptations to which many existing Orthodox political theologies are susceptible, both among "pro-monarchy" and among "pro-democracy" authors.

58. For an extended commentary on the development of the *akakia* and its surrounding rituals, see Gilbert Dagron, "From the Mappa to the Akakia: Symbolic Drift," trans. Jean Birrell in *From Rome to Constantinople: Studies in Honour of Averil Cameron*, ed. Hagit Amirav and Bas ter Haar Romeny (Leuven: Peeters, 2007): 203–19. There is also a gorgeous mosaic in Hagia Sophia (dated to 912 CE) of the Emperor Alexander (+913 CE) holding a cylindrical *akakia*.

59. In his work *Advice to the Emperor Justinian*, Agapetus the Deacon exhorts the Emperor to remember his own mortality (§§4, 14, 67, 71), to remember God's judgment over all (§67 and §69), and to strive to secure the people (§62). See the recent critical edition of the text in *Three Political Voices from the Age of Justinian*, trans. and ed. Peter N. Bell (Liverpool: Liverpool University Press, 2009): 98–122. See also Patrick Henry III, "A Mirror for Justinian: The *Ekthesis* of Agapetus Diaconus," *Greek, Roman and Byzantine Studies* 8, no. 4 (Winter 1967): 281–308.

60. The text within this icon translates as follows: "Sisoes, the great ascetic, stood before the tomb of Alexander the Great, Emperor of the Greeks who of old had shone with glory. Astonished and horrified by the inexorable passing of time and the vanity of this transient world, he cried out: 'Beholding thee, O grave, I fear the Judgment of God and I weep, for the common destiny of all mankind comes to mind. How can I cope with such an end? O Death! Who can escape thee?'" For an analysis of the image, see George Galavaris, "Alexander the Great Conqueror and Captive of Death: His Various Images in Byzantine Art," *Revue d'Art Canadienne/Canadian Art Review* 16, no. 1 (1989): 12–18.

61. Stanley Hauerwas, *A Community of Character: Toward a Constructive Christian Social Ethic* (Notre Dame, Ind.: University of Notre Dame Press, 1981), 109–10.

62. See the discussion in John A McGuckin, "The Legacy of the 13th Apostle: Origins of the Eastern Christian Conceptions of Church and State Relations" *St. Vladimir's Theological Quarterly* 47:3–4 (2003): 251–88.

63. Sir Winston Churchill, *Hansard,* 11 November 1947.

64. See Epicurus, *Fragments*, Vatican Collection 31, cited above.

"I Have Overcome the World"

The Church, the Liberal State, and Christ's Two Natures in the Russian Politics of *Theosis*

Nathaniel Wood

In his recent book *The Mystical as Political,* Aristotle Papanikolaou has drawn attention to the thought of the Russian Orthodox philosopher-theologians Vladimir Soloviev (1853–1900) and Sergius Bulgakov (1871–1944) as an indispensable resource for Christian theologians working out the political implications of the doctrine of *theosis,* or deification, in liberal democratic contexts.[1] Their writings present what is arguably the most significant attempt yet to develop a "politics of *theosis*" in Orthodoxy, the tradition most closely associated with the doctrine. As Papanikolaou shows, examinations of *theosis* in connection to political theology have often tended to set the doctrine in opposition to the liberal democratic politics of the modern West. Papanikolaou cites John Milbank as a major example of this trend, while figures like Soloviev and Bulgakov are noteworthy exceptions to it. The latter two thinkers endorse what is essentially a Christian liberalism, justified on the basis of a distinctively theological conception of the human person as a being created for communion with God. They could at times offer strikingly optimistic appraisals of liberal democratic societies. Bulgakov, for example, would go as far as to call the United States, with its commitment to liberal values, "the regime most favorable to the Church, most normal for it."[2]

At the same time, such glowing remarks exist alongside much more sobering assessments of liberalism. In the vein of contemporary antiliberal political theologians such as Milbank, Soloviev and Bulgakov often treat secular politics as a heresy that denies the transcendent end of the human person and the human community. The Church, as the locus of true community, therefore stands at odds, at least in some ways, with the liberal democratic state. It is "only the Church that possesses the principle of true social order," Bulgakov tells us, and so the secular order must in the end be "overcome and dissolved in *ecclesial* life."[3]

How, then, can these two sides of their thought be reconciled? How can the Church resist the "heresy" of secular politics while also acknowledging that the liberal democratic state is "the regime most favorable" to its mission?

In what follows, I argue that Soloviev and Bulgakov resolve this tension through the theme of "inward overcoming" that runs throughout their work, and that is ultimately rooted in their treatments of the union of Christ's divine and human natures. Both thinkers understand the incarnation as an inward overcoming of humanity's alienation from God: the kenotic immersion of God into the depths of human consciousness in order to raise it up and deify humanity from within, by its own free activity. This approach to the incarnation stands behind a Christological politics focused similarly on the Church's inward overcoming of the secular order. The resulting political theology does not posit a strict opposition between the Church and the liberal democratic state that necessitates the Church's complete withdrawal from democratic politics into some sort of ecclesiocentric "counter-politics," nor does it defer to secular social theory as an adequate and complete description of supposedly immanent, "purely natural" laws of human social relations. The Russian politics of *theosis* celebrates liberal democracy as a genuine advancement toward a free, creative, dignified humanity whose full development will be realized only in *divine-*humanity, *theosis*, the collective incarnation of Christ in society; yet it also recognizes the innate danger of secular society to slide toward an exclusive, atheistic humanism that cuts this development short. In the politics of *theosis*, the Church, imitating Christ, immerses itself within the structures of liberal democracy in order to raise it up to a higher purpose from within, giving it new theological significance as a *free* instrument of the world's deification, without abandoning the liberal commitment to human freedom or reverting to a theocratic privileging of the Church. What we are left with is a Christian politics that affirms some of the core insights of contemporary antiliberal critique, but that ultimately rejects the more strictly oppositional stance associated with someone like Milbank and resists the twin dangers of ecclesiastical triumphalism over the liberal state and ecclesiastical withdrawal from the state.

It should be made clear, finally, that the following argument does not attempt to align the Russian politics of *theosis* straightforwardly with American-style liberal democracy. Despite Bulgakov's occasional praise for the American system, the Russian liberal tradition has its own distinct history that is sometimes very different from the American tradition. Nevertheless, the basic political-theological motifs that Soloviev and Bulgakov developed can be applied to the American context, and I have done my best in this essay to present their political theology in broadly applicable terms.

The Incarnation as a Political Task

While the twentieth century witnessed a spectacular revival of original Orthodox reflection on the doctrine of deification and its implications for our understanding of the human person, the specifically political dimensions of the doctrine have received far less attention from Orthodox theologians; when *theosis* has been explored in connection to political theology, it has tended to be set in opposition to the liberal democratic politics of the West. For the tradition of Russian Orthodox thought represented by Soloviev and Bulgakov, however, the doctrine was always inescapably political. Political challenges drove their turn to *theosis*, particularly the need to find a third way between the false dichotomy of tsarist theocracy and the positivism and materialism of the secular intelligentsia, both of which Soloviev and Bulgakov believed to be incompatible with the Christian humanism on which a successful political order must be based. Thus, the theological recovery of the particular human person as a bearer of "absolute, divine significance,"[4] as one in whom the whole created order will realize its proper communion with the transcendent God, a theme that has become central to contemporary Orthodox theology, is at its origin bound up with political theology—and not just any political theology, but one marked by an openness toward at least some forms of liberal democracy.

We can find evidence of that openness already in Soloviev's early works of the 1870s and 1880s, a time when he still held out hope for the viability of an institutional Christian theocracy. The "free theocracy" that Soloviev advocated reimagined Orthodoxy's theocratic heritage along more liberal, even if not quite democratic, lines, affirming key liberal commitments like the freedom of conscience, freedom of religion, and the absolute dignity of the individual. If by the 1890s he had abandoned hope for the realization of a genuine theocracy in history, he remained committed to a vision of politics rooted in the promise of *theosis* as divine-human communion, which had begun to look very much like a full-fledged Christian liberalism in his most important later work, *The Justification of the Good*, published in 1897.[5] Several of Soloviev's successors, including Bulgakov and S. L. Frank, would carry forward the liberal aspects of his thought, crafting their own "free theocratic" systems that were explicitly and unapologetically theological and yet remarkably receptive to the influence of Western liberal democratic thought. Thus Bulgakov, caught up in the spirit of the Revolution of 1905, could express hope in his political pamphlet *An Urgent Task* for a "worldwide United States," arguing that the most hospitable form of government for a Christian politics is not tsarist autocracy but "the federative democratic republic, as the English dissidents who emigrated to America understood so well in their time."[6] It was thirty years later, in a book written for Western audiences, that he would restate the same sentiment by identifying the American system as the one "most favorable" to the Church's mission.

As I noted above, however, such statements do not indicate an uncritical endorsement of liberalism. For these Russian thinkers, liberalism was never an end itself, but was always subordinate to an all-embracing cosmic vision of divine-human communion, centered on the person and work of Christ. While that vision could in some cases lend provisional support to certain features of liberal democracy as instruments of the Church's mission, certain other aspects of the liberal tradition stand in tension with a politics of *theosis*.

Take, for example, these thinkers' denial of a division between nature and grace, or between creation and deification. In same spirit as Milbank and other recent critics of liberalism, the Russians reject the notion of a "pure nature" that is not intrinsically oriented toward participation in God. For them, then, creation reveals itself only in the light of the incarnation, because creation is predestined to become God's glorified and deified body, in which God will be "all in all." The "cosmic" incarnation of Christ, the historical realization of universal "God-manhood" or "divine-humanity" (*bogochelovechestvo*), is thus "the inner foundation of creation, its *entelechy*."[7] Such is the promise of the Christian gospel, which imposes on its human recipients a religious task: to assist created nature in the unfolding of its inner ontological momentum (resisted by the forces of sin), to labor in history to extend the incarnation into every corner of the world, to "regard *all* things" in light of Christ and to allow Christ to "become incarnate in *all* things."[8]

Here one can see the basic "theocratic" character of the Russian politics of *theosis*. Created nature's intrinsic orientation toward transcendence calls into question any sphere of human activity—whether economic, political, scientific, or any other—that becomes closed in on the autonomous pursuit of its own immanent ends. The promise and task of deification must possess an "all-embracing, central significance"; it must serve as the organizing principle of all human activity.[9] "There must be nothing that is in principle 'secular,'" as Bulgakov argues, nothing that is neutral or indifferent to the historical realization of divine-human communion.[10] Both the economy and the state exist to serve a higher goal that is *given* to them from beyond themselves—by the Church, which, as Christ's collective body, is also the telos of world history. Thus the Church, Soloviev argues, must "subordinate secular society to itself by raising it up to itself, by spiritualizing it, by making the secular element its instrument and means" for incarnating Christ in all things.[11]

Certainly, if Christ's earthly body is his Church, then to speak of incarnating Christ in all things requires us to speak in a certain sense of the "churching" of society. In this sense, the Russians share Milbank's desire for a political theology that is "first and foremost an *ecclesiology*, and only an account of other societies to the extent that the Church defines itself, in its practice, in continuity or discontinuity with these societies."[12] More so than Milbank, the Russians affirm a tremendous degree of continuity between the politics of the Church and the politics of liberal democracy, especially with respect to liberalism's safeguarding of the free development of human personality. Nevertheless, they are also aware of a profound *discontinuity* between the Church and the secular state, because for them, the secular state is founded on a false anthropology: namely, the Feuerbachian heresy of "mangodhood" (*chelovekobozhestvo*), the immanent self-deification of humanity, a parodic reversal of Christ's Godmanhood. Without a theological corrective, a liberal democracy that remains strictly secular, even while securing a space for free human development, is incapable of directing that development toward its proper divine-human end. Instead, to the extent that liberalism encourages the human will and human social activity to remain turned in on themselves and to fail to recognize a goal transcendent to themselves, the liberal democratic state confronts the Church as a rival pseudotheocracy, a competing pseudospiritual society rooted in mangodhood. Consider, for example, Bulgakov's critique of the secular democratic state in his 1917 book *Unfading Light*. There he argues that with the advent of secularism, the state does not cease to be "theocratic" but merely shifts its sacred foundation from the transcendent will of God to the immanent will of the people. "For the democratic religion of deified humanity, the state is the highest form of life—a pseudo-church," he argues. "Even more than that: humanity, organized in a state, is an earthly god."[13]

Unsurprisingly then, like Milbank, the Russians sought to develop a distinctive "Christian sociology" to counter secular accounts of society.[14] Soloviev had begun this project already in his earliest works, such as *The Philosophical Principles of Integral Knowledge* (completed in 1874), in which he located the "principle of social union" within the sacramental life of ecclesial society.[15] Bulgakov followed Soloviev on this point, and in his 1932 essay, "The Soul of Socialism," writes that

> Christianity too recognises that there is a real human unity-in-plurality—the *Body of Christ*, which consists of distinct, individual living members (1 Cor. 12.12–27)—i.e. personalities; and in this dogma concerning the Church there is sufficient basis for developing the principles of a Christian sociology.[16]

Bulgakov then immediately identifies "this dogma" as the Slavophile doctrine of the Church's *sobornost*, the free, harmonious "all-togetherness" of Christians united by their mutual love for each other and their common love for the same transcendent values.[17] The social unity of *sobornost*, in which alone human personality can freely and fully develop in all its potential, is founded on the principle of mutual self-renunciation. "All members of society must set a limit to their exclusive self-assertion and must adopt the point of view of self-denial," Soloviev argues. "They must renounce and sacrifice their exclusive will."[18] This kenotic stance sets ecclesial society at odds with political liberalism, whose founding mythologies give ontological priority to the self-assertion of the individual will. The Church, on the other hand, is founded on the sacraments, whose fundamental feature is humanity's *receptivity* to a divine grace that humanity does not possess of itself. In this way, Soloviev suggests, the sacraments remind us that the foundations of a true social order must be "*divinely-human and not humanly-divine*," or put differently, must be located in humanity's kenotic openness to God's kenotic descent rather than in the temptation of human egoism to seize absoluteness for itself from within itself.[19] For the Russians, this turn to transcendence is necessary if human persons are to enact a genuinely *social* unity, a unity based in the interpenetration of all by all rather than on the coercive power of an externalized legal authority erected to manage the competing wills of self-interested individuals.

The Church thus exists in a state of theopolitical rivalry with every political order founded on the heresy of mangodhood and its denial of transcendence, and it is the political task of the Church to "overcome" this heresy. But, as I stated above, their acknowledgment of this rivalry does not lead either Soloviev or Bulgakov to the more wholesale antiliberalism seen in figures like Milbank. As I have suggested, their ability to hold together their negative and positive appraisals of liberal politics stems from their Christology, where the "overcoming" motif finds its more fundamental theological meaning. In the hypostatic union of Christ's two natures, Christ overcame the egoistic self-assertion of humanity, by which human beings had alienated themselves from God, deifying his humanity by uniting it to himself. In the original incarnation event, Christ won this victory in the "true center of the universe, i.e., in Himself," but history still awaits the communication of this victory to "the circumference of the world, i.e., in the collective whole of humanity."[20] If the Church in history is Christ's collective body in process, then the manner in which it "overcomes" the secular order and incarnates Christ in human society must correspond to that original overcoming accomplished in Christ's own person. Because the deification of the world organically "grows out of the God-man,"[21] the Church's relationship to secular society must conform to the manner in which Christ, as God, united himself to his own humanity, raised it up to himself, and made it into an instrument of divine action in history. The politics of *theosis* must therefore be a Christological politics, a politics that spans the time between the incarnation in Bethlehem and the eschatological incarnation of God in all things.

With these considerations in mind, I will now offer a brief summary of their approaches to the divine-human unity of the incarnate Christ, followed by a more substantial description of their Christological politics.

The Divine-Human Unity of Christ

Hans Urs von Balthasar has rightly suggested that Soloviev's Christological outlook is most deeply informed by the Greek patristic tradition running through Maximus the Confessor, who saw the Chalcedonian formula as "the foundation upon which the entire structure of natural and supernatural reality in the world is erected."[22] For patristic theologians like Maximus and John of Damascus, the unity of Christ involves more than just an external "adhesion" of the divine and human natures, as if they were two wholly discrete objects standing side by side and held together by the "glue" of the one hypostasis. Instead, the divine and the human "interpenetrate" or "mutually indwell" one another in the person of Christ, giving rise to a new *divine-human* mode of personhood, a "theandric operation" that completely unites (albeit without confusion) the two natures' respective characteristics. John's *Exact Exposition of the Orthodox Faith* summarizes this position with particular clarity:

> We do not say that the operations are separated and that the natures act separately, but we say that they act conjointly, with each nature doing in communion with the other that which it has proper to itself. [Christ] did not perform the human actions in a human way, because He was not a mere man, nor did He perform the divine actions in a divine way, because He was not just God, but God and man together.[23]

John continues:

> Thus, the theandric operation shows this: when God became man, that is to say, was incarnate, His human operation was divine, that is to say, deified. And it was not excluded from His divine operation, nor was his divine operation excluded from his human operation. On the contrary, each is found in the other.[24]

John's statements highlight the coactive character of Christ's incarnate activity, showing that Christ, as God, could never act apart from his humanity nor bypass the limitations of his human nature. For the incarnation to be fully realized, Christ's humanity had to be brought into free correspondence with his divinity, had to be deified, so that by its own properly *human* capacities it could become the instrument of God's self-revelation and redemptive activity.

We can see clear influence of the Christological tradition that John summarizes on Soloviev's and Bulgakov's own accounts of Christ's divine-human unity. We see the idea of the theandric operation expressed, for instance, in Bulgakov's claim that in Christ, "there is nothing that is only Divine or only human; the one in and through the other is Divine-human."[25] Both he and Soloviev would deepen this traditional understanding of Christ's divine-human *perichoresis* by examining the historical-ascetical realization of the two natures' interpenetration within the dynamics of Christ's incarnate consciousness. The incarnation was not accomplished *at once* in the stable at Bethlehem, but was, in Bulgakov's words, a "ceaselessly continuing process of the attainment of the divine in the human and the human in light of the divine" across the whole drama of Christ's earthly life.[26]

In his treatment of the incarnation in his *Lectures on Divine-Humanity,* Soloviev argues that Christ "attains" his divine-human unity by means of a double *kenosis,* or the mutual self-limitation of the divine and human natures. As God, Christ cannot deify his human nature unilaterally, but only by eliciting his humanity's free participation in his salvific work. For this reason, Soloviev finds the dogma of Christ's two wills indispensable, because in order for there to be a real synergy between the divine and the human in Christ, Christ's humanity must possess "a will that is distinct from the divine will and that, through the rejection of any possible contradiction with the divine will, freely submits to the latter and brings human nature into complete inner harmony with Divinity."[27] The human will's independence depends on an act of divine *kenosis:* becoming incarnate, Christ renounces his external sovereign power over humanity and submerges his own divinity within the limitations of his human consciousness in order to deify his humanity *from within,* by means of humanity's own free and conscious activity. The divine *kenosis* liberates Christ's humanity to enact its own *kenosis,* to renounce its autonomy and subordinate itself freely to the divine will. As Soloviev puts it, "Christ, as God, freely renounces the glory of God and thereby, as a human being, acquires the possibility of *attaining* that glory."[28] Of course, Christ's humanity attains this glory not as its own stable possession, but only by adopting the posture of ongoing active receptivity to the divine, by acting out its innate human potentialities in constant coordination with the divine will.

Bulgakov's Christology, articulated most fully in his late masterpiece *The Lamb of God,* deepens Soloviev's kenoticism. Following Soloviev, he posits

a mutual limitation of the two natures. In Christ there was "no consciousness of anything divine *apart from* the human," because Christ was conscious of himself *as God* only from within the limits of his human
self-consciousness.[29] He writes:

> The divine-humanity consists precisely in such a *correlativeness* of the
> divine and the human: the divine consciousness in Christ is com-
> mensurate with the human consciousness and does not exceed it. This
> relativity of the absolute, this becoming that occurs within the
> limits of the divine consciousness, is precisely *kenosis*.[30]

In the incarnation, Christ "actualizes His divinity for Himself only in inseparable union with the human nature, *as a function of [the human nature's] receptivity*," that is, "only to the extent of the deification of His
humanity."[31] Because the human nature, with its instinctual drive to assert
itself outside God, is not immediately receptive to the divine will, Christ
must *grow into* his divine-human self-consciousness over time, through
an "intense and unceasing struggle" to deify his human nature. But once
again, as for Soloviev, this struggle will not be won by the sheer force of
divine omnipotence, but by eliciting an active *kenosis* from the human will:

> In the God-Man, the fallen and infirm human essence, subjecting
> itself to the divine essence, becomes harmonious with and obedient
> to it. But this occurs not through the coercion of the human nature
> by the divine nature but by the spiritual overcoming of the "flesh"
> through its free subordination to the commands of the hypostatic
> spirit.[32]

That is to say, the divine nature "restrained its manifestation" until the
human nature's opposition to God was "*inwardly overcome*."[33]

Divine-Humanity and the Politics of *Theosis*

The *perichoresis* of the two natures in Christ, as the "inward overcoming"
of the distance between humanity and God, ties the Russians' Christology
to their political theology. Most fundamental here are the implications of
the incarnation for our understanding of divine sovereignty. Because of
the incarnation, "God is enthroned in a *new* way over the world: in man
and through man in the God-Man," Bulgakov argues.[34] Christ's human-

ity has been taken up into his eternal lordship over the world, where the divine and human natures "co-participate in the sitting at the right hand of the Father, for God and man are seated there in the one God-Man."[35] If redeemed humanity, as Christ's collective body, is seated on the heavenly throne, then humanity itself is the instrument through which Christ exercises his lordship. Christ's rule is a *divine-human rule*, established on the free, conscious participation of those who are ruled. "Christ is enthroned not by virtue of Divine omnipotence but through the *inner overcoming* of the world, through the struggle against enemy powers, through victory by persuasion."[36] Just as Christ's divine nature "leads" his human nature without coercing or erasing his human will, so also Christ leads the world as a whole, his universal human nature, to kenotically renounce its autonomy and egoism and to make itself receptive to the light of divine glory. Thus, even while the theocratic element of Christianity demands our unconditional submission to the will of God, God's will does not confront us as the external authority of a transcendent sovereign. In Christ, Soloviev tells us, the human will renounced itself in favor of the divine will as its own "*inner* good"—the transcendent within the immanent.[37] If the incarnation as divine-human communion is "the law of being for natural humanity,"[38] as I have suggested it is, then there can be no contradiction between human freedom and divine sovereignty, because human nature naturally reaches beyond itself to find completion and rest in communion with God. The coming of God's Kingdom is the fulfillment of humanity's own innermost potentialities and the implicit aim of all free human development.

With regard to the church-state relations, this approach rules out any sort of "political monophysitism" in which the Church would simply swallow up the secular state and society. Society must first possess relative independence from the divine principle, must first be allowed to discover its full *humanness*, before it can kenotically renounce its autonomy and be transformed into the human "flesh" of Christ's divine-human rule. This means that the Church, in turn, cannot incarnate the divine principle in secular society unilaterally, but only by *influencing* society and eliciting its free cooperation: "victory by persuasion." The Church relates to the state and society through *kenosis*, by acting as the *conscience* of society and bearing an inner witness to the divine-human ideal toward which society should freely strive. Just as the union of the two natures in Christ's hypostasis depended on the active receptivity of his human will to divine leading, so

also does the Church's eschatological overcoming of secular society de-
pend on the society's receptivity to the Church's witness to *sobornost*. In
this way, "the Church embodies herself in the state only in as much as the
state becomes spiritualized by Christian principles," as Soloviev argues.
"The Church comes down to temporal realities by the same steps up which
the state climbs toward the Church's ideal."[39]

Modeled on the Chalcedonian definition, a properly "theocratic" relationship between the Church and secular society therefore rests on a clear
distinction between the divine and the human, the Church and the state.
But this is not to suggest that the Church remains indifferent to state politics. As Soloviev reminds us, the Church's political task is to fill all things
with the spirit of Christ and order all human relations around the principle of *sobornost*:

> The church is not only an assembly of believers, but also an assembly
> of lovers. . . . Love is a force of limitless expansiveness, and the church,
> founded on love, must permeate the entire life of human society, all
> its relations and activity, descending into everything and elevating
> everything to itself. Existing outwardly in the milieu of civil society
> and the state, the church cannot segregate itself and separate itself
> from this milieu, but must influence it by its spiritual strength, must
> attract state and society to itself and gradually make them like itself,
> convey its principle of love and harmony in all spheres of human life.[40]

The Church carries out this task in two distinct but inseparable ways
that S. L. Frank helpfully identifies as the immediate *"radiation of love,"*
or the direct enactment of the principles of ecclesial communion in personal
encounters with our neighbors, and the *"politics of love,"* the systematic
attempt to embody those principles in political and legal structures through
political and legal means.[41]

The radiation of love takes precedence in the Church's mission, and with
the coming of God's Kingdom all politics and law will be dissolved into the
"anarchy" of *sobornost*. But in the present age, the politics of love assists
the radiation of love, making use of political and legal structures to establish the necessary *external* conditions that allow Christian social principles to flourish and maximize the potential of all human persons to freely
participate in humanity's common task of incarnating Christ in all things.
While state politics can never effect the *inner* harmony between humanity

and God that deification requires and therefore can never build the Kingdom of God on earth, the more modest aim of the politics of love is to use the power of the state to promote "the free development of all human powers which are to be the instrument of the future perfection, apart from which the Kingdom of God could not be realized in humanity."[42]

Frank ensures us that such a Christian politics will often resemble "the wisdom of this world."[43] At the present moment, it may most closely resemble the wisdom of liberal democracy. To the extent that the liberal tradition has championed the rights of individuals and secured an independent social space for the free development of human personality in all its distinctive humanness, Christians can recognize liberalism as a historical outgrowth of the social truth latent in the Christ-event and a providential advancement toward the realization of Christ's divine-human rule. This is certainly the reason that someone like Bulgakov could look to the United States as a beacon of hope for the future of Christian politics. But to the extent that liberalism remains captive to the heresies of immanentism and individualism, it still awaits eschatological "overcoming" by the sacramental society of the Church. Christian politics is therefore never reducible to liberal democratic politics, and the Church's mission never reducible to the interests of the liberal state. Christian politics is possible only when the divine principle toward which society strives is realized "not *in* the state, but *for* it in the Church."[44] Therein lies the significance of theological critiques of "Constantinianism," or what Soloviev called the "medieval worldview"[45]: If the Church is to spiritualize secular society, it must bear witness to a *different* Kingdom established on the basis of kenotic love and sacramental receptiveness to God's self-gift (which is, at the same time, God's gift to us of our own selves).

In an important sense, then, liberal church-state separation is a positive development for Christian politics, precisely because it allows the Church and the state to each develop its respective divine or human distinctiveness so that the two might become partners in a *divine-human* activity without division or confusion. Christians who take seriously the "theocratic" character of their faith can and should work within the liberal democratic structures in which they find themselves, not for the sake of undermining liberalism's historical successes (for example, by exploiting the democratic process to secure legal privileges for Christianity) but to assist liberalism in the further unfolding of its innate potential to serve as a human instrument of Christ's rule. That will mean developing the *human* aspect of the liberal tradition to its fullest extent, not only through the use of the state's coercive power to restrain all manifestations of evil that are "dangerous to the very existence of society,"[46] but also by taking positive steps toward a more just and equal society through the promotion of human rights, social welfare, education and healthcare, access to both meaningful labor and leisure, and other measures that foster the development of free human persons who can become agents of Christ's divine-human activity—all of which can be accomplished entirely through the means of liberal democratic politics. While the Church is driven toward these goals by its own theological commitments rather than by the interests of secular statecraft, it nevertheless can and should make use of liberal means to accomplish the goals in a way that involves the maximum cooperation of secular society itself.

At the same time, the Church will also have to bear witness to its own distinctive "counter-politics" through the living-out of its communal, sacramental life, challenging the heterodoxy of the liberal tradition and calling into the question the liberal state's pseudotheocratic ultimacy. In the radiation of the love, the Church bears witness to a higher mode of life toward which secular society must freely aspire, the divine telos of collective human activity. But in the same way that divine nature of Christ brings positive fulfillment to his human nature and *humanizes* his humanity, the Church reveals its own social principles as the *inner goal* of liberalism, the fulfillment of liberal society's own deepest humanistic commitments. While the liberal tradition has been remarkably successful at securing the rights and freedoms of human persons, it stands in opposition to Christ's rule to the extent that it drives human freedom toward the pursuit of private and collective self-interest, depriving human freedom of any absolute content through the attainment of which the human person might realize his or her "absolute, divine significance." In its radiation of love, on the other hand, the Church "discloses to man the sphere in which his freedom can find positive realization, and his will actual satisfaction."[47] It is precisely the *humanism* of liberal democracy that demands it be receptive to that which is beyond the human, that in relation to which alone humanity can become itself. The Church that "overcomes" liberal democracy is not a separate sovereign entity standing over against the state but the completion of the state's own humanistic work, liberal society in self-transcendent, self-realizing communion with God.

Conclusion

If we approach the politics of *theosis* in the way that I have described, then the Church's eschatological overcoming of the secular can only be an *inward* overcoming. This approach affirms that all Christian politics must begin and end in the sacramental life of the Church, the divine ideal for secular society, but it also suggests that the Church must enter kenotically into liberal democracy to lead toward that ideal from within, without overstepping the limits of liberalism, just as Christ's deification of his human nature never overstepped the limits of his human will and its receptivity to the divine. In its communal life, the Church embodies those social principles that will someday be freely incarnated in human society as a whole, and in its political activity the Church helps prepare the material and structural conditions that make that incarnation possible. On this view, the Church can both appreciate the accomplishments of liberal democracy as providential advancements in salvation history while also insisting that the liberal state can never be an end itself, since the very humanity that liberalism champions will only be fully humanized when it is fully deified, when it looks beyond itself to discover itself in communion with God.

Notes

1. Aristotle Papanikolaou, *The Mystical as Political: Democracy and Non-Radical Orthodoxy* (Notre Dame, Ind.: University of Notre Dame Press, 2012), especially 32–43.

2. Sergius Bulgakov, *The Orthodox Church*, translation revised by Lydia Kesich (Crestwood, N.Y.: St. Vladimir's Seminary Press, 1988), 163.

3. Bulgakov, "The Soul of Socialism," 264.

4. Vladimir Solovyov, *Lectures on Divine-Humanity*, trans. Peter Zouboff and revised by Boris Jakim (Hudson, N.Y.: Lindisfarne Press, 1995), 17.

5. For more on the development of Soloviev's liberalism, see Andrzej Walicki, *Legal Philosophies of Russian Liberalism* (Oxford: Clarendon, 1987), 165–212.

6. Sergius Bulgakov, "An Urgent Task," in *A Revolution of the Spirit: Crisis of Value in Russia, 1890–1924*, ed. Bernice Glatzer Rosenthal and Martha Bohachevsky-Chomiak (New York: Fordham University Press, 1990), 144.

7. Sergius Bulgakov, *The Lamb of God*, trans. Boris Jakim (Grand Rapids, Mich.: Eerdmans, 2008), 173.

8. Vladimir Solovyov, *The Justification of the Good*, trans. Nathalie Duddington and ed. Boris Jakim (Grand Rapids, Mich.: Eerdmans, 2005), 169.

9. Solovyov, *Lectures,* 1.

10. Quoted in Aidan Nichols, "Wisdom from Above?: The Sophiology of Father Sergius Bulgakov," *New Blackfriars*, vol. 85 (2004), 602.

11. Solovyov, *Lectures,* 16.

12. John Milbank, *Theology and Social Theory: Beyond Secular Reason*, 2nd ed. (Malden, Mass.: Blackwell, 2006), 382.

13. Sergius Bulgakov, *Unfading Light: Contemplations and Speculations,* trans. Thomas Allan Smith (Grand Rapids, Mich.: Eerdmans, 2012), 414.

14. Milbank, *Theology*, 383.

15. Vladimir Solovyov, *The Philosophical Principles of Integral Knowledge*, trans. Valeria Z. Nollan (Grand Rapids, Mich.: Eerdmans, 2008), 27.

16. Sergius Bulgakov, "The Soul of Socialism," in *Sergii Bulgakov: Towards a Russian Political Theology*, ed. Rowan Williams (Edinburgh: T & T Clark, 1999), 259–60. See also his "Social Teaching in Modern Russian Theology" in *Orthodoxy and Modern Society*, ed. Robert Bird (New Haven: The Variable Press, 1995), 5–25.

17. See *On Spiritual Unity: A Slavophile Reader*, trans. and ed. Boris Jakim and Robert Bird (Hudson, N.Y.: Lindisfarne, 1998).

18. Solovyov, *Lectures,* 7.

19. Solovyov, *Justification,* 377.

20. Solovyov, *Justification,* 169

21. Solovyov, *Justification*, 168.

22. Hans Urs von Balthasar, *The Glory of the Lord: A Theological Aesthetics, Volume 3:Studies in Theological Style: Lay Styles*, trans. Andrew Louth et al. (San Francisco: Ignatius, 1986), 287.

23. John of Damascus, *Writings*, trans. Frederic H. Chase Jr. (Washington: Catholic University of America Press, 1958), 322.

24. John of Damascus, *Writings*, 323.

25. Bulgakov, *Lamb,* 251–2.

26. Bulgakov, *Lamb*, 238

27. Solovyov, *Lectures,* 159.

28. Solovyov, *Lectures,* 161.

29. Bulgakov, *Lamb,* 250

30. Bulgakov, *Lamb*, 251.

31. Bulgakov, *Lamb*, 256.

32. Bulgakov, *Lamb*, 243.

33. Bulgakov, *Lamb*, 238.

34. Bulgakov, *Lamb*, 418.

35. Bulgakov, *Lamb*, 399.

36. Bulgakov, *Lamb*, 429.

37. Solovyov, *Lectures,* 161.

38. Bulgakov, *Lamb,* 435.

39. Vladimir Solovyev, *God, Man, and the Church: The Spiritual Foundations of Life,* trans. Donald Attwater (Cambridge: James Clarke, 1974), 180.

40. Vladimir Soloviev, "On Spiritual Authority in Russia," in *Freedom, Faith, and Dogma,* trans. and ed. Vladimir Wozniuk (Albany, N.Y.: SUNY Press, 2008), 18.

41. S.L. Frank, *The Light Shineth in Darkness: An Essay in Christian Ethics and Social Philosophy,* trans. Boris Jakim (Athens: Ohio University Press, 1989), 149.

42. Solovyov, *Justification,* 392.

43. Frank, 151.

44. Solovyov, *Justification,* 393.

45. For his most incisive critique of the "medieval worldview," see "On the Decline of the Medieval Worldview," in Wozniuk, ed., *Freedom, Faith, and Dogma,* 159–70. See also "Byzantinism and Russia," 191–227 of the same volume.

46. Solovyov, *Justification,* 323–24.

47. Solovyov, *Justification,* 374.

CONSTANTINE'S SHADOW: HISTORICAL PERSPECTIVES

EMPERORS AND BISHOPS OF CONSTANTINOPLE (324–431)

Timothy D. Barnes

Constantine, the first Christian ruler of the Roman Empire, casts a long shadow over all the subsequent history of Christian churches everywhere in the world up to the present day. But Constantine's relations with the Christian Church were shaped by an existing framework of attitudes and beliefs formed in a pagan Roman Empire that first formally recognized Christianity as a legitimate religion in 260, little more than a dozen years before the future emperor was born.[1] It was quite natural, therefore, for the supporters of Maiorinus in a disputed episcopal election in Carthage to appeal to Constantine in April 313 shortly after he had announced his conversion to Christianity and had exempted from curial duties their opponents ("those belonging to the worldwide church [in Carthage], over whom Caecilianus presides"),[2] just as it had been natural for bishops who had condemned and deposed Paul of Samosata, the bishop of Antioch, in the late 260s, to petition a pagan emperor to enforce their verdict of deposition.[3] For from the age of the apostles onwards, Christians had believed that Roman emperors were appointed by God to judge all disputes among their subjects. In the late second century, for example, Theophilus of Antioch answered the imputation of disloyalty to the emperor as follows: "You will say to me, 'Why do you not worship the emperor?' Because he was not made to be worshipped, but to be honoured with legitimate honour. He is not God, but a man appointed by God, not to be worshipped but to judge justly."[4] Constantine was proclaimed emperor in 306 and rose to supreme power in an ideological milieu in which emperors were regarded by all as supreme arbiters over all matters terrestrial, including the Christian Church, and it was only during the course of the fourth century that it became possible for Christians to argue that ecclesiastical affairs lay outside the jurisdiction of a Roman emperor. In Constantinople, however, the successors of Constantine exercised an effective and unchallenged control over the appointment and dismissal of bishops of the imperial city.

Alexander had been bishop of the ancient Greek city of Byzantium for a decade or more when Constantine defeated Licinius and gained control of the East in 324.[5] Hence, when Constantine razed Byzantium to the ground and built a new and wholly Christian city on its site, Alexander automatically became bishop of the new city of Constantinople, whose boundaries Constantine marked out on 8 November 324, and that he formally dedicated on 11 May 330. About Constantine's relations with Alexander only one thing is known, but it is very significant. In 336 a council of bishops met in Constantinople, readmitted Arius to communion on the recommendation and with the support of Constantine and was about to attempt to compel Alexander to accept Arius into communion when Arius suddenly collapsed and died.[6] Constantine died within a year on 22 May 337, but Alexander outlived him by only a few weeks, dying in the summer of 337 at the advanced age of ninety-eight.

Paul, Eusebius, and Macedonius (337–360)

After the death of Alexander, who had not appointed or co-opted a successor, a contested election ensued. The priest Paul was supported by those among the clergy and laity of Constantinople who fully accepted the creed drawn up at the Council of Nicaea, while those who were sympathetic to the theological views of the recently deceased Arius and his party supported the deacon Macedonius. The adherents of Paul elected and consecrated him bishop without waiting, as was required by the canons of the Council of Nicaea, for their choice to be ratified by the bishops of adjacent sees. When Emperor Constantius arrived in the city, he convened a council of bishops from the surrounding area that deposed Paul and replaced him with Eusebius, the bishop of nearby Nicomedia. Constantius then returned to Antioch.

Such is the clear and straightforward account of Paul's election and almost immediate deposition given by Socrates and repeated with rhetorical embellishment by Sozomen.[7] The date can be determined almost precisely. Athanasius reveals not only that he was in Constantinople when Paul was accused prior to his deposition, but also that Macedonius was both a priest under Paul and supported his bishop on that occasion.[8] Now Athanasius had been in Constantinople twice during the lifetime of Constantine (in the winter of 331–32 and the autumn of 335),[9] but after the emperor died he set foot in the city only once. He passed through Constantinople during his journey from Trier to Alexandria in 337, when the sons of Constantine allowed all the Eastern bishops deposed under their father to return to their sees. Athanasius was still in Trier on 15 June 337, and he entered Alexandria on 23 November of the same year. He traveled overland through the Balkans, and at Viminacium he had an audience with Constantius, presumably shortly before 9 September 337, when the three brothers Constantinus, Constantius, and Constans were jointly acclaimed Augusti by the Roman army in Pannonia. Paul was elected bishop of Constantinople during Constantius's absence in the Balkans and deposed when the emperor returned to Constantinople, but before he departed for Antioch, where he spent the winter of 337–38. Although Socrates explicitly dates both Paul's election and his replacement by Eusebius of Nicomedia to the year 340 or later, the precise circumstantial details that he provides exclude any date later than around October 337, since Constantius, who had left Antioch in the spring of 337 when he discovered that his father was fatally ill, returned to Antioch in the autumn of 337 and did not visit Constantinople again for several years.[10]

Eusebius died late in 341.[11] On his death, his ecclesiastical supporters, including bishops from surrounding regions, elected Macedonius as the new bishop of Constantinople. However, those who had supported Paul in 337 invited him to return from Pontus, where Constantius had exiled him, and again installed him as bishop of the city. When Constantius, who was in Antioch, heard the news, he ordered the general Hermogenes to expel Paul en route to taking up his new military command in Thrace. When Hermogenes attempted to remove Paul from the church that he had occupied, Paul's adherents resisted, a mob burned the house where Hermogenes was lodging, dragged him out, and lynched him. Constantius thereupon traveled posthaste across Asia Minor, expelled Paul, punished the city by reducing the amount of free bread distributed daily from 80,000 to 40,000 *modii,* and returned to Syria, leaving Macedonius as bishop of Constantinople. Once more Socrates, who is followed and rewritten by

Sozomen, provides a precise and detailed narrative, and this time his consular date of 342 for the murder of Hermogenes is confirmed by other evidence.[12]

Macedonius's tenure of the see of Constantinople was insecure, since the bishops of the West, who had the political support of the Western emperor Constans, who had been sole emperor in the West since 340, recognized Paul as the legitimate bishop of the city. In 343, Paul was restored to his see by the Council of Serdica: that is, by a council of Western bishops meeting separately from their Eastern counterparts, who assembled and formed a counter-council at Philippopolis. But when Paul returned to Constantinople in the autumn of 344, his second attempt to reoccupy his see was suppressed by Constantius's new praetorian prefect Philippus, who acted with guile in order to avoid meeting the same fate as Hermogenes. Philippus summoned Paul to a private interview in the baths of Zeuxippus, where he had him arrested and then secretly bundled on board a ship, which took him to Thessalonica, which was in the territory of Constans and Paul's native city, and forbade him to reenter the territory of Constantius.[13] Once in the territory of Constans, Paul betook himself to the court of the Western emperor and persuaded him to take up his cause. Constans wrote to his brother threatening war if Constantius did not restore both Paul and Athanasius, who were with him, to their sees in Constantinople and Alexandria.[14] In 346 Constantius bowed to the political, diplomatic, and military pressure from his brother and allowed the restoration of all the exiled Eastern bishops who had been vindicated by their Western compeers at the Council of Serdica. In the summer of 346, therefore, Paul returned to Constantinople, and Macedonius was compelled to yield his place as bishop.

So far Socrates was well informed about ecclesiastical events in Constantinople itself, even though he sometimes set individual episodes in a false chronological context. I have, however, added some details to the narrative of Socrates, who is followed and rewritten by Sozomen, from a very slippery passage in Athanasius's highly polemical *History of the Arians*, written in 357, which now needs to be analyzed in detail. Athanasius's account of Paul of Constantinople reads as follows:

About Paul the bishop of Constantinople, I think that no-one is ignorant. For the more famous the city, the less hidden is what actually happened. Even against Paul a false charge/excuse [*prophasis*] was invented. For his accuser Macedonius, who is now bishop after replacing Paul, remained in communion with him when he was accused and served as a priest under the same Paul, when I myself was present. Nevertheless, since Eusebius was watching with greedy eyes because he wished to usurp the bishopric of the city [of Constantinople] (he had been translated from Berytus to Nicomedia in the same sort of way), the false charge was retained and they did not desist from their plot, but continued to slander him. On the first occasion, Paul was exiled to Pontus by Constantius [*para Konstantiou*]; on the second, he was shackled in iron chains and exiled to Constantius [*para Konstantion*] in Singara in Mesopotamia, then transferred from there to Emesa, and on the fourth occasion to Cucusus in Cappadocia next to the deserts of the Taurus [Mountains], where, as those who were with him have reported, he was throttled by them[15] and died.

After doing this, those who never tell the truth showed no shame even after his death when they again invented the falsehood [*prophasis*] that Paul had died from illness, even though all those who dwell in that region know the facts. For Philagrius, who was then *vicarius* of that area and disingenuously [*hypokrinomenos*] accepted whatever they wished, was nevertheless surprised at this, and perhaps distressed because someone other than himself had performed the evil deed, announced to many others known to me and in particular to the bishop Serapion that Paul had been shut up by them in a very small, dark place and left to die of starvation, but that subsequently six days later, when they entered and found him still breathing, they then set upon the poor man and throttled him.

This was the end of Paul's life on earth.[16]

The first sentence of this passage fixes the date of Paul's first deposition as autumn 337, since Athanasius was in Constantinople when Paul was accused and deposed for the first time. What of Paul's second, third, and fourth exiles? Paul was indeed expelled from Constantinople four times, as Athanasius acknowledges. But the details that Athanasius supplies relate only to Paul's first and last expulsions from the city. Athanasius supplies the place to which Paul was exiled in 337, which is not known from any other source. On both the second and third occasions, however—that is, in 342 and 344—Paul went to the West, an important historical fact that

Athanasius wished to conceal. The places that he names as the places to which Paul was exiled for the second and the third time are in fact (and can only be) places to which Paul was sent after his fourth and final expulsion from Constantinople.

It is for this reason that the text must be emended on the basis of two observations, one literary, the other historical. First, the preposition *para* plus the genitive case to express agency is Athanasius's normal usage; *hypo* is an Atticizing corruption of a common type, which replaces *para* with a stylistically superior synonym. Second, Athanasius cannot have been mistaken about the identity of the emperor who sent Paul to Pontus in 337. He was Constantius. The transmitted *Konstantinou* must accordingly be emended to *Konstantiou*.[17] But to repeat *para Konstantiou* would be lame and pointless, and both Singara in Mesopotamia and Emesa in Syria, to which Paul was successively sent, are places in an area where Constantius is independently known to have been between 348 and 350.[18] As for the council of bishops that deposed Paul for the fourth time, it can hardly be other than the Council of Antioch, which met and deposed Athanasius in 349, probably in the autumn,[19] after which Constantius sent his praetorian prefect Philippus to Egypt to arrest the bishop of Alexandria.[20]

Eudoxius and Demophilus (360–380)

The Council of Constantinople, which promulgated the *homoean* creed in January 360, replaced Macedonius with Eudoxius, who occupied the see of Constantinople for a full decade. Eudoxius weathered the "persecution" which Julian the Apostate directed against the *homoeans*, was left unmolested by Jovian, and then enjoyed the support of Emperor Valens, who sustained the *homoean Reichskirche* in the East from his accession in 364 until his death on 9 August 378. When Eudoxius died in the spring of 370, the *homoeans* installed Demophilus as his successor. This was an obviously partisan choice, since Demophilus had been bishop of Beroea in Thrace in the reign of Constantius before he and a number of other bishops were condemned and deposed by the Western Council of Ariminum in 359 because they "refused to anathematize the Arian doctrine.'"[21] Demophilus occupied the see until Emperor Theodosius entered Constantinople on 24 November 380, and immediately demanded that Demophilus accept the creed of Nicaea, and expelled him from the city when he demurred.[22] Although Demophilus continued to lead a conventicle of "Arians" outside the gates of Constantinople until he died in 386,[23] the Nicenes took possession of the main churches of the city that had been in the hands of the "Arians" for many years.[24]

Gregory of Nazianzus (379–381)

When Valens was defeated and presumed dead at the Battle of Adrianople on 9 August 378, the *homoean Reichskirche* that he had sustained in Asia Minor, the Syrian region, and Egypt rapidly collapsed.[25] It was probably in the autumn of 378 that Gregory, the bishop of the insignificant small town of Sasima in Cappadocia, came to Constantinople to support orthodoxy in the city, though not initially as bishop.[26] Gregory of Nazianzus, as he is normally known from the name of his later see, had been urged by Basil of Caesarea, who died on 1 January 379,[27] and by many other bishops in Asia Minor and their congregations, to defend orthodoxy in Constantinople, and, against his better judgment, he acceded to their plea. After some time had elapsed, Gregory was elected bishop, according to Socrates "by the vote of many bishops"—which implies that he was consecrated as bishop of Constantinople by the Council of Antioch, which met in the autumn of 379.[28] Within Constantinople itself, however, Gregory's position only became secure after Theodosius expelled Demophilus on 26 November 380.[29]

Earlier in 380 an attempt had been made to supplant Gregory. A group of bishops sent by Peter, the bishop of Alexandria, started one night to consecrate an itinerant philosopher from Egypt, whom had Gregory initially welcomed to the city as a supporter, as the Nicene bishop of Constantinople. (His name is stated as both Hero and Maximus, often with a sobriquet as Maximus the Cynic.)[30] By a fortunate accident, the attempted consecration was interrupted before the ceremony could be completed and Maximus was expelled from Constantinople. From there he traveled to Thessalonica, where he was rebuffed by Theodosius, then returned to Alexandria.[31] From Alexandria, Maximus went to Italy, where he sought and gained support in the West: He convinced the Council of Aquileia in September 381, which was dominated by Ambrose of Milan, that he was still the legitimate bishop of Constantinople, with the result that after the council Ambrose wrote to Theodosius in his own name and that of "the rest of the bishops of Italy" demanding that Maximus be restored to the see of Constantinople, which had been usurped by others, whom

Ambrose names as Gregory and his successor Nectarius.[32] This Western
démarche had no effect whatever in the East.

This Council of Constantinople, which is traditionally called "the Second Ecumenical Council," was a purely Eastern affair. About one hundred
and fifty Eastern bishops gathered in Constantinople at the behest of Theodosius in the summer of 381 under the presidency of Meletius, the bishop
of Antioch. But Meletius died suddenly and unexpectedly with the council's business far from complete. Gregory took Meletius's place, with
unforeseen consequences. The Egyptian bishops, who had arrived in
Constantinople after the council opened, lodged an objection not merely
to Gregory's presidency over the council, but to the validity of his consecration as bishop of Constantinople. Both the fifteenth canon of the Council of Nicaea in 325 and the twenty-first of the canons ascribed to the
"Dedication Council" of Antioch in 341 expressly forbade the transfer of
a bishop from one see to another,[33] and, although the rule was disregarded
whenever it was politically convenient to do so,[34] it could always be invoked
when ecclesiastical politics required a plausible reason for deposing a bishop,
as it was against Gregory. Since Gregory had been consecrated bishop of
the unimportant town or village of Sasima in 372,[35] the Egyptian bishops
argued that his consecration as bishop of Constantinople by the Council
of Antioch in 379 was invalid. After listening to insults and abuse directed
at him, which filled him with disgust, Gregory decided to stand aside without contesting the issue and obtained Theodosius's permission to resign.[36]
On 30 June 381, while he was still "bishop of the catholic church in Constantinople," Gregory drew up a will, which observed all the technical for-
malities required by Roman law and left all his property to the Church of
Nazianzus, of which he must therefore have known that he was about to
become bishop.[37] Gregory subsequently subscribed to the canons of the
council as bishop of Nazianzus.[38]

Nectarius and John Chrysostom (381–404)

Nectarius occupied the see of Constantinople for sixteen years from the
summer of 381 until his death on 27 September 397, carefully avoiding
controversy or, as was later alleged, energetic action of any sort.[39] His death
produced yet another contested election. Theophilus, the bishop of Alexandria, made strenuous efforts to secure the election of Isidore, a priest of
Alexandria under him, whom he expected to be pliant and subservient as

bishop of Constantinople, but Eutropius, who was then the chief minister of Arcadius, persuaded the emperor to summon John, whom he had met in Antioch while organizing resistance against a Hunnic invasion, and install him as Nectarius's successor. Since John was already well known in the imperial capital as an outstanding teacher, preacher, and exegete of holy scripture and as a staunch supporter of Nicene orthodoxy, this was duly done, and a council of prominent Eastern bishops met, elected and consecrated John on 15 December 397, thus providing ecclesiastical and canonical ratification of what was effectively an imperial appointment.[40]

In the present context, it would be superfluous to describe John's tumultuous tenure of the see of Constantinople even in brief compass. It will suffice to note that, although John initially enjoyed the firm support of Emperor Arcadius and his consort Eudoxia, within six years he had alienated Eudoxia, who had the ear of her husband, and in the late summer of 403 John was condemned and deposed by the so-called Council of the Oak and bundled into exile, and that, though the imperial pair recalled John almost immediately, they played a large part in John's permanent exile in June 404.

We are unusually well-informed about John's troubled time as bishop of Constantinople. In addition to important information preserved in later texts such as the ecclesiastical histories of Socrates, Theodoretus, and Sozomen, and the chronicle of Marcellinus, we possess two detailed accounts written shortly after John had perished from maltreatment on a forced march ordered by Emperor Arcadius. The first is the funerary speech delivered in a city near Constantinople by one of John's followers as soon as news arrived of his death in distant Comana Pontica on 14 September 407.[41] Despite its discovery in 1895, this *Funerary Speech* was first edited critically by Martin Wallraff in 2007, together with an Italian translation by his wife Cristina Ricci.[42] It presents our earliest and fullest surviving account of John's activities in Constantinople and of the opposition that he encountered or provoked with emphasis on the role played by Eudoxia.[43] The slightly later *Historical Dialogue of Palladius, bishop of Helenopolis, on the Life and Conduct of the blessed John, bishop of Constantinople, called Golden Mouth*, which survives in a single manuscript of the eleventh century (Laurentianus IX.14), has been known to scholars for centuries. Palladius composed this dialogue between two anonymous interlocutors styled "the bishop" and "the deacon" in exile at Syene in Upper Egypt in 408 and gave it a dramatic date earlier in the same year. Palladius's theological standpoint and his purpose and method in composing the *Historical Dialogue* can be defined quite precisely: Palladius was an "Origenist monk and bishop"; he wrote in defense of John as an advocate for the recently deceased bishop; he produced "a highly structured composition" in John's defense using the traditional rhetorical form of a narration followed by arguments; and he wrote primarily for a Roman audience, though also for supporters of John in both Antioch and Constantinople.[44] But it was not Palladius's *Dialogue* that "fixed John in the popular consciousness as both hero and innocent victim," as has recently been claimed.[45] For Palladius's John corresponds very closely with the John whom the *Funerary Speech* had described several months earlier.

Arsacius, Atticus, and Sisinnius (404–427)

A mere five days elapsed between John's expulsion from Constantinople for the second time and the election of Arsacius as his successor (on 26 June 404). The rapidity of this election and its political context point to imperial intervention, and it is significant that a few weeks later the city prefect Optatus ordered John's noble and wealthy supporter Olympias to acknowledge Arsacius as the rightful bishop of Constantinople and imposed a heavy fine on her when she refused.[46]

Arsacius died on 11 November of the following year. After his death another contested election ensued, and Atticus, an ascetic from Sebasteia in Armenia, was finally consecrated bishop in March 406. The *Funerary Speech* identifies Atticus as one of the leading enemies of John and alleges that he had only allowed Arsacius to become bishop of Constantinople after John because he knew that Arsacius would soon die.[47] On the other hand, Socrates gives Atticus a very favorable presentation, commending him especially for his protection of the schismatic sect of the Novatians, to which Socrates himself belonged.[48] Hence it must be suspected that when Socrates reports that the pious Atticus "was advanced to position of bishop" after a delay of four months,[49] the vague and decorous phrasing conceals imperial involvement in his election.

Atticus lived on until 23 October 425. After his death a hotly contested election again ensued. According to Socrates the two main candidates were the ecclesiastical historian Philippus of Side and Proculus, who was to become bishop nine years later, both of whom were priests in charge of churches inside the city. The Christian laity of Constantinople, however, unanimously favored Sisinnius, the priest of a suburban parish, who was duly elected on 26 February 426—which was the fortieth anniversary of the ordination of John Chrysostom as a priest in Antioch. It may be presumed that "all the people" and "the laity" who, according to Socrates, carried the election of Sisinnius included the younger Theodosius and his imperial sisters.

Nestorius

Sisinnius died on 24 December 427. On the following 10 April, Nestorius was installed as bishop of Constantinople by the ministers of Emperor Theodosius II. Socrates describes the role of the imperial court quite explicitly:

> After the death of Sisinnius those in power were determined that no-one from within the church [of Constantinople] should be advanced to the position of bishop through the efforts of lobbyists (*dia tous kenospoudastous*), although many were urging that Philippus, many that Proclus be elected. Instead they wished to summon an external candidate from Antioch. For there was there someone named Nestorius, a native of Germanicia who spoke fluently and elegantly. For this reason they decided that he was very suitable as a teacher and accordingly resolved that he be summoned. So when three months had passed Nestorius was brought from Antioch.[50]

The role of Theodosius in the deposition and exile of Nestorius, which was preceded by complicated political maneuvers, is equally clear.[51] The so-called Third Ecumenical Council of 431 at Ephesus was in reality no such thing. Although both met in the same city, there were two parallel and opposing councils, just as there had been in 343, when the Western and Eastern bishops assembled separately in Serdica and Philippopolis. On 22 June 431, despite the protests of both many bishops from the diocese of Oriens and the *comes* Candidianus, whom Theodosius had sent to keep order at the council that he had convened, Cyril of Alexandria, assisted by Juvenalis of Jerusalem and Memnon of Ephesus, presided over a gathering of bishops that deposed Nestorius on the grounds that he had refused to appear before it. Another group of bishops met under the presidency of John of Antioch on 29 June and deposed Cyril and Memnon. Envoys from both groups of bishops then scurried to the emperor in Constantinople: After some delay, Maximianus was consecrated as bishop of Constantinople on

25 October 431 as the successor of Nestorius, who had resigned,[52] and Theodosius allowed the bishops who had assembled in Ephesus five to six months earlier to return home, thus implicitly confirming Cyril and Memnon in the possession of their sees and allowing the Cyrillian council retrospectively (and quite anachronistically) to acquire the cachet of the "Third Ecumenical Council."

A clear picture emerges. With one possible exception, it was the will of the emperor that determined the election of bishops of the city of Constantinople from its foundation onwards, even though he played no formal role in either their election or their consecration: Elections were made either by the clergy and laity of the Church of Constantinople or by a council of bishops, and consecrations could only be performed by bishops of other cities, who sat as a church council when replacing a bishop whom they had just deposed. Depositions, it seems, were a different matter. Theodosius unceremoniously expelled Demophilus from Constantinople without waiting for him to be condemned by a council of bishops, and Arcadius similarly sent John into exile in June 404 without waiting for a council of bishops to condemn him for an infraction of canon law, for which he himself was responsible. In Constantinople at least, therefore, there was an unambiguous answer to the question famously posed in the West in the fourth century: What has the emperor to do with the church?[53] In Constantinople it was everything.

Appendix One: Bishops of Constantinople, 337–431

(1) Bishops who were formally consecrated:
PAUL
337 elected, then deposed and exiled to Pontus
342 attempts to resume possession of his see on the death of Eusebius, but is expelled from Constantinople, flees to the West, and goes to the court of Constans in Trier
343 reinstated as bishop of Constantinople by the Council of Serdica
344 attempts again to regain his see, but is deported to Thessalonica
346 finally allowed by Constantius to resume possession of the see of Constantinople

349 deposed by a council of bishops meeting in Antioch and taken to the court of Constantius, who exiles him to Cucusus

350 dies in prison at Cucusus

EUSEBIUS OF NICOMEDIA

337 replaces Paul after the intervention of Constantius

341 dies in office

MACEDONIUS

341 succeeds Eusebius

346 replaced by Paul

360, Jan. deposed by the Council of Constantinople

EUDOXIUS

360, Jan. elected by the Council of Constantinople

370 dies in office

DEMOPHILUS

370 installed as bishop as the successor of Eudoxius

380, Nov. 26 expelled from the city by Theodosius, but continues to lead conventicles of "Arians" outside the city gates of Constantinople

386 dies

GREGORY

378, autumn probably comes to Constantinople

379 probably elected and consecrated by a council of bishops meeting in Antioch

381, June resigns and is consecrated bishop of Nazianzus

NECTARIUS

381, June-July elected and consecrated by the Council of Constantinople, over which he then presides

397 dies in office

JOHN CHRYSOSTOM

397, autumn summoned from Antioch by imperial order

397, Dec. 15 consecrated bishop of Constantinople

403, ca. Sept. deposed by the "Council of the Oak," sent into exile, then recalled by Arcadius

404, June 20 expelled from Constantinople and exiled to Cucusus

407 Arcadius orders John to be transported to Pityus on the northeast coast of the Black Sea

407, Sept. 15 John dies at Comana Pontica during a forced
   march north through Asia Minor

ARSACIUS

404, June 26 consecrated bishop

405, Nov. 11 dies in office

ATTICUS

406, March elected and consecrated bishop

425, Oct. 10 dies

SISINNIUS

426, Feb. 28 consecrated bishop

427, Dec. 24 dies in office

NESTORIUS

428 summoned from Antioch by imperial order

428, April 10 consecrated bishop of Constantinople

431, late June condemned and deposed by the a council of
   bishops meeting in Ephesus on the initiative of Cyril of
   Alexandria, after which he requests permission from
   Emperor Theodosius to resign

431, August Nestorius's deposition confirmed by Theodosius; he retires to his monastery of St. Euprepius near
   Antioch

436 exiled to Petra, and later (perhaps in 438 or 439) moved to
   Upper Egypt

451 recalled by Emperor Marcian in order to be rehabilitated
   at the Council of Chalcedon, but dies on the journey

451, Oct. definitively condemned as a heretic by the Council of
   Chalcedon

(2) Schismatic bishops:

MARCIANUS Novatianist   died 395, Nov. 27 (Socrates, *HE*
   6.1.8)

DOROTHEUS Arian   died 407, Nov. 6 (Socrates, *HE* 7.6.1)

CHRYSANTHUS Novatianist   died 419, Aug. 26 (Socrates,
   HE 7.17.1)

BARBAS Arian   died 430, June 24 (Socrates, *HE* 7.30.7)

(3) Rejected Names:

EVAGRIUS 370

According to Socrates, *HE* 4.13.3–15.3, followed by Sozomen,
HE 6.13.3–4, when Eudoxius died in 370, the supporters of the

homoousion elected one Evagrius, who shared their theological views, and he was consecrated by Eustathius, the bishop of Antioch, but the emperor Valens arrested both Eustathius and Evagrius as soon he heard of the consecration and exiled both men: Eustathius to Bizye in Thrace and Evagrius "to another place"[54]
MAXIMUS   380
Maximus was never formally consecrated bishop of Constantinople

Appendix Two: The Last Will and Testament of Gregory of Nazianzus

The last will and testament, which Gregory drew up on 30 June 381, while he was still bishop of Constantinople, survives complete because it was deposited in the Church of Nazianzus, to which he bequeathed his entire estate. It conforms perfectly to the technical requirements of Roman law[55] and is in fact the earliest Roman will to survive complete in its original form.[56] A critical edition was published by Joëlle Beaucamp in 1998,[57] which was unfortunately unknown to Brian Daley when he published an English translation of the superseded text printed by the Abbé Migne (PG 37.389–396) eight years later.[58] I have therefore supplied a new translation, carefully noting whenever I adopt a reading different from that printed by Beaucamp.

Copy of the Will of Saint Gregory the Theologian, transcribed from the original document, in which the handwritten subscriptions are preserved of both [Gregory] and the witnesses who subscribed.

In the consulate of Flavius Eucherius and Flavius Evagrius, *viri clarissimi*, on the day before the kalends of July[59]

(1) I, Gregory, bishop of the catholic church in Constantinople, being alive and of sound mind, have, with a healthy judgment and unimpaired reason, drawn up this my will, which I order and desire to be valid and effective in every court of law and before every [judicial] authority.

(2) I have already made my intention clear and have consecrated all my estate to the catholic church in Nazianzus for ministering to the poor who are dependent on the said church. Accordingly, because of this intention of mine I previously appointed three sustainers of the poor—the deacon and monk Marcellus, the deacon and monk Gregory, who was born in my own household,[60] and the monk Eustathius,

who was also himself born in my household. Now too, preserving the same sentiment toward the holy church in Nazianzus, I hold to the same course of action.

(3) If it happens, therefore, that I reach the end of my life, let the sole heir of all of my property, both movable and unmovable, which I possess anywhere, be the aforementioned deacon and monk Gregory, who was born in my household and whom I freed long ago, and let everyone else be disinherited—on this condition, however, that he transfer all of my property, both movable and unmovable, to the holy catholic church in Nazianzus, abstracting nothing whatever except what I may leave in this my will to anyone personally by way of legacy (*legatum*) or *fideicommissum*, but carefully preserve everything, as I have said, for the church, having the fear of God before his eyes and in the knowledge that I have instructed all my estate to be applied to ministering to the poor of the same church, and that I have instituted him as heir for the precise purpose that through him everything may be preserved for the church without diminution.

(4) In respect of the slaves whom I have freed, whether on my own initiative or as a result of instructions from my deceased parents, I wish both that all of them remain free and that the *peculium* of each of them remain firmly and without contestation in their possession.

(5) In addition, I desire that my heir Gregory the deacon, together with the monk Eustathius, who were both born in my household, receive the landed property in Arianzos[61] which came to me from the estate of Reginus. And I desire that all the mules and sheep that I had some time ago, when I was there, ordered to be given to them and had entrusted them with both their maintenance and ownership, remain theirs without contestation with the legal right of ownership.

(6) In addition, I particularly desire that Gregory, the deacon and my heir, who has nobly served me, receive fifty gold pieces with right of ownership.

(7) To the most venerable virgin Rousiane, my relative, I ordered to be given stated sums of money each year so that she could live honorably; these sums I desire and order to be given to her promptly each year according to the schedule that I drew up. About her residence, I gave no instructions on that occasion, since I did not know where it would be most agreeable for her to live. Now, however, I de-

sire that a house suitable for a respectable person and appropriate for the virtuous way of life of a virgin be built for her in whatever place she may choose. This house, to be clear, she shall have for her use and enjoyment during her lifetime without contestation; after this, however, she shall transfer it to the church. And I desire that two girls of her choice be assigned to her, so that the girls remain with her for the duration of her lifetime; and that, if she were to show them gratitude, that she have the power to honor them with freedom; but if she does not, that they belong to the same church.

(8) Theophilus, the young slave who lodges with me, I have already freed. I now desire, therefore, that five *solidi* be given to him as a legacy (*legatum*).

(9) His brother Eutaxius I desire to be free and that he be given on account of a legacy (*legatum*) five gold *solidi*.

(10) I also desire that my secretary Theodosius be freed and be given on account of a legacy (*legatum*) five gold *solidi*.

(11) As for my sweet daughter Alypiane (for little heed [need be paid] to the others, Eugenia and Nonna, whose very [way of] life is reprehensible), I desire her to pardon me for lacking the capacity to leave her anything, because I have already promised everything to the poor or rather have followed the promise of our blessed parents, whose decision I do not consider it either holy or safe to set aside. However, I desire that all that is left of garments of silk, linen or wool or waggons[62] among the effects of my deceased brother Caesarius belong to her children, and that neither she nor her sisters trouble either my heir or the church in any matter.

(12) Let Meletius, my relative by marriage, be aware that he is wrongly occupying the property at Apenzesus,[63] which belongs to the estate of Euphemius. On this matter I have often in the past written to Euphemius, denouncing his fecklessness for not reclaiming what is his; now too I call on all, both magistrates and nonmagistrates, to witness that Euphemius is being wronged, for the property ought to be restored to Euphemius.

(13) The purchase of the estate of Kanotala[64] I desire to be restored to my venerable son, the bishop Amphilochius. For it is in my papers and all know that the contract has been discharged, that I have received the price and that I have long ago turned over the administration and the ownership of the property.

(14) To the deacon Evagrius, who has shared many of my sufferings and concerns and has shown his loyalty in even more ways, I confess my gratitude before God and men. God will recompense him with greater [rewards]; but so that even small tokens of friendship not be lacking on my part, I desire that he be given one double woolen cloak,[65] one tunic, two ordinary cloaks[66] and thirty gold *solidi*.

(15) Similarly I desire that sweet Theodoulos, who was a deacon with me, be given one double woolen cloak, two tunics from those in my home city and twenty gold *solidi* from the sum kept in my home city.

(16) To Elaphius the secretary, who is of good character and has nobly comforted me during the time that he has served me, I desire to be given one double woolen cloak, two tunics, three ordinary cloaks, a vestment[67] that is in my home city and twenty gold *solidi*.

(17) This my will I desire to be valid and effective in every court of law and before every legal authority. But even if it were not to have legal force as a will, I desire that it have legal force as an expression of my wishes or a codicil (*codicillum*). Anyone who attempts to overturn it will account for his actions at the Day of Judgment and will [need to] justify himself in the name of the Father, the Son and the Holy Ghost.

I, Gregory, bishop of the catholic church in Constantinople, have read my will, satisfied myself with all that is written therein, have subscribed with my own hand and order and desire it to have legal effect.

I, Amphilochius, bishop of the catholic church in Iconium, being present at the will of the most venerable bishop Gregory at his invitation, have subscribed with my own hand.

I, Optimus, bishop of the catholic church in Antioch,[68] being present at his invitation when the most venerable bishop Gregory made his will as it is written above, have subscribed with my own hand.

I, Theodosius, bishop of the catholic church in Hyde,[69] being present at the will of the most venerable bishop Gregory at his invitation, have subscribed with my own hand.

I, Theodoulos, bishop of the holy catholic church in Apamea,[70] being present at the will of the most venerable bishop Gregory at his invitation, have subscribed with my own hand.

I, Hilary, bishop of the catholic church in Isauria, being present at his invitation when the most venerable bishop Gregory made his will as it is written above, have subscribed with my own hand.

I, Themistius, bishop of the holy church of God in Adrianople, was present at the will of the most venerable bishop Gregory at his invitation and have subscribed with my own hand.

I, Cledonius, priest of the catholic church in Iconium, being present at the will of the most venerable bishop Gregory at his invitation, have subscribed with my own hand.

I, Johannes, reader and *notarius* of the most holy church of Nazianzus, made the copy of the divine will of the holy, glorious theologian Gregory, which is deposited in my most holy church, and have published it.

Transcribed from the original document deposited in the church of Nazianzus.

(*CPG* 3033)

Appendix Three: The Date of Gregory's Will

The true historical significance of Gregory's will has been obscured by the widespread adoption of an erroneous date. The edition reproduced by J.-P. Migne (PG 37.389) gives the date of 31 December 381 (πρό μιᾶς καλανδῶν Ἰανουαρίων) as if this date were the sole date with manuscript attestation. This date has traditionally been rejected as impossible, for the obvious reason that Gregory had ceased to be bishop of Constantinople several months earlier, though Brian Daley has recently defended it as correct and deduced that even at the very end of 381 Gregory could not bring himself to accept that he was no longer bishop of Constantinople.[71] Hence the diurnal date of 31 December has normally been emended to 31 May (πρό μιᾶς καλανδῶν Ἰουνίων).[72] Indeed, so entrenched did the date of 31 May become that the only critical edition of Gregory's will printed the emendation (πρό μιᾶς καλανδῶν Ἰουνίων) in preference to the date of 30 June, which also has manuscript attestation.[73]

Gregory's will is transmitted in some thirty manuscripts, of which a slight majority are manuscripts of Gregory, while the rest are legal manuscripts. In her critical edition of 1998, Joëlle Beaucamp identifies three main groups of manuscripts, one comprising four manuscripts of Gregory, of which three have the date of 31 December 381. One manuscript, however, which was copied in Constantinople in 1062, to which Beaucamp assigns the siglum **A**, and which has the date of 30 June 381 (πρό μιᾶς καλανδῶν Ἰουλίων), stands apart from the rest. Beaucamp's assessment of its value is that, apart from some false readings shared with other manuscripts, "A apparaît, par ailleurs, comme un témoin d'une grande qualité: le nom du mois (1.5) y est le plus proche de l'original, et les noms propres des souscriptions y sont exacts; les leçons propres à A ne sont pas très nombreuses et une seule est manifestement erronée (1.86: τῆςφιλοσοφίαςσύμβολα)."[74] According to the normal criteria of textual criticism, the reading of A deserves to be accepted as correct unless there is strong countervailing evidence. In fact, it entails a new interpretation of the circumstances surrounding Gregory's resignation as bishop of Constantinople.

On 30 June 381 Gregory was still bishop of the imperial city, but he knew that he would soon be bishop of Nazianzus. That implies that Gregory had already requested to be allowed to resign as bishop of Constantinople and that his resignation had been accepted before 30 June 381. In turn this implies that an arrangement had already been made, with the approval of Emperor Theodosius, that on his resignation as bishop of Constantinople, Gregory would immediately be transferred to the see of Nazianzus, and that by 30 June it was already known that Gregory would be replaced as bishop of Constantinople by Nectarius, the *praetor urbanus* in Constantinople. Nectarius had not yet been baptized when he was selected as bishop of Constantinople in succession to Gregory,[75] but, like Ambrose in Milan seven years earlier,[76] he was advanced rapidly through the clerical ranks and presided over the final sessions of the Council of Constantinople, which probably concluded on 27 July 381, although two different dates are also attested for its closure.[77]

It has normally been assumed that the bishops subscribed the canons of the council on 9 July 381, since that is the date stated in the heading to the council's address to Emperor Theodosius and the canons of the council as printed by Mansi in the eighteenth century:

ἐν ὑπατείᾳ Φλαβίου Εὐχερίου καὶ Φλαβίου Εὐαγρίου
τῶν ἐκλαμπροτάτων πρὸ ἑπτὰ εἰδῶν Ἰουλίων[78]

In the more recent edition by Périclès-Pierre Joannou, however, the date is stated very differently and from a different manuscript source as

ἐν ἰνδικτιῶνι θ' ὑπατείᾳ Εὐχερίου καὶ Εὐαγρίου,
πρὸ ς'. καλανδῶν αὐγούστων ἔτους Ἀντιοχείας υκθ'.[79]

Now Theodosius, whose presence is attested close to Constantinople in Heraclea/Perinthus from 9 to 30 July 381,[80] added his imprimatur to the council's decisions at the request of the bishops on 30 July.[81] The date of

27 July should surely therefore be preferred to 9 July for the closure of the council.[82] The bishops who subscribed its canons included Nectarius, who presided as the newly elected bishop of Constantinople and hence subscribed first, while both Gregory of Nyssa and Gregory of Nazianzus subscribed together with another four bishops from Cappadocia.[83]

Notes

1. For proof that this important step occurred in 260, not half a century later, see Timothy D. Barnes, *Early Christian Hagiography and Roman History*, Tria Corda 5, Jena Lectures on Judaism, Antiquity and Christianity (Tübingen: Mohr Siebeck, 2010), 100–105.

2. The three relevant documents (Eusebius, *HE* 10.7.1–2; Augustine, *Ep.* 88.2; Optatus, 1.22) are conveniently reproduced together in Hans von Soden and Hans Lietzmann, *Urkunden zur Entstehungsgeschichte des Donatismus*, Kleine Texte für Vorlesungen und Übungen 122 (Berlin: Walter de Gruyter, 1950), nos. 9–11. On their dates, see Timothy D. Barnes, *The New Empire of Diocletian and Constantine* (Cambridge, Mass.: Harvard University Press, 1982), 240–41.

3. On these two appeals and their historical background, see especially Fergus Millar, "Paul of Samosata, Zenobia and Aurelian: The Church, Local Culture, and Political Allegiance in Third-Century Syria," *Journal of Roman Studies* 61 (1971): 1–17, reprinted in his *Rome, The Greek World and the East*, vol. 3, *The Greek World, the Jews and the East* (Chapel Hill: University of North Carolina Press, 2006), 243–74, esp. 267–71; Fergus Millar, *The Emperor in the Roman World (31 BC–AD 337)* (London: Duckworth, 1997), 584–90; Timothy D. Barnes, *Constantine and Eusebius* (Cambridge, Mass.: Harvard University Press, 1981), 145 and 54–61.

4. Theophilus, *Ad Autolycum* 1.11, modified slightly from the translation by Robert M. Grant, *Theophilus of Antioch: Ad Autolycum* (Oxford: Clarendon Press, 1970); the passage was quoted and its profound implications noted by Millar, *Emperor*, 507.

5. Socrates, *HE* 2.6.1; Theodoret, *HE* 1.3.3–4, identifies the Alexander who received an undated letter, which he quotes in full (*HE* 1.4.1–61), from Alexander of Alexandria denouncing Arius at some date before September 324, as bishop of Byzantium, and there is no good reason to identify him instead as Alexander of Thessalonica, as do H.-G. Opitz, *Athanasius Werke*, Bd. 3, Tl. 1, *Urkunden zur Geschichte des arianischen Streites (318–328)* (Berlin & Leipzig: 1934–), 19 (heading to *Urkunde* 14) = H. C. Brennecke, U. Heil, A. von Stockhausen, and A. Wintjes, *Athanasius Werke*, Bd. 3, Tl. 1, *Dokumente zur Geschichte des arianischen Streites 3* (Berlin: Walter de Gruyter, 2007), 91 (heading to *Dokument* 17). On the date, addressee, and context of the letter,

see F. Winkelmann, "Die Bischöfe Metrophanes und Alexander," *Byzantinische Zeitschrift* 59 (1966): 47–71; Barnes, *Constantine and Eusebius*, 205–6, and 373–74n151.

6. For the Council of Constantinople in 336, see Timothy D. Barnes, "Emperor and Bishops, A.D. 324–344: Some Problems," *American Journal of Ancient History* 3 (1978): 53–75, here 64–65; Barnes, *Constantine and Eusebius*, 241–42; Timothy D. Barnes, "The Exile and Recalls of Arius," *Journal of Theological Studies*, NS 60 (2009): 109–29, here 119–24.

7. Socrates, *HE* 2.6.1–8.1; Sozomen, *HE* 3.4.1–5.1.

8. Athanasius, *History of the Arians* 7.1 (translated and discussed below).

9. Timothy D. Barnes, *Athanasius and Constantius: Theology and Politics in the Constantinian Empire* (Cambridge, Mass.: Harvard University Press, 1993), 20–25.

10. The recent critical edition of Socrates Scholasticus by Günther Christian Hansen supplies the correct dates in its annotation on the passage: *Sokrates Kirchengeschichte* (Berlin: Akademie Verlag, 1995), 96.

11. Socrates, *HE* 2.12.1.

12. Socrates, *HE* 2.13–14; Sozomen, *HE* 3.7; see Libanius, *Orat.* 59.94–97; *Descriptio consulum* 342.2; Jerome, *Chronicle* 235f; see Barnes, *Athanasius*, 214, 219.

13. Socrates, *HE* 2.16; Sozomen, *HE* 3.9. Socrates again puts his account of events in Constantinople into a false context: he places the episode before (not after) the Council of Serdica and imagines that Paul had been restored to his see through the intervention of Julius, the bishop of Rome (*HE* 2.15.3).

14. Socrates, *HE* 2.17.30, 22.5.

15. That is, by those whom Athanasius stigmatizes as "Arians."

16. Athanasius, *History of the Arians* 7.1–6 (Opitz, 186.9–187.1); my translation, which supplies proper names for some of Athanasius's pronouns and incorporates my emendation of the second transmitted "Κωνσταντίνου" to "Κωνσταντιόν" (Barnes, *Athanasius*, 21).

17. Eduard Schwartz, *Gesammelte Schriften*, vol. 3, *Zur Geschichte des Athanasius* (Berlin: Walter de Gruyter, 1959), 274–75n6, falsely claimed that Montfaucon had restored the manuscript reading "παρά Κονσταντίνου" in the Benedictine edition of Athanasius (Paris, 1698). In fact, "Κωνσταντίου" is one of many misprints in Migne's nineteenth-century reprint of Montfaucon, betrayed as such by the fact that the Latin translation, which Migne prints in parallel, has "*a Constantino*" (see Barnes, *Athanasius*, 309–10n17).

18. Barnes, *Athanasius*, 220.

19. This council is explicitly recorded by Sozomen, *HE* 4.8.3–4, who found its date surprising. It has been ignored or misdated by most modern scholars:

see Barnes, *Athanasius,* 94–100; Timothy D. Barnes, "The New Critical Edition of Athanasius' *Defence before Constantius,*" *Zeitschrift für Antikes Christentum* 11 (2007): 378–401, here 395–97.

20. Athanasius, *History of the Arians* 51.4 (Opitz, 212.25–28), see Barnes, *Athanasius,* 104.

21. Athanasius, *De Synodis* 9.3 (236.10 with Opitz's note ad loc.); Socrates, *HE* 2.37.14, 28, 51.

22. Socrates, *HE* 5.7.10 and 5.12.6, see Ammianus Marcellinus, *Res Gestae,* a. 380; see Ludwig August Dindorf, *Chronicon Paschale,* Corpus Scriptorum Historiae Byzantinae (Bonn: Weber, 1832), 561 = Michael Whitby and Mary Whitby, *Chronicon Paschale 284–628 A.D.,* Translated Texts for Historians 7 (Liverpool: Liverpool University Press, 1989), 50.

23. Socrates, *HE* 5.7.9, 12.6.

24. Socrates, *HE* 5.7.3–11.

25. H. C. Brennecke, *Studien zur Geschichte der Homöer: Der Osten bis zum Ende der homöischen Reichskirche,* Beiträge zur historischen Theologie 73 (Tübingen: Mohr, 1988), 158–242; Timothy D. Barnes, "The Collapse of the Homoeans in the East," *Studia Patristica* 29 (1997): 3–16.

26. Gregory, *On His Life,* 595–651. On Gregory's struggles in Constantinople, see Rosemary Radford Ruether, *Gregory of Nazianzus: Rhetor and Philosopher* (Oxford: Clarendon Press, 1969), 42–48; Justin Mossay, "Gregor von Nazianz in Konstantinopel (379–381 A. D.)," *Byzantion* 47 (1977): 223–38; Neil B. McLynn, "A Self-Made Holy Man: The Case of Gregory Nazianzen," *Journal of Early Christian Studies* 6 (1998): 463–83, at 474–82; Jean Bernardi in *Saint Grégoire de Nazianze: Œuvres Poétiques* 1.1, *Poèmes personnels* II, 1, 1–11, by A. Tuilier, A. Bady & J. Bernardi (Paris: Les Belles Lettres, 2004) xxiv–xli, 162–208.

27. Gregory, *Orat.* 43.2; see Barnes, "Collapse of the Homoeans," 6–13.

28. Socrates, *HE* 4.26.13–15, 5.5.8–6.1; see Hansen, *Sokrates Kirchengeschichte,* apparatus to 277.18–19.

29. Socrates, *HE* 5.6.6.

30. Gregory, *Orat.* 25.34; see Marie Madeleine Hauser-Meury, *Prosopographie zu den Schriften Gregors von Nazianz,* Theophaneia 13 (Bonn: P. Hanstein, 1960), 119–21.

31. Described in some detail by Gregory, *On His Life,* 750–1014.

32. Ambrose, *Ep. extra collectionem* 9 [13M].3–7 (CSEL 82.202–204). ·

33. Perikles-Petros Joannou, *Discipline Générale Antique: IIe–IXe,* 1.1, *Les Canons des Conciles Œcuméniques,* Ecclesia Catholica Commissio ad Redigendum Codicem Iuris Canonici Orientalis, Series 1.9.1.1 (Grottaferrata, Rome: Tipografia Italo-Orientale "S. Nilo," 1962), 36–37; *Discipline Générale Antique:*

IVe–IXe, 1.2, *Les Canons des Synodes Particuliers* (Grottaferrata, Rome: Tipografia Italo-Orientale "S. Nilo," 1962), 121.

34. Thus Eusebius of Nicomedia had first been bishop of Berytus, then bishop of Nicomedia, for nearly twenty years before he was installed as bishop of Constantinople in the early autumn of 337. See Opitz, *Urkunde* 4b.4 = Brennecke, Heil, von Stockhausen & Wintjes, *Dokument* 6.4; Athanasius, *Defense against the Arians* 6.6; Socrates, *HE* 1.6.33. 2.6–7.

35. Gregory, *On His Life*, 495–525.

36. Gregory, *On His Life*, 1818–1904.

37. The will is translated below in Appendix 2 and its date discussed in Appendix 3.

38. Cuthbert Hamilton Turner, *Ecclesiae Occidentalis Monumenta Iuris Antiquissima* 2.3 (Oxford: Clarendon Press, 1939), 446–47n64.

39. See Timothy D. Barnes and George Bevan, *Funerary Speech for John Chrysostom: Translated with an Introduction and Brief Commentary*, Translated Texts for Historians 60 (Liverpool: Liverpool University Press, 2013), 48, § 17.

40. The best account of John's appointment and the role of Eutropius and Asterius is given by Palladius, *Dialogue* 5; See J. N. D. Kelly, *Golden Mouth: The Story of John Chrysostom—Ascetic, Preacher, Bishop* (London: Duckworth, 1995), 104–7.

41. The date of the speech is conjectured to be "perhaps around the second week of November" by Demetrios S. Katos, *Palladius of Helenopolis: The Origenist Advocate* (Oxford: Oxford University Press, 2011), 90, n.135. The published version was presumably completed during the winter of 407/408.

42. Martin Wallraff, *Oratio Funebris in Laudem Sancti Johannis Chrysostomi: Epitaffio attribuito a Martirio di Antiochia (BHG 871, CPG 6517)* (Spoleto: Fondazione Centro Italiano di Studi sull'Alto Medioevo, 2007). Wallraff's edition was unfortunately not yet available for Peter Norton's otherwise valuable study *Episcopal Elections 250–600: Hierarchy and Popular Will in Late Antiquity* (Oxford: Oxford University Press, 2007), but it is inexcusably overlooked in the pretentious essay by Peter van Nuffelen, "Episcopal Succession in Constantinople (381–450 CE): The Local Dynamics of Power," *Journal of Early Christian Studies* 18 (2010): 425–51.

43. See now Barnes and Bevan, *Funerary Speech*, 24–32, 45–111, § 13–132.

44. Katos, *Palladius*, 9–32.

45. Katos, *Palladius*, 34.

46. *Funerary Speech*, § 131, with the notes by Barnes and Bevan.

47. *Funerary Speech*, § 115; see also § 134.

48. Socrates' sympathy for the Novatianists has often been observed; for proof that he actually belonged to the sect, see Martin Wallraff, "Geschichte

des Novatianismus seit dem vierten Jahrhundert im Osten," Zeitschrift für Antikes Christentum 1 (1997): 251–79; Martin Wallraff, Der Kirchenhistoriker Sokrates: Untersuchungen zu Geschichtsdarstellung, Methode und Person, Forschungen zur Kirchen- und Dogmengeschichte 68 (Göttingen: Vandenhoeck & Ruprecht, 1997), 235–57, 275–78. According to the Funerary Speech § 137, Atticus' behavior changed completely when he heard that John was dead.

49. Socrates, *HE* 6.20.2.

50. Socrates, *HE* 7.29.1–3 (my translation).

51. Now elucidated in the masterly analysis of George Bevan, *The New Judas: The Case of Nestorius in Ecclesiastical Politics, 428–451 CE* (Leuven: Peeters, forthcoming), Chapter 3.

52. Socrates, *HE* 7.37.19.

53. A question asked of imperial envoys by Donatus, according to Optatus, *Against the Donatists*, 3.3.

54. Brennecke, *Studien zur Geschichte der Homöer*, 225; Eustathius dead before 362; see Schwartz, *Gesammelte Schriften*, vol. 3, 173n1; Socrates, *HE* 4.14.2–4.15.3.

55. Max Kaser, *Das Römische Privatrecht*, vol. 2, *Die Nachklassischen Entwicklungen* (Munich: Beck, 1971), 478n5; 479n18; 481n27.

56. Edward Champlin, *Final Judgments: Duty and Emotion in Roman Wills, 200 B.C.–A.D. 250* (Berkeley: University of California Press, 1991), 29n1, citing the edition of Gregory's will by J. B. Pitra, *Iuris ecclesiastici graecorum historia et monumenta*, vol. 2 (Rome: Typis Collegii Urbani, 1868), 153–60.

57. Joëlle Beaucamp, "Le testament de Grégoire de Nazianze," *Fontes Minores* 10 (Frankfurt-am-Main, Löwenklau Gesellschaft, 1998), 1–100, at 30–40.

58. Brian E. Daley, *Gregory of Nazianzus* (London, 2006), 184–88.

59. 30 June 381. The name of the second consul was in fact Syagrius: As in many other sources, the initial sigma has been corrupted to epsilon; see R. S. Bagnall et al., *Consuls of the Later Roman Empire* (Atlanta: Scholars Press, 1987), 296–97.

60. That is, "who was born a slave in my household" (Daley, *Gregory of Nazianzus*, 186n9).

61. In Cappadocia: see Richard J. A. Talbert, ed., *Barrington Atlas of the Greek and Roman World* (Princeton: Princeton University Press, 2000), Map 63, E4; see Friedrich Hild and Marcell Restle, *Tabula Imperii Byzantini 2, Kappadokien*, Denkschriften 149 (Wien: Verlag der Österreichischen Akademie der Wissenschaften, 1981), 150–51. Beaucamp ("Le Testament," 30) prints the plural "ἔν Ἀριάνζοις" with the majority of the manuscripts.

62. The manuscripts have "βουριχαλίοις" LSJ 326 states the meaning of the word as "senator's ox-cart," citing John the Lydian, *De magistratibus* 1.18; G. W. H. Lampe, *A Greek Patristic Lexicon*, (Oxford: Clarendon Press,

1968), 304 gives "a kind of carriage," citing this passage and the *Chronicon Paschale*, 309. Beaucamp renders the noun as "calèches," but Daley translates it as "ponies" (188).

63. The manuscripts attest the name of this so far unidentified place, which is generally agreed to be in Cappadocia, as Apenzesos, Apezesos, Apinzesos, and Apinzisos (Beaucamp, "Le Testament," 36, apparatus to line 73); Richard J. A. Talbert et al., *Barrington Atlas of the Greek and Roman World Map-by-Map Directory*, vol. 2 (Princeton: Princeton University Press, 2000), 992, cites William Mitchell Ramsay, *The Historical Geography of Asia Minor* (London: John Murray, 1890), 307.

64. Also in Cappadocia: *Barrington Atlas*, Map 63, E4.

65. Beaucamp ("Le Testament," 37) translates "κάμασος" as "*chemise*"; LSJ 872 merely adduces the gloss "ἀμφίμαλλος" for which it gives the meaning "woolly on both sides" (92),and the Late Latin "*camasus*"; while Lampe, 700 cites this passage among others for the meaning "garment, perh[aps] shirt."

66. For "πάλλιον" as a transliteration of the Latin "*pallium*," see Lampe, 999.

67. The meaning of "σιγιλλιῶνα," which appears to be a *hapax legomenon*, is quite uncertain: LSJ offers no opinion; Lampe, 1232 glosses it as "plain or short garment" and Beaucamp ("Le Testament," 37) translates as "un vêtement léger."

68. Optimus is well attested as bishop of Antioch in Pisidia (see *Barrington Atlas*, Map 35, D1).

69. For Hyde, a small city in Lycaonia, see *Barrington Atlas*, Map 66, D2; S. Mitchell, *Barrington Atlas, Map-by-Map Directory*, vol. 2, 1016, cites G. Laminger-Pascher, "Das lykaonische Koinon und die Lage, der Städte Barata, Dalisandros und Hyde," *Anzeiger Wien* 123 (1986): 238–60.

70. Presumably Apamea in Pisidia (see *Barrington Atlas*, Map 65, D1), not the distant Apamea in Syria (Daley, *Gregory of Nazianzus*, 257n33).

71. Brian E. Daley, "Who is the Real Bishop of Constantinople? A Reconsideration of Gregory of Nazianzus' Will," *Studia Patristica* 47 (2010): 147–52.

72. Baronius, *Annales ecclesiastici* 41 & 42; Papebroch, AASS, Mai. 3 (Antwerp, 1680), 410E; G. Rauschen, *Jahrbücher der christlichen Kirche unter dem Kaiser Theodosius dem Großen. Versuch einer Erneuerung der Annales Ecclesiastici des Baronius für die Jahre 378–395* (Freiburg im Breisgau, 1897), 111; O. Seeck, *Regesten der Kaiser und Päpste für die Jahre 311 bis 476 n. Chr. Vorarbeit zu einer Prosopographie der christlichen Kaiserzeit* (Stuttgart, 1919), 257.

73. Beaucamp, "Le Testament," 30.

74. Beaucamp, "Le Testament," 18.

75. Rufinus, *HE* 11.21; Socrates, *HE* 5.8.12; Sozomen, *HE* 7.8.1–2; Photius, *Bibliotheca* 257.

76. Paulinus, *Vita Ambrosii* 9.3.

77. Mansi, *Sacrorum Conciliorum Nova, et Amplissima Collectio* 3 (Florence, 1759), 568, 569; Turner, *Ecclesiae Occidentalis Monumenta Iuris Antiquissima* 2.3, 434–35n1; see also note 81 below.

78. J. D. Mansi, *Sacrorum Conciliorum Collectio* 3, 557.

79. Joannou, *Les canons des conciles œcuméniques*, 45, where the insertion of "ἰνδικτιῶνιθ'" after instead of before the preposition "ἐν" shows that the consular and Roman date is primary while both the indiction year and the era of Antioch have been added later.

80. Otto Seeck, *Regesten der Kaiser und Päpste für die Jahre 311 bis 476* (Stuttgart: J. B. Metzler, 1919), 257.

81. *Codex Theodosianus* 16.1.3.

82. Joannou, *Les canons des conciles œcuméniques*, 43, repeats the traditional date in his introductory note.

83. Mansi, *Sacrorum Conciliorum Collectio* 3, 568, 569; Turner, *Ecclesiae Occidentalis Monumenta Iuris Antiquissima* 2.3, 434–35n1; 446–47n60, 64.

STEPPING OUT OF CONSTANTINE'S SHADOW

Peter Iver Kaufman

Beginning in 1970 and continuing for forty years thereafter, Robert Markus informed and enlivened discussions of Constantinian Christianity. His impressive erudition still illumines our understanding of the period "during which Christian Romans came slowly to identify themselves with traditional Roman values, culture, practices, and established institutions."[1] Markus identifies the world in which that assimilation slowly occurred as "the secular." Accustomed to hearing about assimilation of that sort when conversations turn to Christianity's affirmations of—or accommodations to—democratic structures or, more pointedly, to civil religion, we may consider Markus politically correct. Yet because he conscripted Latin Christianity's prolific paladin, Augustine of Hippo, into the service of the secular, as it were, Markus invites us to question whether he was, on that count, historically correct.[2]

According to Markus, Augustine subscribed neither to his faith's repudiation nor to its usurpation of the political cultures around it. What required repudiation, Markus's Augustine claims, was—and is—the profane or unacceptable. The "neutral realm of the acceptable" was "secular." The Christians of the late fourth and early fifth centuries—living in Constantine's shadow and especially after Emperor Theodosius I emphatically proscribed pagan worship—found it difficult to conceive of municipal or imperial politics as alien or, to borrow Markus's terms, to perceive the secular as profane; the empire "had become the vehicle of their religion and its natural political expression." Participation in political culture was hardly compulsory. "Christians could treat [it] as secular," Markus allowed, "perhaps distancing themselves but without feeling a need to disown and condemn" political practice.[3]

What of the other options, usurpation and repudiation? Markus associated the first with the medieval papacy, making Pope Gregory I responsible for the desecularization of the secular. Gregory purportedly inspired his successors in Rome, papal hierocratic theorists, and the canon lawyers who posted precedents for the theorists' intentions to "swallow . . . up the world."[4] As for resistance, repudiation, and repudiators, Markus could have nominated the usurpers' medieval and early modern critics but cited instead several twentieth-century evangelical protests against Gregorian Christianity, particularly those of John Howard Yoder who alleged that "the church desert[s] its vocation" whenever it celebrates its "Constantinian status"—that is, whenever it forgets that it is a community that ought to be in critical relation to "the sword"—to the political.[5]

We shall start in 314, by assessing that status and celebration shortly after Constantine's apparent conversion to Christianity. We will consider what Markus and his Augustine believe to be the secular spaces Constantinian changes opened between the sacred and profane. My aim is to raise several questions about the Church's mission, to ask why the Church should agitate in the world and whether and how it can do so without losing its distinctiveness. Perhaps "agitate" is too strong a term, yet disturbances probably seemed inevitable when moral clarity, which faith ostensibly imparts to the faithful, was released into the secular where, according to historian and ethicist Charles Mathewes—from whom I've borrowed the use of the word "agitate"—situations always are "morally ambiguous," at best, and, at worst, the world is infectiously wicked, as Augustine once claimed. The bishop could be quite unflattering when he bridled at and wrote about the conditions in this wretched world, *in hoc saeculo maligno*.[6]

Soon after he was attracted to Christianity, Emperor Constantine came to the conclusion that the African Christian clerics, who stubbornly opposed Bishop Caecilian of Carthage, were malevolent (*qui vis malignitatis in eorundum pectoribus perseverat*).[7] Caecilian's critics had challenged the validity of his appointment and consecration and, in effect, seceded from other African Christian churches, whose bishops believed their accusations against Caecilian libelous. But before seceding, they had urged Proconsul Anulinus to deny Caecilian and his partisans the exemptions Constantine awarded his new faith's clergy. Anulinus fretted, referring the matter to the emperor who, in turn, directed Miltiades, bishop of Rome, to confer with selected Italian prelates and to investigate the petitioners' accusations. He complied, assembled eighteen colleagues, probed the cause of the dissidents' discontent—notably Caecilian's alleged collaboration with Christianity's persecutors in the past—and vindicated the accused. Still, Miltiades hoped to avoid further recrimination and to appease the discontented by coupling Caecilian's acquittal with a declaration that bishops ordained by his critics were not to be denied authority. According to the proposal formulated in Rome, wherever opposition to Caecilian in Africa divided a church, seniority rather than partisanship would dictate which of the rival bishops remained in his see. The less senior would relocate. The dissidents thought the Roman compromise reprehensible. They defiantly demanded that their original complaints be reevaluated. Constantine acquiesced and set aside the decisions reached by Miltiades and the bishops he had summoned to Rome, but a second council in Arles in 314 reconfirmed the Caecilianists' position. Thereafter, the emperor considered the rage against Caecilianists irrational. The secular had weighed in, endorsing the resolution of a crisis that the sacred seemed unable to contain. Few, if any, better examples of Constantinianism—not as the church's capitulation to, but as its collaboration with, "the state"—could be found. Yet the endorsement failed to have the desired effect. The Arles verdict and imperial approval were expected to marginalize if not to douse dissent. But dissidents soon capitalized on an outpouring of African sentiment against Roman occupation and landlords to fortify their coalition, consecrating as bishop of Carthage Donatus, a resourceful leader who masterminded a campaign that, within a century, gave the secessionists' churches— the *pars Donati* or Donatists—a commanding position in several African provinces.[8]

Donatist successes during the fourth century—when they mattered most to Augustine during the 390s and thereafter—will concern us shortly, but first we need to reemphasize the perceived appropriateness of Constantine's involvement in combatting what he took as the *vis malignitatis*, the "wickedness," from which the African schism originated. He was said by his biographer to have deliberated with the bishops, if not at Rome in 313, then at Arles the next year. Eusebius imagined that collaboration; generations later, Augustine repeated the story.[9] The evidence, however, suggests that Constantine did little more than nominate a few bishops to participate in the Roman conversation, which may have been in Trier when the

Council of Arles met. The wisest course, I suspect, is to follow Brent Shaw's lead and to surmise that the bishops at Rome and Arles, regardless of the emperor's whereabouts, vindicated Caecilian and condemned his African critics at Constantine's prompting.[10]

But Constantine's prompting and the Church's councils failed to suppress African dissent. Nearly eighty years later, when Augustine resettled in Africa, the Donatist Christians outnumbered the Caecilianists. The emperor had promised to go to North Africa to make clear "what sort of devotion" pleased God, and compel the dissidents to conform to "the most perfect faith." He explained that statesmen had no greater obligation than to eradicate religious error and encourage the faithful to defer to their legitimate bishops' authority.[11] But he never went, and the immediate outcome in situ was not what he (or what became the North African Catholic Church) expected. For the Donatists were durable, intransigent, and unsparing in their criticism of their rivals. They made the religious situation terribly untidy in one of the empire's strategically important regions.

Doubts about Constantine's motives linger. He seems to have believed that God's favor was conditional, that God entrusted him with all earthly affairs, *terrena omnia*, including Church controversies about cultic practices, and that God would continue to favor his family and his rule as long as he sensibly ordered his realm's religious life. The secular and sacred were one.[12] Yet Peter Brown's generalization about the effect of Constantine and his successors on religious disputes applies well to the untidiness across the Mediterranean in the fourth and fifth centuries: "Far from bringing doctrinal controversies to an end [the emperors' pronouncements] were usually the opening shot in a campaign for the mastery of public opinion." "The shambling Roman Empire," Brown continues, "was far from being like a modern state, and the so-called Catholic Church was a loose-knit confederation of local churches, which resembled in no way the papal monarchy of later centuries."[13] So, once the "opening shot[s]" were fired, Augustine took it upon himself to arrange conversations with local Donatist bishops, circulate records of what was said, and master public opinion without inviting zealots who seemed eager to upstage statesmanlike conferees and without attracting the unwanted attention of secular authorities. One could argue that Augustine—on this count, and for a time—was trying to step outside Constantine's shadow.[14]

From the late 390s into the next century, he tried to reason with the secessionists, content to offer rules of engagement that had the prospect of restoring unity to North African Christianity. His subsequent reliance on imperial decree and on coercive measures to end the schism represented "a decisive volte-face."[15] It followed his disillusionment with attempts to appease Donatist moderates who, like Bishop Proculeianus, appeared irenic (*in te praeeminent placidoris mentis indicia*) and able to dissuade Donatists from stubborn resistance to reunion.[16] Only gradually (and grudgingly, it seems) did Augustine realize that many Donatists remained certain of the truth of the charges that had failed to convince the prelates at Rome and Arles of Caecilian's unsuitability for office in the early fourth century. And many other dissidents were too uninformed to argue intelligently, yet appeared ghoulishly to take pleasure in recycling the accusations against Caecilian and his long-dead colleagues to smear their current Catholic critics.[17]

In 403, Augustine collaborated with Bishop Aurelius of Carthage on a proposal to enlist the help of local magistrates, who might serve as referees and keep conversations from turning into nasty confrontations.[18] Augustine also favored conferring in small villages where neither faction had established a church. Neutral sites seemed perfect places to pore over passages in sacred texts and to reconcile rival interpretations.[19] But by 406, Augustine had issued a veiled ultimatum, suggesting that the Donatists would soon be faced with a decision either to agree to reconcile with him or to confront government officials bent on their suppression.[20]

During this period and into the next decade Augustine harped on about the difficulties that Catholic Christians in Africa were facing from the Donatist thugs, called *circumcellions*. If we believe Augustine, they were paramilitary ruffians whom militant Donatist bishops used as enforcers. Augustine circulated reports of their atrocities and called on the emperor's deputies in Africa to remove local officials who tolerated the terror. The *circumcellions* were "men of blood . . . armed and active everywhere."[21] To assume that moderate dissidents could bridle them was unrealistic. The moderates were in a tight spot; they could hardly appear severe when so many of their colleagues—and not a few of those among them—owed their basilicas to *circumcellions*, who had frightened away Catholic congregations and left their rivals in possession. Augustine complained that Donatist prelates were the thugs' driving force—*agonistices*—inciting *circumcellions* to "arm themselves against the law." Hence, Catholic Christians were justified calling in the law, Augustine explained, in effect raising the stakes, overstating the militants' malevolence, and overdramatizing Africa's purported

plunge into anarchy.[22] His recourse to force was "fundamentally defensive," Charles Mathewes says, and in no way "an exemplary case of Constantinianism," and, understandably, many of his contemporary admirers
found it "alarming."[23]

Alarmed Augustinians may find little comfort from this reconstruction
of the perception of the crisis that led Augustine himself to subscribe to
his colleagues' appeals for government assistance. The context does not excuse
the miscue. And I fear that what remains of this essay will not comfort
the alarmists who sift Augustinian sources for "an ethic of democratic
citizenship," inasmuch as I want to trawl in a few of Augustine's texts to
catch a modus operandi that might be construed as his alternative to
Constantinian Christianity.

He had not been looking for one earlier in his career. His *Confessions*
confides that he had hoped for a place at court and traveled to Italy to cultivate influential friends, flatter officials, and make an advantageous marriage.
His progress was professionally promising but personally unfulfilling. He
grew apprehensive. He came to believe that the happiness he sought was
specious, that street people were better off, and that his quest for patron-
age had turned him into a bootlicking beggar.[24] Years later, composing
his memoir, he recalled that he and several friends contemplated forming a community of scholars "far removed from crowds." The project
called for the appointment of a bursar or two so that others, undistracted
by the business end of their colloquy could devote themselves to studies
and learned conversations. Yet several wives withheld consent, so the plan
was abandoned.[25] Its attraction for Augustine, who was unwed, seems com-
prehensible. He had been drawn to the Manichees years before, in part
because he valued the companionship and conversations in the sect's cells.
He was also intrigued by the promise that Manichaean specialists would
explain cosmology and Christian theology. Even after he grew disillusioned
with their "utterly confused" explanations and found their conduct unbe-
coming (which, he scowled, they egregiously explained away by referring
to the sinners reckoned as righteous in several of Christianity's sacred texts),
he was loath to leave the Manichees.[26] Peter Brown suggests that Augustine's "decades of shared religious intensity . . . as a Manichee [and as] a
pioneer of a philosophical commune" led him to withdraw to a country
estate outside Milan for a few months with his mother, his son, and some
others—"a community of like-minded souls," Brown says—and then led
him to return to North Africa, with a "party of retired bureaucrats and

failed would-be courtiers," "a closed religious group" or company of Christian intellectuals intent on prayer, reading, and discussion.[27]

Apparently Augustine was satisfied that his small companies of Christians could encourage the self-inquiry and colloquy (*interius cogitando et loquendo*) he thought necessary as preparation to approach what he called "the edge of eternity."[28] Most studies of his *Confessions* emphasize the introspection, but Gaetano Piccolo, in a lengthy discussion of interiority, concedes the importance of self-analysis, and especially memory, in the reception of God's revelations. The inner life, if overemphasized, often disorients, becoming the principal obstacle to *convivenza civile*.[29] Augustine seems to have anticipated Piccolo's counsel. When describing his party's pastimes, he added *loquendo* as if to signal that the Christian community's piety and fellowship were due to discourse as well as to sighs, studies, and prayers. As he came under the influence of the call for personal reform found in the gospels and the writings of the apostle Paul, Augustine elsewhere and increasingly advised that colloquy, which he called "a surface activity," was an aid to contemplation. Nonetheless, as Phillip Cary notes, "the privacy of the inner self is a temporary phenomenon." Augustine looked forward to a time when the "inmost selves" of the faithful would "be open to each other's gaze, as they were always meant to be."[30]

Memory was critical: *ego sum qui memini*.[31] Their memories constituted Christians. Memory probed and processed experiences and, in Augustine's memoir, memory molded experience into what Brian Stock calls "the West's first fully developed narrative philosophy."[32] The tenth and eleventh books of the *Confessions* are its display cases. Significantly, the latter starts speaking "plurally and communally," Charles Mathewes notes; for nine books, readers watch Augustine, alone, measuring time, but after that "we are in the church," a church that remembered Constantine's conversion, but not necessarily as a watershed: that is, as a political turning point that accommodated Christianity—or assimilated the Church—to the political structures of the empire.[33]

Faithful Christians in the Church were on pilgrimage in time, Augustine explained later, when he realized that politicized Christianity was unsturdy in theory and practice. After he wrote his memoirs—but before his day seemed so disjointed, following rebellion and riots in Africa and the sack of Rome in 410—he associated pilgrimage with tears. Weeping, he claimed, was the appropriate response to the faithful's estrangement from the celestial city.[34] Despite the consolations on offer in time (rationality, vitality, and the Church with its sacraments), pilgrims needed to be re-minded that their true home was elsewhere, and that their purpose on earth, in large part, was to yearn for it. The Church was also the repository for memories and for their authoritative interpretation. Both the memories and their interpretation reinforced the pilgrims' sense of mission to pro-claim their citizenship in the celestial city together with their longing for it. Augustine learned as much in the 380s. In the *Confessions* he recalled being told a story by Simplicianus, who succeeded Ambrose as bishop of Milan. Simplicianus reported coaxing a widely respected rhetorician, Victorinus, into the Church. Victorinus eventually admitted that he found truth and comfort in Christianity, but he resisted public disclosure. He declined Simplicianus's invitation to come to church (arguing that it was preposterous to suppose that walls made the faithful any more faithful) until God unexpectedly moved him to make a conspicuous and celebrated confession of his adopted religion and to join "God's gentle flock."[35]

The Church was custodian of memories and stories such as that of Sim-plicianus. Retelling the stories of conversions instructed prospective con-verts. Conceivably, Augustine was thinking of that possibility when he drafted his memoirs and added his odyssey to the Church memory bank. Possibly he had this prospect in mind when he strategically deployed the Church's recollections in his *City of God*. Rehearsing martyrs' ordeals, he suggested to Christian pilgrims what they could expect from authorities, even after the Constantinian settlement, since many pagans continued to blame Christianity for their empire's unnerving setbacks in 387, when Em-peror Valens died defending the frontier, and in 410, when Alaric chased Emperor Honorius from Rome. The Christians were blamed for abandon-ing Rome's old gods who protected cities in return for worship rendered by leading citizens. Pilgrims learned from martyrs that they lived precari-ously and as captives on earth and that they should stand ready to embrace the promise of redemption rather than cultivate civic pride and accumu-late possessions associated with an unwholesome secular life.[36] Pagans cre-ated and preserved memories for related reasons, using them to encourage civic solidarity. In a recent study, Patrice Cambronne infers that Augus-tine adapted their approach to the Church's purposes. Alleging that the pagans' storytellers were charlatans, he relayed his memories of martyrs to bind pilgrims to their Church over their cities, and to the Christian prom-ise of redemption.[37]

Binding pilgrims to each other as well as to a repository of their faith's stories and memories, Augustine steps outside our frame of reference, which, as Martin Claussen says, takes pilgrimage "as a somewhat solitary exercise." For Augustine this was not the case, and pilgrimage was rather "something the whole community . . . does together."[38] Entering the community, catechumens were given history lessons. They began with the Old Testament's saga of creation, fall, and flood. They recalled the apostles' ordeals and concluded with a short tribute to the martyrs, who attested the truth of their faith until "the neck" of their persecutors' pride had been snapped. The Church, as Joost van Neer says, makes its memories come alive "to build up the faith."[39]

On Augustine's watch, memories were crafted and conveyed to make the Church's story and prospects so much more appealing than those of the secular world. His *City of God* sets out the history (and pre-history) of the Church after commenting somewhat favorably on old Rome's achievements. Contestable interpretations of those comments and of several passages elsewhere suggest that Augustine imagined that secular regimes could be more or less just; readings of the *City*'s fourth book, for example, justify Rome's territorial expansion by referring to the unruly conduct of the neighbors it absorbed. But the lust for domination, which Augustine deplored, is the proper explanation—his explanation, according to which such lust made political equilibrium impossible. That the *City* defines a republic without reference to justice and that it endorses the complaints of one of Cicero's characters in *De re publica*, who maintained that political practice requires unjust behavior, appear to be irrelevant to scholars devoted to discovering Augustine's optimism or sources for political optimism in his *City* that would enable them to come to comfortable terms with liberal democracy.[40]

Thomas Martin's essay on the politics of monasticism seems to me a more sensible application of Augustine's reflections on solidarity and civic piety. Martin relates Augustine's take on fairness and meaningful reciprocity to "the republic of grace" in convents. Monasticism was *peregrinans* and "far from perfect," yet it represented humanity's best efforts—and best bet—*in hoc saeculo maligno* to get just results. "The monastic community does witness to the art of the possible," Martin says, to "what can be done while still on pilgrimage."[41] As for Christian magistrates and soldiers, who cannot responsibly retire from the secular world and who must reconcile themselves to their secular duties, which amount to damage control, Augustine told them to pray for their deliverance, fret about the inconsistency between their political practice and their piety, and to repent. Ideally, they can find scope for an uncompromising exercise of virtue in their churches.[42]

The world is to be used but not improved by Christian pilgrims and their Church, which is the context in which operative and cooperative grace improves relations among the faithful and the relations between them and their creator and redeemer. Pilgrims are taught to expect celestial rewards, properly to weigh the value of temporal rewards, and to pay forward God's love in their love for neighbors. But pilgrims are not to propose a new religious foundation for municipal moral order. Augustine did not politicize piety. For him, piety's proper arena was, according to John Rist, "unpolitical"—not apolitical, but unpolitical—and what Francesco D'Agostino identifies as Augustine's *antigiuridismo* demonstrates just that. It surfaces in several skirmishes with Pelagians who depicted law as grace, when, insisting that a Christian's freedom to obey the law was implicit in the very existence of law, they supposed the laws of God were reflected in the laws of civil society. To Augustine, their supposition was preposterous.[43]

So it would be foolish to look for any significant slab of the optimism resembling Eusebius of Caesarea's euphoria in Augustine's remarks on political leadership or jurisprudence. Perhaps we should we refer to Augustine, in the words of Christoph Horn, as "a political functionalist," one who acknowledges the normativity of institutions and laws, while accepting that prevalent political practices serve useful yet occasionally immoral purposes? After all, Augustine would have conceded that institutions, laws, and practices in the terrestrial city, *in hoc saeculo maligno*, were normative to a point. But "normativity" meant relatively little in the long run for Augustine or, to put his likely perception in more precise terms, calling the prevailing patterns of political behavior normal or normative did little to relieve the distress that "everywhere filled" what he knew of human experience in this wicked world (*ubique impleverunt*); temptations and suspicions afflicted what passed as ordinary lives. For Augustine, the secular was sinful; whatever there was of his functionalism was trumped by his "moralism."[44] In Augustine's *City of God* political behavior and, more importantly, political institutions invariably succumb to "the universal sway of antagonism." That phrase, "universal sway of antagonism," is John Milbank's and is quite controversial, but, as James Wetzel admits, Milbank has "an exegetical basis in the *City of God* for conjoining sin, secularity, and paganism."[45]

The Church supplied some refuge and relief from the wreckage of creation that we have been calling "the secular." The Church had a distinctive
calling, which distinguished it from—and called for unremitting criticism
of—political settlements. That criticism neither required nor commended
active participation in political deliberations. In Augustine's judgment,
the compassion of Christians was better spent in their churches than in
senates, better spent paying forward God's love for the pilgrims' celestial
city in their love for neighbors. *Opera misericordiae*, expressions of tender-
ness, were sacrifices that assuredly pleased God, Augustine warranted, and
might even snatch up (*rapere*) neighbors whose behavior had been objec-
tionable and change them into effective executors of God's love.[46] To change
or reform others, of course, required that one be reformed, which, for
Augustine, meant losing the form of secular desire (*formam concupiscentiae
saecularis amittat*), having it consumed by the fire of God's love. That fire
was kindled by submission to God. Pilgrims' passions for the celestial city
began with self-inquiry, which Luigi Alici dubs "spiritual reconnaissance,"
developed with their submission, and contributed to constituting churches
as pride-free zones in which aversion to contention eventually, and ideally,
douses the self-love and lusts that inflame contentious spirits.[47]

"Zoning" the Church in this fashion returns us to Augustine's opposition to the Donatists. To his mind, the Donatists' claims to superior
righteousness—their purported libels against their first critics, the Caecilianists, and their resistance to reconciliation—exhibited an all-too-human
lack of compassion and an addiction to contention. Augustine believed the
Pelagians were similarly disposed. He chided them as well for conceit, inasmuch as their claims to please God without special divine assistance
drove them, he said, from the certainties of faith to idolatry.[48] Pride played
itself out in assertions of "moral self-sufficiency, religious superiority, and
political domination," according to J. Patout Burns—"pride was the principal obstacle to overcome." One function of the law was "to dissolve a
person's sense of self-reliance," Patout Burns goes on, but it was also the
Church's function to challenge members' self-satisfaction. The churches
consequently contributed to a process by which the celestial city was "constantly being formed by the reform (*mutatione*) of the wicked."[49] Augustine acknowledged that there would be heavy lifting ahead. Professed
Christians in the Church could be indecisive, and "many live[d] lives un-
worthy of the baptisms they received." They crowded into the circus rather
than into the basilica. They set up shops on holy days and grew irritable if

trade on those days was restricted.[50] Augustine urged that the faithful help
coreligionists whose determination was unequal to the challenges that
Christian standards posed for them. The most motivated pilgrims should
help the least to "cross the Red Sea," he said, and get wet enough to wash
away the residue of their sinful lives—to accept God's promises, and put
the temptations of this wicked world into perspective.[51] In the same sermon, preached sometime during the first decade of the fifth century or
shortly after Rome's humiliation in 410, Augustine concluded that Christians might also assist those "dregs" (*amurca*) who tempted pilgrims into
the *saeculum* and have them participate as incurious and uncomplaining
citizens of this wicked world; maybe the faithful should bring that "slag"
to church along with those susceptible to their tempters' touting civic pride,
Augustine suggested, trusting that tempters and tempted alike might be
inspired by the memories of martyrs and the stories of converts as well as
by self-reconnaissance, and colleagues' compassion—inspired to step out
of Constantine's shadow.[52]

Notes

1. Robert Markus, "The Secular in Late Antiquity," in *Les frontières du
profane dans l'antiquité tardive*, ed. Éric Rebillard and Claire Sotinel (Rome:
École Française de Rome, 2010), 358. For secularization as liberation, see
Robert Markus, *Saeculum: History and Society in the Theology of St. Augustine*,
2nd ed. (Cambridge: Cambridge University Press, 1988), 173. Contemporary
commentary on civil religion accepts that the acculturation of Christianity
thrives after the "break up" of "religious monopolies . . . into precisely a free
market of countless small entrepreneurs," as Ronald Beiner explains, paraphrasing
Adam Smith. Robert Bellah, too infrequently cited by Beiner, is largely
responsible for the civil religion's relevance to rituals and rhetoric in the United
States ("Europe is Egypt; America, the promised land where a new sort of social
order . . . shall be a light unto all nations"). See Ronald Beiner, *Civil Religion: A
Dialogue in the History of Political Philosophy* (Cambridge: Cambridge University
Press, 2011), 243–44 and Robert Bellah, "Civil Religion in America," *Daedalus*
96.1 (1967), 7–8. For the term's early modern (and influential) meaning,
consult Jean-Jacques Rousseau, *Du contrat social ou princeps du droit politique*,
ed. Jean-Marie Fataud and Marie-Claude Bartholy (Paris: Bordas, 1972),
209–19.

2. Charles Taylor, *A Secular Age* (Cambridge, Mass.: Belknap Press, 2007),
86–88 traces to the late Renaissance the "disciplined reordering of life and
society," which disenchanted the world, distinguished the elite's ideals of piety

and civility from those of ordinary Christians, and made possible the new self-understandings and practices, which, to his mind, define secularity.

3. Markus, "Secular in Late Antiquity," 253–59.

4. Robert Markus, *Christianity and the Secular* (Notre Dame, Ind.: University of Notre Dame Press, 2006), 86.

5. Markus, *Christianity and the Secular*, 24–28. Here, as in the sixth article of the Schleitheim Confession, "the sword" refers to "an ordering outside the perfection of Christ." Yoder's works have been profoundly influential. His *Täufertum und Reformation im Gespräch* (Zurich: EVZ Verlag, 1968) chronicled the early opposition to the Constantinianism of the magisterial reformation. For relatively recent commentary, see the essays by Waldemar Janzen and J. Alexander Sider in *The Church Made Strange for the Nations: Essays in Ecclesiology and Political Theology*, ed. Paul G. Doerksen and Karl Koop (Eugene: Wipf and Stock, 2011).

6. Augustine, *De civitate Dei* 18.49. Readers may check references to (and my translations from) the Latin on-line at http://www.augustinus.it/latino/cdd/index2.htm (accessed 2 August 2014), which contains texts from the relevant volumes of Jacques-Paul Migne, *Patrologia Cursus Completus: Series Latina* (PL). I have consulted relevant volumes of the *Corpus Scriptorum Ecclesiasticorum Latinorum* (CSEL). For the church's (or Christians') interventions as "agitation," see Charles Mathewes, *The Republic of Grace: Augustinian Thoughts for Dark Times* (Grand Rapids, Mich.: Eerdmans, 2010), 214–15. For alternative evaluations of the secular in Augustine's *City*, see, in addition to Markus, *Christianity and the Secular*, Paul J. Griffiths, "Secularity and the Saeculum," in *Augustine's "City of God": A Critical Guide*, ed. James Wetzel (Cambridge: Cambridge University Press, 2012): 32–54.

7. Documents related to the origins of the African schism are conveniently printed in *Le Dossier du Donatisme*, vol. 1, ed. Jean-Louis Maier (Berlin: Akademie Verlag, 1987); for "*vis malignitatis*" see Constantine's epistolary response to the Arles determinations, 169. The Council of Arles and its immediate aftermath are discussed in W. H. C. Frend, *The Donatist Church: A Movement of Protest in Roman North Africa* (Oxford: Clarendon, 1985), 151–56.

8. Donatus was long after known as the prelate who purged Carthage of practices associated with undisciplined versions of the Christian faith imported from Rome; see Augustine, *Contra Cresconium* 3.56.

9. "Über das Leben des Kaisers Konstantins," in *Die griechische christliche Schriftsteller der ersten Jahrhunderte, Eusebius Werke* 1.1, ed. Friedhelm Winkelmann (Berlin: de Gruyter, 1991), 1.44; and Augustine, *Epistolae* 43.5.

10. Brent D. Shaw, *Sacred Violence: African Christians and Sectarian Hatred in the Age of Augustine* (Cambridge: Cambridge University Press, 2011), 62; H. A. Drake, *Constantine and the Bishops: The Politics of Intolerance*

(Baltimore: Johns Hopkins University Press, 2000), 218–19, details the emperor's and Miltiades's influence on participation in 313; Timothy Barnes, *The New Empire of Diocletian and Constantine* (Cambridge, Mass.: Harvard University Press, 1982), 71, reconstructs Constantine's itinerary for 314.

11. Maier, *Dossier*, 195–96.

12. See, for example, Constantine's Letter to Aelafius, in Maier, *Dossier*, 157–58.

13. Eric Brown, "Emotion and Peace of Mind: From Stoic Agitation to Christian Temptation," *Philosophical Books* 43 (2002): 195–96. On this connection, see H. A. Drake, "The Impact of Constantine on Christianity," in *The Cambridge Companion to the Age of Constantine*, ed. Noel Lenski (Cambridge: Cambridge University Press, 2006): 11–36; and Claudia Rapp, *Holy Bishops in Late Antiquity: The Nature of Christian Leadership in an Age of Transition* (Berkeley: University of California Press, 2005), especially 236–52.

14. See Augustine's Letter to Donatist Proculeianus (396), *Epistolae* 33.4.

15. Émilien Lamirande, "Aux origines du dialogue interconfessionnel: Saint Augustin et les donatistes, vingt ans de tentatives infructueuses (391–411)," *Studia canonica* 32 (1998), 205. See also Pierre Cazier, "La *compelle intrare* d'Augustin, mise en perspective," in *Violence et Religion*, ed. Pierre Cazier and Jean-Marie Delmaire (Villeneuve d'Ascq: Université Lille, 1998), 29–31 and Shaw, *Sacred Violence*, 141–45.

16. Augustine, *Epistolae* 33.1.

17. Augustine, *Epistolae* 43.15.

18. Lamirande, "Origines," 222–24.

19. Augustine, *Epistolae* 44.14.

20. See Augustine's Letter to Donatist Bishop Januarius (406), *Epistolae* 88.10.

21. Augustine, *Enarrationes in Psalmos* 54.26: "[N]on quiescent armati ubique Circumcelliones." Also see Cécile Barreteau-Revel, "Faire l'unité dans l'Église d'Afrique du Nord: la réintégration des donatistes des IVᵉ et Vᵉ siècles," *Les Pères de l'Église et les dissidents: Dissidence, exclusion et réintégration dans les communautés chrétiennes des six premiers siècles*, ed. Pascal-Grégoire Delage (La Rochelle: Caritas Patrum, 2010), 236–37; Peter Iver Kaufman, "Donatism Revisited: Moderates and Militants in Late Antique North Africa," *Journal of Late Antiquity* 2 (2009): 131–42; and Shaw, *Sacred Violence*, especially 634–37, 646–47, 656–59, and 702–4.

22. See Augustine's Letter to Macrobius (409), *Epistolae* 108. Also, for Augustine's overstatements, consult Emin Tengström, *Donatisten und Katholiken: Soziale, wirtschaftliche, und politische Aspekte einer nordafrikanischen Kirchenspaltung* (Göteborg: Acta Universitatis Gothoburgensis, 1964), 84–87; and Peter Iver Kaufman, *Incorrectly Political: Augustine and Thomas More* (Notre Dame, Ind.: University of Notre Dame Press), 86–90.

23. Charles Mathewes, *The Republic of Grace: Augustinian Thoughts for Dark Times* (Grand Rapids, Mich.: Eerdmans, 2010), 49–51. For "alarming," see Eric Gregory, *Politics and the Order of Love: An Augustinian Ethic of Democratic Citizenship* (Chicago: University of Chicago Press, 2008), 305.

24. Augustine, *Confessions* 6.6.9 and 6.11.18–19. Also see Claude Lepelley, "*Spes saeculi*: Le milieu social d'Augustin et ses ambitions séculières avant sa conversion," *Studia ephemerides Augustinianum* 24–26 (1987), 112–13.

25. Augustine, *Confessions* 6.14.24. If Claude Lepelley is correct, the plan would have surprised some members of his family who had come to Milan to participate in Augustine's success. See Claude Lepelley, "Un aspect de la conversion d'Augustin: La rupture avec ses ambitions sociale et politiques," *Bulletin de Littérature ecclésiastique* 88 (1987), 243.

26. Augustine, *De utilitate credendi* 14.31 and 18.36; Augustine, *De moribus ecclesiae catholicae et de moribus Manichaeorum* 19.72. Also see François Decret, *L'Afrique Manichéisme dans l'Afrique Romain* (Paris: Études Augustiniennes, 1970), 219–21; J. Kevin Coyle, *Manichaeism and Its Legacy* (Leiden: Brill, 2009), 244–48; and Jason David Beduhn, *Augustine's Manichaean Dilemma: Conversion and Apostasy, 373–388 C.E.* (Philadelphia: University of Pennsylvania Press, 2010), especially 241–43.

27. Peter Brown, *Through the Eye of a Needle: Wealth, the Fall of Rome, and the Making of Christianity in the West, 350–550 AD* (Princeton: Princeton University Press, 2012), 166–67.

28. Augustine, *Confessions* 9.10.24.

29. Gaetano Piccolo, *I processi di apprendimento in Agostino d'Ippona* (Rome: Aracne, 2009), 228–34.

30. Phillip Cary, *Augustine's Invention of the Inner Self* (Oxford: Oxford University Press, 2000), 121–22. Also see Brian Stock, "Self, Soliloquy, and Spiritual Exercises in Augustine and Some Later Authors," *The Journal of Religion* 91 (2011), 11–12; Brian Stock, *Augustine's Inner Dialogue: The Philosophical Soliloquy in Late Antiquity* (Cambridge: Cambridge University Press, 2010), 190–91; and Anton Van Hoof, "Die Dialektik der Umkehr," in *Die "Confessiones" des Augustinus von Hippo*, ed. Norbert Fischer and Cornelius Mayer (Freiburg: Herder, 1998), 365–66.

31. Augustine, *Confessions* 10.16.25. See Paula Fredriksen, *Sin: The Early History of an Idea* (Princeton: Princeton University Press, 2012), 118–19, for Augustine on time, language, and "the integrative function of memory." And, for memory as "the ground for a constant link between the faculties of the soul and God" and for the importance of "spiritual attentiveness" to oneself and God through memory, see Paige E. Hochschild, *Memory in Augustine's Theological Anthropology* (Oxford: Oxford University Press, 2012), especially 139–49 and 166–67.

32. Stock, *Augustine's Inner Dialogue*, 181–82 and 213–14.

33. Charles Mathewes, "The Liberation of Questioning in Augustine's *Confessions*," *Journal of the American Academy of Religion* 70 (2002), 554.

34. Augustine, *Sermones* 31.5.

35. Augustine, *Confessions* 8.2.5.

36. Augustine, *De civitate Dei* 19.17: "apud terrenam civitatem velut captivam vivam." Also see *De civitate Dei* 1.29.

37. Patrice Cambronne, *Saint Augustin: Un voyage au Coeur du temps*, vol. 1 (Bordeaux: Presses Universitaires de Bordeaux, 2010), 90–96.

38. M. A. Claussen, "*Peregrinatio* and *Peregrini* in Augustine's *City of God*," *Traditio* 46 (1991), 43–44.

39. Augustine, *De catechizandis rudibus* 24.44; Joos van Neer, "Bouwen aan het geloof: De twee modeltoespraken in *De Catechizandis rudibus*," *Lampas* 43 (2010), 356.

40. I raise objections to the findings of several of the most conspicuous devotees of Augustine's political optimism in Kaufman, *Incorrectly Political*, 99–132 and Kaufman, "Christian Realism and Augustinian(?) Liberalism," *Journal of Religious Ethics* 38 (2010): 699–723. But see the interpretations of *De civitate Dei* 4.4 and 4.15 in Paul J. Cornish "Augustine's Contribution to the Republican Tradition," *The European Journal of Political Theory* 9 (2010): 133–48, at 139–40. For Cicero and injustice in the City, see Augustine, *De civitate Dei* 2.21.

41. Thomas Martin, "Augustine and the Politics of Monasticism," in *Augustine and Politics*, ed. John Doody, Kevin L. Hughes, and Kim Pfaffenroth (New York: Lexington, 2005), 183–84.

42. See Augustine, *Epistolae* 220 and Augustine, *De civitate Dei* 19.6. But compare Christoph Horn, "Augustinus über politische Ethik und legitime Staatsgewalt," in *Augustinus: Recht und Gewalt*, ed. Cornelius Mayer (Würzburg: Zentrum für Augustinusforschung, 2010), 53–57; Peter Burnell, *The Augustinian Person* (Washington: Catholic University of America Press, 2005), 144–54; and Robert Dodaro, *Christ and the Just Society in the Thought of Augustine* (Cambridge; Cambridge University Press, 2004), 206–14. A few lines of wishful thinking in one of Augustine's several letters to government authorities intimate that Christianity's precepts might overhaul ("consecrate") political culture, but no program for the improvement of Constantinian Christianity or for reconstituting the government develops from them. See Augustine, *Epistolae* 138.10.

43. See John Rist, *Augustine: Ancient Thought Baptized* (Cambridge: Cambridge University Press, 1994), 214–15; and Francesco D'Agostino, "L'antigiuridismo di S. Agostino," *Rivista internazionale di filosofia del diritto* 64 (1987), 31, 35–36, and 40–41.

44. Augustine, *De civitate Dei* 19.5; Horn, "Staatsgewalt," 65–67.

45. See John Milbank, *Theology and Social Theory: Beyond Secular Reason* (Oxford: Blackwell, 1990), 389; and James Wetzel, "Splendid Vices and Secular Virtues: Variations on Milbank's Augustine," *The Journal of Religious Ethics* 32 (2004), 280–81.

46. Augustine, *Sermones* 90A.11 and Augustine, *De civitate Dei* 20.24.2.

47. Augustine, *De civitate Dei* 10.6. For "autoriconoscimento spirituale" see Luigi Alici, "Storia e salvezza nel *De civitate Dei*," in *La fine dei tempi: storia e escatologia*, ed. Mario Naldini (Fiesole: Centro di Studi Patristici, 1994), 87–90. This is obviously quite different from what Augustine describes as *amor sui* or from what Charles Mathewes calls "morbid self-consciousness"; see Augustine, *De civitate Dei* 14.28 and Charles Mathewes, "A Worldly Augustinianism: Augustine's Sacramental Vision of Creation," *Augustinian Studies* 41 (2010), 337.

48. Augustine, *De spiritu et littera ad Marcellinus* 18.11–19.12.

49. Augustine, *Enarrationes in Psalmos* 61.7; J. Patout Burns, "Augustine on the Origin and Progress of Evil," *The Journal of Religious Ethics* 16 (1988), 24.

50. Augustine, *Enarrationes in Psalmos* 80.2.

51. Augustine, *Enarrationes in Psalmos* 80.8: "Nihil ergo aliud significabit transitus per mare, nisi Sacramentum baptizatorum."

52. Augustine, *Enarrationes in Psalmos* 80.11.

"YOU CANNOT HAVE A CHURCH WITHOUT AN EMPIRE"

POLITICAL ORTHODOXY IN BYZANTIUM

James C. Skedros

At the end of the fourteenth century, the Byzantine Empire had been reduced to a handful of possessions consisting of the depopulated city of Constantinople, a few port towns in nearby Thrace, the independent empire of Trebizond on the southern coast of the Black Sea, some northern Aegean islands, and parts of the Greek Peloponnesus. The grandeur, military might, and economic dominance that once had made Byzantium the envy of the medieval world was gone. By 1371, Emperor John V Palaiologos had begun to pay an annual tribute to the more powerful Ottomans. It is rather remarkable that Byzantium would survive for another three generations. Yet, even within such a bleak political and military existence, the rhetoric of empire continued. In 1393, Anthony, patriarch of Constantinople, penned a letter to Basil I, grand prince of Moscow. Anthony had learned that the Muscovite prince was not offering the liturgical commemoration of the Byzantine Emperor Manuel II Palaiologos (1391–1425).[1] In this oft-quoted letter, Patriarch Anthony expresses his dismay at such an oversight and expresses the conventional imperial ideology of Byzantium:

> My son, it is not possible for Christians to have a Church and not have an empire. Church and empire have a great unity and community. It is not possible for them to be separated from one another. For the holy emperor is not as other rulers and the governors of other regions are; and this is because the emperors, from the beginning,

established and confirmed true religion (*eusebia*) in all the inhabited world (*oikoumene*). They convoked ecumenical councils . . . and [they] struggled hard against heresies.

Though not part of the imperial orbit of the dwindling eastern Roman Empire, Moscow was, at the very least, a member of the larger Christian Orthodox world, the Orthodox *oikoumene* that had already begun to replace the soon-to-be-defunct political entity on the Bosporus, and as such, Moscow, in Patriarch Anthony's view, ought to remember and pray for the emperor. In a clear reference to the first Christian emperor, Anthony argued that emperors had always been involved in defining orthodox doctrine over against misguided teachings. Though written within the context of ecclesiastical relations between Constantinople and the metropolitanate of Russia, Anthony's letter offers a succinct exposition of the imperial responsibility as defender of Orthodoxy.

Byzantine emperors had a long tradition as defenders and protectors of the faith dating back to the enshrined deeds of the first Christian emperor, Constantine. Imperial proclamations in support of the early Ecumenical Councils make this role abundantly clear. Emperors were generally required to profess their doctrinal orthodoxy at their coronation, the first attestation of such a profession being that of Anastasios I (491–518).[2] The Byzantine emperors had the authority and right to call ecumenical councils and to enforce synodal and canonical decisions made by the Church. Further, emperors, most famously Justinian I (527–65) and Leo VI (886–912), promulgated legislation that was directly related to the affairs of the Church. Regarding issues of dogma, emperors were expected to defend the Church against the encroachment of heresy. Though key concepts in the self-definition of the Christian Church, the constructs of heresy and orthodoxy were not exclusive domains of the Byzantine Church but were at work in creating and sustaining imperial ideology as well. In this paper, I suggest that the concept of "orthodoxy" was as much, if not more, important to the political and cultural identity of Byzantium as to the defense of the proper teachings of the Christian faith. This "political orthodoxy," especially from the eleventh century onwards, became critical to Byzantine political identity in ways that it had not been in the earlier period.[3]

Byzantine Political Theory

Before defining what is meant by "political orthodoxy," three relatively undisputed and rather prosaic observations about church and state in Byzantium are in order. First, Byzantium lacked detailed or systematic political treatises defining the theoretical foundations of its political legitimacy.[4] There was no constitution per se, nor did any great thinker produce the equivalent of a *City of God* as Augustine had done in the West. Rather, in the East it was politics as usual. That is, the imperial office (and its holder) was the justification for and the legal basis of the Byzantine political machinery. Even the dynastic principle, though at times operative during the history of Byzantium, was unnecessary to validate authority. Imperial legitimacy rested primarily on the imperial office itself, and whoever held the office of emperor held absolute authority.

Second, the Byzantine emperor played a significant role in the life of the Byzantine Church. The emperor possessed longstanding privileges: He presided at Church councils and gave them the weight of civic (imperial) law; he could formulate rules for the proper governing of the ecclesiastical hierarchy; and he had the right to be involved in the election of bishops to vacant sees as well as to initiate episcopal transfers, most significantly that of the see of Constantinople. His right to appoint and remove the patriarch of Constantinople was never seriously challenged. In addition, he held lesser (perhaps merely symbolic) liturgical rights: He could cense the altar in Hagia Sophia as well as the tombs in the Church of the Holy Apostles; he could preach on certain occasions; he could commune himself (at the very least, on the day of his consecration); and as affirmed in the well-known Canon 69 of the Council in Trullo (690–91), he was the only layman who was officially allowed in the bema of a church (*thysiasterion*).[5]

Third, the boundaries between church and state were blurred. Although employing these two institutional identities (i.e., church and state) already prejudices the discussion, divisions between or harmony among the spiritual and the temporal, the *hierosyne* and *basileia*, and the kingdom of heaven and the political *oikoumene*, continuously informed the history of Byzantium. It is wrong to assume that Byzantine society did not recognize differences between church and state; the two often came into conflict. Yet to set up the two in opposition to each other already introduces into the discussion preconceived ideas of the "theory of the two powers" that was prevalent in the West from Pope Gelasius onwards but failed to make solid inroads in the East.[6]

This is not the place to address the question of Byzantine caesaropapism. How one views Byzantium and the role of its emperor in the life of the Church is often related to the observer's own political and ecclesial views. Whether Byzantium was or was not caesaropapist is of no import for the present discussion. Whether we view Byzantine society as the best possible combination of the two powers—the *symphonia* or harmony of the priestly and imperial powers in the language of Justinian's sixth novella— or as the Church surrendering to worldly authority, there can be no doubt that civic and religious life in Byzantium were intertwined.

The Byzantine Church absorbed the legacy of Constantine in a variety of ways. Throughout its millennial existence within the political orbit of the Roman Empire, the Church dealt often in a realpolitik approach to the challenges that imperial authority posed. At times, concessions or af- filiations granted to the *imperium* raised the ire of many a Church leader and observer. At other times, the Church of Constantinople was more than willing to pursue a policy of accommodation toward imperial authority as long as it furthered the goals of the Church. In one area, however—that of political orthodoxy—imperial and ecclesial authorities joined forces in both policy and rhetoric. Defining the message and the language appro- priate for the expression of the Christian gospel was as old as the evangeli- cal message itself. What was new from Constantine onwards was the involvement of the state in this process. Constantine set the precedent and it continued down to the end of the empire. Within this relationship between the state and the Church that transpired over centuries and as Byzantine ecclesial identity and doctrinal content were being defined, there emerged not only the definition of orthodoxy but the utilization of this construct for political purposes. Political orthodoxy describes the adoption and defense of orthodox dogma as well as the cultural and political iden- tity that helped to define it. As a construct, political orthodoxy differs from "political theology" or "political Christianity"—the former referring in gen- eral to the adoption of Christianity for political purposes (á la Constan- tine) and the latter constructing a theological view to support political authority (á la Eusebius).[7] Political orthodoxy moves beyond these, though informed by both. Adhering to orthodox doctrine and practice, political orthodoxy expresses these in terms of cultural and institutional identity. It places orthodoxy in the service of defining oneself against someone else.

Certainly the categories of heresy and orthodoxy had been doing this kind of work for centuries. Political orthodoxy encompasses the definition of religious orthodoxy and places it in the service of the larger emerging ethno-political identities of the Eastern Roman Empire. To defend orthodoxy is thus to defend these identities as well.

Defender of Orthodoxy

In the first half of the fifteenth century, Symeon, archbishop of Thessaloniki (1416–29), noted that the emperor held an ecclesiastical rank equivalent to that of *depotatos* (*deputatus*) as well as the title of defender (*defensor*) of the Church.[8] Both titles and the several privileges given to the emperor were, according to Symeon, derived from the fact that the emperor at his coronation was anointed by the patriarch with chrism—that is, the same *myron* used in baptism. Physical anointing of the Byzantine emperor was a late innovation, and can be attested with certainty only with the coronation of John III Vatatzes in 1221, who was crowned Byzantine emperor at Nicaea.[9] The Western influence of such anointing cannot be doubted. Yet the political reality of the loss of the city of Constantinople a few years earlier to the Fourth Crusade, along with the breakup of the empire into three competing centers of authority (Trebizond, Epirus, and Nicaea), led to the diminishing of the political legitimacy of the imperial office. The use of chrism reflects the increased authority of the Church, as does the addition, during the Palaiologan period, of a profession of faith and proclamation by the emperor to defend the Church.[10]

As protector and defender of the Church, the function of the emperor was well defined and had a long history. Justinian placed the following edict at the beginning of his codification of law:

> It is our will that all peoples who are ruled by the administration of Our Clemency shall practice that religion which the divine Peter the apostle transmitted to the Romans. . . . We command that those persons who follow this law shall embrace the name of Catholic Christians. The rest, however, whom we judge demented and insane, shall sustain the infamy attached to heretical dogmas.[11]

This imperial responsibility is repeated again and again in our sources, perhaps most famously by Photios in the second title of the *Epanagoge*, a law book published in 886 that served as an introduction to the late ninth-century comprehensive collection of laws known as the *Basilika*. Photios writes, "The emperor is presumed to enforce and maintain, first and foremost, all that is set out in the divine scriptures; then the doctrines laid down by the seven holy Councils."[12] The role of defender of the faith is reflected more dramatically by the actions of Emperor Alexios I Komnenos (1081–118). In the second year of his reign, in March 1082, Alexios timed the condemnation of John Italos, head of the school of philosophy in the imperial capital, to coincide with the Feast of Orthodoxy, which was celebrated each year on the first Sunday of Lent.[13] The Feast of Orthodoxy celebrated the final victory of Orthodoxy over Iconoclasm that had occurred in 843. Each year on this feast day the *Synodikon of Orthodoxy* was read out. The *Synodikon*, a quasiliturgical/canonical text that affirmed the reinstatement and veneration of images, had remained substantially unaltered. Alexios changed all this, and added to the *Synodikon* anathemas against Italos for his apparent philosophical musings that did not sit well with ecclesiastical authorities. The condemnation of Italos and the reading of the anathemas against him on the Feast of Orthodoxy transformed the traditional role of the *Synodikon*. From Alexios's time onwards, additions to the *Synodikon* would continue to be made. The *Synodikon* no longer remained identified with the victory over Iconoclasm but was now seen as "an authoritative statement of orthodoxy."[14] Alexios's expanded role as defender of orthodoxy would be repeated throughout the remainder of the empire.[15]

The imperial defense of doctrinal orthodoxy did not necessarily translate into recognition of a particular emperor's sanctity. It is true that all the emperors of Constantinople who convened an ecumenical council are commemorated in the tenth-century *Synaxarion of Constantinople*. This does not mean, as Hippolytus Delehaye noted over a century ago, that inclusion in the *Synaxarion*, an official collection of brief notices of saints commemorated in the liturgical calendar in Constantinople, was equivalent to recognition of sanctity.[16] Interestingly, the majority of the imperial recognitions made in the *Synaxarion* do not use the adjective *hagios* or *hagia*, but rather rely on formula that make reference to an individual's piety (most often using the word *eusebia* [εὐσέβια]). Several *augusta* show up as well (Flacilla Eudokia; Pulcheria; Ariadne, the wife of Zeno (and later Anastasios); Theodora, the wife of Justinian). With the exception of the saintly Theophano, the first wife of Leo VI, and Constantine and his mother Helena, the *Synaxarion of Constantinople* is cautious in acknowledging the sanctity of imperial office holders. This may have more to do with a broader view of what it means to "remember" the pious monastic, the steadfast martyr, the great theologian, or the effective emperor. The "memory" (*mnēmē*) is what is called upon; and remembrance does not necessarily equate with sanctity. Yet, it is significant that the *Synaxarion* remembers only those emperors who were defenders or supporters of orthodoxy; conspicuously, and not surprisingly, absent are the seventh-century emperors associated with monotheletism and those of the Icono-clastic period.

Political Orthodoxy

The task of defining and defending religious orthodoxy continued to oc-cupy a variety of constituencies in Byzantine society. Yet it was in the wake of a series of political, ecclesiastical, and military crises that the understand-ing in Byzantium of the role of orthodoxy shifted. With the exception of the Palamite controversy of the mid-fourteenth century, the fundamental doctrinal content of orthodoxy had not changed since the conclusive re-buttal of Iconoclasm. Yet, we can point to three major catastrophes that required responses: schism with Rome in the eleventh century; the arrival and settlement of Turks in Asia Minor (the Seljuks at the end of the elev-enth century, followed by the Ottomans at the beginning of the fourteenth); and the eastward extension of Western feudal power, culminating in the sack of Constantinople during the Fourth Crusade. All of this provided the context for a reevaluation of the function of "orthodoxy." Most dramati-cally the Fourth Crusade fragmented the empire into several competing centers of authority: The Empire of Nicaea, the Despotate of Epiros, and the Empire of Trebizond each tried to fill the political void created in the aftermath of the Fourth Crusade. Although the Empire of Nicaea regained the imperial capital in 1261, the political fragmentation of Byzantium proved irreversible.

It was the period from 1261 until the fall of Constantinople to the Ottoman Turks in 1453, known as the Palaiologan period, that witnessed a subtle but significant shift in the self-consciousness of the Byzantines. This final period of Byzantine history is characterized by an odd combina-tion of territorial and political disintegration in parallel with a cultural re-vival in art and literature. The imperial office survived and continued its ideological claims to the Roman *imperium*. For many of the Palaiologan emperors, the only possible chance for survival was better diplomatic, commercial, and ecclesiastical relations with Western powers, which were realized in three ways: increased economic advantages given to Italian commercial fleets; ecclesiastical reunion with the papacy (the reunion councils of Lyons in 1274 and Florence in 1438–39 are the most tangible expressions of this policy); and military assistance from Western armies. One of the results of this westward-looking policy was an intense debate among intellectuals, churchmen, and others about what constituted their own political, cultural, and religious identity. It is during this time that the notion of political orthodoxy emerges definitively in opposition to the West and the irreversible Ottoman expansion.

Coinciding with this new understanding of "orthodoxy," and under its influence, was the flourishing of Hellenic *paideia* that occurred during the Palaiologan period. The flowering of cultural Hellenism at this time paralleled a new understanding of what it meant to be a Hellene. The term "Hellene" was now being used in varying frequency to refer to the eastern Roman population. The threat posed by the Latins and the Turks was not simply territorial but cultural. By this time, the Byzantines had sufficient experience living under both Turks and Latins, and although both might allow for the continuation of Byzantine culture, there was intense pressure (economic and personal) to adopt the culture of the overlords. It is in this context that the Byzantines reasserted their identity in terms of the ancient Greeks and an expanded understanding of orthodoxy. Although the concept of orthodoxy had been around since the earliest days of the empire, it was now being used as a cultural and national marker of identity.[17]

At the twilight of the Byzantine Empire, political orthodoxy, once the sole purview of imperial leadership, had found a home among opponents of ecclesiastical reunion with the Latin Church. Both the pro- and anti-unionist camps had accepted it as well, though it does seem that the anti-unionists were more inclined to adopt it. The ardent fifteenth-century pro-unionist John Argyropoulos referred to his contemporary Constantine XI, who, unknown to Argyropoulos at the time, would be the last emperor of Byzantium, as the God-appointed "emperor of the Hellenes" and considered him the defender of "the freedom of the Hellenes."[18] Yet, unsurprisingly, the pro-unionist Argyropoulos never makes use of the adjective "orthodox" nor of its derivative noun "orthodoxy." For pro-unionist Byzantines it was the ancient Hellenes and not Byzantium's Orthodox Christian roots that provided for a new self-definition.

It was the opponents of reunion with the Roman Church who elevated the construct of orthodoxy to the level of a self-conscious marker of identity in contrast to the heretical West. One of the earliest examples of this comes from the pen of Germanos II, patriarch of Constantinople in exile at Nicaea (1223–40) and a strict anti-unionist. In several of his letters to Latin ecclesiastical leaders, Germanos identifies his Orthodox flock with those *Graikoi* (Γραικοί) living both within and outside of the Nicaean Empire.[19] Joseph Byrennios, a monk and fervent anti-unionist, while addressing a synod in Constantinople in the year 1412, stated that Orthodoxy "is our riches, it is our past glory, it is our nation."[20] For Byrennios, the Byzantines were an "Orthodox race (τὸ ὀρθόδοξον γένοι)."[21] Orthodoxy had now become a marker of national or political identity.

Orthodoxy was not only defined in relation to the Latin West. Isidore Glabas, twice metropolitan of Thessaloniki during the last two decades of the fourteenth century, witnessed firsthand the challenges Orthodox Christians faced living under Ottoman rule. In 1387 he traveled to Asia Minor to negotiate a political treaty with the Turks on behalf of the empire. He encouraged the Christians he met with the following words: "Let us be sure above all, my brothers, that with all our energy and power we keep Orthodoxy unstained, even if it be necessary to this end that our worldly wealth be dissipated, our country enslaved, our limbs mutilated, our bodies tortured, our lives violently extinguished. Let us endure all this with joy if it means that our flawless religion be not betrayed."[22]

Doukas, who composed a history of the Empire covering the period from 1341 to 1462, reports how George Scholarios, the onetime pro-unionist turned staunch anti-unionist, responded to the Council of Florence. In his description of the reception of the Greek delegation upon its return to Constantinople from Florence, Doukas describes how the anti-unionists visited the cell of George Scholarios, who had now become the monk Gennadios. The group asked Gennadios how they should react to the union proclaimed at Florence. Gennadios penned his response and placed it on the door of his cell. According to Doukas, the note read: "Wretched Romans, how you have gone astray! You have rejected the hope of God and trusted in the strength of the Franks; you have lost your piety, along with your city which is about to be destroyed." Doukas continues his narrative: "Then all the nuns, who believed themselves to be pure and dedicated servants of God in Orthodoxy, in accordance with their own sentiments and that of their teacher Gennadios, cried out the anathema, and along with them the abbots and confessors and the remaining priests and laymen."[23]

An odd shift has taken place. It is generally agreed by historians of Byzantium that the authority and prestige of the patriarch of Constantinople reached its zenith during the Palaiologan period—that is, from the recapture of Constantinople from the Latins in 1261 to the fall of the city in 1453. As the political stature of the Byzantine Empire and its emperor diminished, the importance and authority of the patriarch expanded. Demographically, more Orthodox Christians were under the ecclesial jurisdiction of Constantinople than were under the political control of the Byzantine emperor. It was no longer enough for the emperor simply to be a defender of orthodox doctrine; his prestige needed a boost, so he was now to be seen as the defender of political orthodoxy. The Roman *imperium*, by all measures except rhetoric, was dead. It was in need of a redefinition. The *imperium* was the protector of Orthodoxy: a concept that signified not only a theological body of doctrine, but a cultural expression of Christianity that was neither Latin nor barbaric. It was neither Western nor Middle Eastern. It was not Roman Catholic, nor was it Islamic. It was Orthodoxy. Political orthodoxy was born within the cultural revival and theological flowering that occurred within the context of the Palaiologan dynasty and amid the political upheaval that would signify the end of the empire.

Conclusion

For Byzantine society prior to 1204, "orthodoxy" primarily referred to adherence to a set of dogmatic beliefs and religious practices. During the period between the end of Iconoclasm and the Fourth Crusade, this "religious orthodoxy" began to expand as a concept to include cultural identity in addition. The Komnenian dynasty, especially under Alexios I, helped direct this development as it continued its employment of "orthodoxy" in aid of the state. The shift from "religious orthodoxy" to "political orthodoxy" is most dramatic during the final two centuries of Byzantium. Yet the move was never fully complete. For some, "orthodoxy" remained a referent to the pristine expression of the person of Christ, his message of salvation, and the manner in which one should worship him. For others, "orthodoxy" was a political orientation as well. Patriarch Anthony's claim that one cannot have a Church without an emperor has less to do with traditional religious orthodoxy than it does with a new self-definition of

Christian Byzantine (Roman) identity. The fall of Byzantium was one of many moments in the complicated history of Byzantine "orthodoxy" which served as a catalyst for the further development of political orthodoxy. In fact, the transition from pristine Christian orthodoxy to political orthodoxy continued after 1453, and found a permanent home among the Orthodox faithful under Ottoman rule.

Political orthodoxy, therefore, was a marker of identity that developed at a time when the very political and cultural foundations of Byzantium were threatened by forces that were not Orthodox. Orthodoxy, as a construct vis-à-vis heterodoxy, was as old as Christianity itself; and Byzantine Christianity was never able to divorce itself from this reality. For the Byzantines and their identity, political orthodoxy comes into focus in the decades following the end of Iconoclasm, not as some scholars have argued in response to the internal Orthodox debate over Iconoclasm, but in response to the Latin West. It gained fuel in the eleventh-century distancing of the two churches; it was defended by the faithful Komnenian emperors; it became more prominent following the catastrophe of the Fourth Crusade; and it became entrenched in the anti-unionist responses to the pro-Latin ecclesiastical policies of the Palaiologans. It was the political failure of the Byzantines to reassert their once-great imperial authority and prestige among their neighbors that caused a reassessment of their own identity. Orthodoxy provided the Byzantines with an identity that, although extending beyond the shrinking political boundaries of *Romania*, was in need of the cultural and political legacy that Byzantium had imparted to the Church. Political orthodoxy is the culmination of a long process of self-identity set in motion by the actions of and reactions to the first Christian emperor.

Notes

1. See John Meyendorff, *Byzantium and the Rise of Russia* (Cambridge: Cambridge University Press, 1981), 254–58 for a partial translation of the letter and interpretation. The letter is found in Franz Miklosich and Joseph Müller, *Acta et diplomata graeca medii aevi sacra et profana*, vol. 2, (Vienna, 1862) 188–92.

2. Theophanes the Confessor, *Chronographia*, vol. I, ed. C. de Boor (Leipzig, 1883) 136; see Dimiter Angelov, *Imperial Ideology and Political Thought in Byzantium, 1204–1330* (Cambridge: Cambridge University Press, 2007), 411–14.

3. Recent work on the post–Fourth Crusade Byzantine political context have used the adjective "political" to articulate the close connection between the church and the state; see, for example, Kristina Stoeckl, "Political Hesychasm? Vladimir Petrunin's Neo-Byzantine Interpretation of the Social Doctrine of the Russian Orthodox Church," *Studies in Eastern European Thought* 62 (2010) 125–33; and Dimiter Angelov's use of "political ecclesiology" in *Imperial Ideology*, 351ff.

4. Gilbert Dagron, *Emperor and Priest: The Imperial Office in Byzantium*, trans. J. Birrell (Cambridge: Cambridge University Press, 2003), 15–18.

5. The most detailed rationale for allowing the emperor access to the altar area is given by the Byzantine canonist Theodore Balsamon (c. 1130–c. 1195) in his commentary on Canon 69; see Georgios Rhalles and Michael Potles, *Syntagma ton theion kai hieron kanon*, vol. 2 (Athens, 1852) 466–7.

6. Gelasius, *Epistle* 12 (see Dagron, *Emperor and Priest*, 300–301).

7. For a discussion of "political Christianity" and "political theology" see Dagron, *Emperor and Priest*, 286ff.

8. Symeon of Thessaloniki, *De Sacro Templo* 142–50, PG 155.352–56 (reference taken from Dagron, *Emperor and Priest*, 280).

9. Angelov, *Imperial Ideology*, 388n129.

10. For a translation of the oath, see P. Charanis, "Coronation and its Constitutional Significance in the Later Roman Empire," *Byzantion* 15 (1941), 57–58.

11. Justinian, *Codex Justinianus* I.1.1 (quoted in Cyril Mango, *Byzantium: The Empire of New Rome* [New York: Scribner, 1980], 88).

12. Quoted in Ernest Barker, *Social and Political Thought in Byzantium* (Oxford: Clarendon Press, 1957), 90; for the Greek text, see Photios, *Epanagogue* II.4 (in Ioannes Zepos, *Jus Graecoromanum*, vol. 2 [Athens, Greece, 1931], 241).

13. For a fuller discussion, see Michael Angold, *Church and Society in Byzantium under the Comneni, 1081–1261* (Cambridge: Cambridge University Press, 1995), 50ff.

14. Angold, *Church and Society*, 51; see Jean Guillard, "Le Synodikon de l'Orthodoxie," *Travaux et Mémoires* 2 (1967) 253–85.

15. The memory of the "praised and blessed" Emperor Andronikos III (1328–41), even with his questionable moral behavior, is noted in the Synodikon along with "all those who struggled in defense of Orthodoxy" (Guillard, "Synodikon," 91, l. 714–16).

16. Hippolyte Delehaye, ed., *Synaxarium Ecclesiae Constantinopolitanae*, Propylaeum ad Acta Sanctorum Novembris (Brussels, 1902) lxxv; for a more complete analysis of imperial sanctity, see Dagron, *Emperor and Priest*, 149–57.

17. For a differing view on the importance of Hellenism in late Byzantium, see Cyril Mango, "Byzantinism and Romantic Hellenism," *Journal of the*

Warburg and Courtauld Institutes 28 (1965) 29–43. I have adopted the view of Anthony Kaldellis, *Hellenism in Byzantium: The Transformations of Greek Identity and the Reception of the Classical Tradition* (Cambridge: Cambridge University Press, 2007), 82–100.

18. Quoted in Apostolos Vacalopoulos, *Origins of the Greek Nation: The Byzantine Period*, trans. I. Moles (New Brunswick: Rutgers University Press, 1970), 183; see Spyridon Lambros, *Argyropouleia* (Athens, Greece, 1910), 45, 47.

19. Angelov, *Imperial Ideology*, 95–96.

20. Quoted in Vacalopoulos, *Origins of the Greek Nation*, 102.

21. Joseph Bryennios, *Epistle* 24, l. 25, E. Boulgares, ed., *Ioseph monachou tou Vryenniou: ta heurethenta* (Leipzig, 1768).

22. Quoted in Vacalopoulos, *Origins of the Greek Nation*, 94–95; see Spyridon Lampros, "Isidōrou mētropolitou Thessalonikēs oktō epistolai" *Neos Hellēnomnēmōn* 9 (1912), 389.

23. Vasile Grecu Doukas, *Historia Turco-byzantina (1341–1462)*, Scriptores Byzantini 1 (Bucharest, 1958), 315, 317; quoted in Deno Geanakoplos, *Byzantium: Church, Society and Civilization Seen through Contemporary Eyes* (Chicago: University of Chicago Press, 1984), 225.

ROMAN CATHOLICISM AND DEMOCRACY: THE POSTCONCILIAR ERA

J. Bryan Hehir

The goal of this essay is to provide a synthetic statement of the understanding of democracy in the Roman Catholic Church after Vatican II. This will be achieved in two stages: first, some background information to elucidate the state of the question before the Council; second, an examination of (1) the Conciliar era, (2) the pontificate of John Paul II (1978–2005), and (3) the pontificate of Benedict XVI (2005–13).[1]

A Clash of Cultures: Catholicism and Democracy

If one takes the quite different examples of the American and French Revolutions as a baseline for the establishment of modern democracy, then the relevant religious background for this essay stretches from the responses of Pope Gregory XVI (1831–46) and Pius IX (1846–78) to that of Pius XII (1939–58). The story has been told often, well, and in great detail by historians and theologians. The purpose here is simply to harvest from their work, and sketch a complex narrative.[2]

The journey from Gregory XVI's description of the modern liberties, upon which democracy is based, as "utter madness," to Pius XII's careful but clear endorsement of democracy in 1944 is not easily summarized. One persuasive account by Paolo G. Carozza and Daniel Philpottl argues for a long, slow process of convergence, which always (even today) produces substantial, but limited, agreement about the political order.[3] A second account, which has achieved among scholars the status of a classic, is the more detailed analysis of John Courtney Murray, SJ, who provides a lucid sense of how conflicted the process of convergence was within the Church and in the political world.[4] The two accounts need not be counterpointed; the first is a broad-brush, but careful narrative; the second, a close reading of texts reaching until the decisive moment of Vatican II. Murray's interpretive essays used a multidimensional analysis of Church teaching to explain that what Gregory XVI condemned is not what Vatican II endorsed even though both were addressing what they understood democratic freedoms to mean. In the nineteenth century, the papacy encountered a two-dimensional threat. First, a philosophical position (Liberalism in its European model) and second, a political movement designed to force the Catholic Church (along with the Ancien Régime) out of the political process. Neither Gregory XVI nor Pius IX saw any room for convergence or compromise with either of these threats, and they reacted by launching a frontal assault on both, and then withdrawing the Church behind the fortress of the Vatican.

The last pope of the nineteenth century, Leo XIII (1878–1903), shared some of the premises of his predecessors, but he did not push them to the same conclusions. In Murray's account Leo is the transitional figure in the narrative; he did not achieve convergence, but he did open the door to developments that he neither imagined nor achieved. Indeed, it is arguable that Murray saw openings in Leo's extensive corpus of political writings that Leo himself did not see.[5] Leo XIII recognized that, by the late nineteenth century, the Church had been backed into a corner with no exit and rapidly declining influence in its primary area of concern—the European state system. The imprisonment was partially coerced and partially chosen. Leo had more confidence in the intellectual resources of Catholicism than his immediate predecessors;[6] he was committed also to playing a vigorous diplomatic role, even with limited possibilities of success. Murray depicts Leo as engaging his surroundings at the philosophical level and the political level simultaneously. Leo XIII died after a long pontificate, but with a very unfinished agenda. He created space for the Church to assert itself in a changing political context, but his successors were not prepared to carry the process of development forward. The term of the process Leo began arrived only with the pontificate of Pius XII.

Like Leo XIII, Pius XII was a conservative intellectual diplomat, determined to provide the Church with a voice and status in the world of states. For both of them, it is necessary to distinguish their view of Liberalism as a philosophical position and democracy as a political regime. Convergence with Liberalism has always been a limited enterprise for Catholicism; convergence with democracy, at least the Anglo-American version of it, was simpler and more promising. The disagreements with Liberalism—even recognizing that this philosophy has a pluralism of expressions—have been deep and substantial. They include a conception of the human person (less autonomous and more social in the Catholic view) in the understanding of society (less contractual, more organic), in jurisprudence (rooted in Natural Law), and in a more expansive, normative role for the state and civil law.[7]

In spite of continuing tension with advocates of Liberalism during the pontificate of Pius XII and his successors, Catholic teaching on democracy, after World War II, exhibited a search for common ground and expressions of moral support. This shift from the nineteenth century was the result not only of changing ideas, but also current events. A Church that had often been not uncomfortable with authoritarian regimes found itself faced, in the 1930s, with totalitarian regimes, in whose view the Church was as much an adversary as the Liberals. This experience was a principal element in determining the Church's postwar diplomatic position and eventually its reexamination of democracy. Pius XII, whose entire priesthood was spent in the Vatican diplomatic service, and whose teaching built upon Leo XIII's opening and went beyond it, is a unique case study in the evolution of the Holy See's theology and diplomacy. In his diplomatic service as nuncio to Germany and then secretary of state for Pope Pius XI, then-Cardinal Pacelli was a brilliant, but not innovative, representative of Vatican diplomacy.[8] Neither Liberalism nor democracy were aspects of his statecraft. Elected to the papacy on the threshold of World War II, Pacelli— now Pope Pius XII—moved Catholic social teaching, during the war and during the Cold War, decisively in the direction of support for human rights and recognition of the merits of democracy and the rule of law. The clearest example of the changing dynamic in Catholic social teaching was his 1944 Christmas Address. During the period from 1939–45, the pope used his traditional Christmas Address—a teaching document, not a liturgical homily—to outline the Holy See's position on the postwar international order. After a century of the Church treating democracy as at least suspect, Pius XII dedicated this address to an examination of the requirements of democratic governance and an affirmation of its value. The address focused primarily on the role citizens should play in influencing the shape of civil society. It also acknowledged the Church's standard position that multiple forms of government can exist. But then he turned the address from the citizenry to the structure of the state:

> If then, we consider the extent and nature of the sacrifices demanded of all citizens especially in our day when the activity of the state is so vast and decisive, the democratic form of government appears to many as a postulate of nature imposed by reason itself.[9]

The final phrase is the decisive statement in the address: "A postulate of nature imposed by reason" is the archaic, but recognizable language of Natural Law, the Holy See's substantive discourse in its century-long debate with Liberalism, the "modern liberties," and, to some degree, forms of democracy. Natural Law discourse used rational reflection on human nature and human experience to derive moral norms for human behavior and human institutions like the state, society, and the economy. As is its typical style, when the Holy See is about to alter its public stance on a topic, the appeal here is to say that democracy "appears to many" as a demand of reason. This is beyond Leo XIII's teaching, but a less forceful endorsement than we will find in John XXIII, Vatican II, and the postconciliar teaching of John Paul II and Benedict XVI, but it is the basic turning point for Catholicism and democracy.

The Conciliar Era

The Second Vatican Council ran from October 1962 to December 1965. In this section, while focusing on two documents of the council, *Dignitatis Humanae* (The Declaration on Religious Freedom) of 1965 and *Gaudium et Spes* (The Pastoral Constitution on the Church in the Modern World) of 1965, I also include the 1963 papal encyclical *Pacem in Terris*. Collectively, these documents provide an understanding of the relationship of Catholicism to the idea and institutions of democracy in the 1960s and 1970s.

John XXIII convoked Vatican II and promulgated *Pacem in Terris*. While he did not live to see the two major documents of the council about the Church's public role, his encyclical and his basic posture of promoting a dialogue with the modern world were foundational for the council's work. The encyclical *Pacem in Terris* was a deeply personal initiative of John XXIII in the last months of his life. Working with his close collaborator, Msgr. Pietro Pavan of the Lateran University, the pope wrote this text about peace in the nuclear age as a response to the Cuban Missile Crisis, which had occurred just as Vatican II opened in Rome. While the encyclical was a clarion call for diplomacy rather than war, the pope's basic theme was that peace could be achieved and guaranteed only if the rights and duties of persons and states were respected and promoted. His opening sentence set the theme for the encyclical: "Peace on earth, which all men of every era have most eagerly yearned for, can be firmly established only if the order laid down by God be dutifully observed."[10] That order, the letter asserted, can be understood principally in terms of a fabric of rights and duties that structure and shape the national and international common good.

Pacem in Terris was both thoroughly traditional in substance and fully contemporary in tone. The language of the letter was drawn directly from the Natural Law tradition. The theme of order, however, allowed the classical ideas to be understood in a relational, personalistic, and historically contemporary fashion. Without ever articulating this goal explicitly, John XXIII's interpretation of Natural Law was designed in part to narrow the gap between the centuries-old argument of Natural Law and Natural Rights philosophers. Rather than rehearse that real and significant divide, the encyclical focused on analyzing a modern conception of human rights that owed its heritage to both traditions of discourse. The papal letter endorsed the spectrum of rights found in the United Nations Declaration on Human Rights (1948) and the subsequent implementing documents. The entire tone of the letter sought to build bridges (between the Church and the world, and between East and West) rather than walls, in the context of the still-tense and dangerous atmosphere of the Cold War.

A bridge of some intellectual understanding with Liberalism was possible in terms of human rights, but even with this strip of common ground as a mediating discourse, there remained substantial differences between Catholic teaching and Liberalism. Regarding democracy, the possibility existed for more substantial convergence between Catholic social thought and democratic polity. In his extensive and detailed essay, "Catholicism and Liberal Democracy," Princeton University Professor Paul Sigmund identified *Pacem in Terris* as a unique text in paving the way for Vatican II's endorsement of the right to religious freedom and, beyond this, to democracy. Sigmund points to the encyclical's assertion that, "the dignity of the human person involved the right to take an active part in public affairs and to contribute one's part to the other common good of the citizens."[11] Like other statements in *Pacem in Terris*, this support for democracy is expressed in general terms rather than a clear endorsement, but the encyclical's principles became the foundation for the council's endorsement of both the right to religious freedom and democratic polity.

Vatican II produced sixteen major documents, covering both the internal life of the Church and its relationships to other religious traditions and to the secular world. The two texts that are pertinent to this chapter are *Dignitatis Humanae* and *Gaudium et Spes*. They share some secular themes, but differ in style and character. *Dignitatis Humanae* has a single, important purpose and stands as a culminating moment in the long debate in Catholicism about the meaning of religious freedom. The precise objective of the declaration is stated in its second paragraph: "This Vatican Synod declares that the human person has a right to religious freedom . . . [and] that the right to religious freedom has its foundation in the very dignity of the human person, as this dignity is known through the revealed Word of God and by reason itself."[12] This simple, direct affirmation of a basic human right took centuries of argument to find its place in the social teaching of Catholicism. Some serious opposition to it was sustained throughout the first three years of Vatican II. To affirm this right, however, was to presume that it should be honored in *any* specific form of government or polity. So the question for this chapter remains: What is the relationship of the conciliar declaration to *democratic* polity?

In answer to this question, Fr. Murray, the principal drafter of the declaration, is uniquely helpful. In commentaries after the council, Murray argued that the affirmation of a right to religious freedom was in part the Church's response to two broad themes of modern life: the human person's rising sense of political consciousness, and the desire of citizens to live under a government limited by law and respect for human rights.[13] While these characteristics of civil society (also noted in *Pacem in Terris*) are themes rather than specific arguments, Murray also pointed to the substantive fact that Pius XII and John XXIII had endorsed the concept of the "constitutional state," in a more limited understanding of the power and rights of the state than had characterized Catholic teaching through the pontificate of Leo XIII.[14]

There are different ways to define democracy, but an essential component is a legal system that defines the state's powers and sets precise limits. Within this structure, human rights are central concepts: "The protection and promotion of the inviolable rights of man ranks among the essential duties of government; therefore, government is to assume the safeguard of the religious freedom of all its citizens in an effective manner by just laws and by other appropriate means."[15] In clarifying the Catholic Church's position on democracy, the conciliar declaration relies in its argument for religious freedom on characteristics of government that are central aspects of democracy.

The companion text from Vatican II, *Gaudium et Spes,* is a lengthy reflection on a broader question than religious freedom. It is the theme, as ancient as Augustine, of the relationship of the Church to the world. The "world" here can mean its political, intellectual, legal, scientific, or economic dimensions. *Gaudium et Spes* has a distinctive place in Catholic social thought: It builds on the tradition, but it is more explicitly theological; it also reframes questions (such as war and peace) in new ways. Sigmund rightly argues that in its treatment of democracy, it builds on *Pacem in Terris,* but is even more explicit in its endorsement of this polity. Again, Sigmund identifies a section of *Gaudium et Spes* that he calls a "formal commitment of Catholicism to democracy":

> It is in full accord with human nature that judicial-political structures should, with even better success and without any discrimination, afford all the citizens the chance to participate freely and actively in establishing the constitutional bases of a political community, governing the state, determining the scope and purpose of various institutions, and choosing leaders.[16]

In interpreting these conciliar texts elsewhere, I have argued that it is not only the conceptual support for democracy and human rights that is the measure of Catholic commitment to both, but also the public engagement of the Church, from the papacy to the parish, national episcopal conferences, religious orders, and lay Catholics, within countries and in international forums, that illustrates the contrast between the nineteenth century and our own time.[17] John Paul II's ministry was a unique testimony to the bond linking the Church to democracy.

John Paul II

In his pontificate of twenty-seven years, John Paul II enhanced Catholic social teaching and the Church's public role in a far-reaching fashion. His impact involved both words and deeds: What he did and what he refused to do, what he said and how he said it, made a great difference. In all of his social teaching, he was at pains to stress continuity with the words of his predecessors. But John Paul II also moved Catholic social thought to new frontiers, by word and deed. The reasons for his impact were multidimensional: First, he was a professional philosopher who always extended his reflections to a philosophical-theological contribution; second, the fact that he was a citizen, a priest, and a bishop in a communist state, with a command economy and few political freedoms, gave his teaching a unique perspective and power; third, he played an acclaimed role in the collapse of communism; fourth, he never confined his social critique only to Europe, communism, and Western democracies; rather, he focused substantially also on the fate and future of the Global South.[18] To illustrate his contribution to human rights and democracy, I will refer to three texts: his two addresses to the United Nation (of 1979 and 1995) and his encyclical *Centesimus Annus* (1991).

Pope John Paul II was twice invited to address the General Assembly of the United Nations and did so with a profound sense that he was before what the Yale historian Paul Kennedy has called "The Parliament of Man."[19] His two addresses spanned the collapse of the Cold War. Neither address was specifically focused on democracy, but both were relevant to the theme. The 1979 address was dedicated to a reflection on the United Nations, the UN Declaration of Human Rights, and the Holy See's collaboration with the United Nations. The address served to set the direction of John Paul's pontificate in making the defense of human rights a programmatic theme of his ministry. The pope did not directly address the topic of democracy. His comment on political systems was pitched at a higher level: "It is a question of the highest importance that in internal social life, as well as in international life, all human beings in every nation and country should be able to enjoy effectively these full rights under any political regime or system."[20] In this address, and in other forms of teaching, John Paul made his case that the right to religious freedom should have a unique significance and protection because it served as a foundation for other rights.

The relationship of democracy and human rights is a topic that extends beyond the bounds of religious discourse; human rights as moral claims, based on human dignity and having, therefore, universal validity, are a test for any political regime. There are certainly arguments made on a normative and empirical basis that democracy provides the most secure political context for the protection and promotion of human rights. John Paul did not make this case. In this early address to the question, he stressed the universality of human rights, argued that they needed a solid philosophical foundation, and then provided an original exposition about how the "two kinds" of rights found in the UN Declaration and in its implementing covenants should be understood.

This latter question sounds very theoretical, but in fact was a dividing line at the United Nations throughout the Cold War. Some Western voices argued that only political-civil rights are *truly* rights, whereas socio-economic rights are human needs, but should not be given the status of rights. Voices from the Communist states, and also Western voices, argued for equality in the status of rights. John Paul entered this political thicket by redefining the rights debate by speaking of spiritual and material goods. He clearly held to the position that both claims to rights were valid, but he moved beyond that debate to argue that spiritual goods and the rights to them should be given priority.[21] His argument was that spiritual goods are not limited and do not lead to conflict about how many people seek to possess them. Material goods by definition are limited in supply; they are surely necessary, but pursuit of them is more likely to lead to conflict in society. It is important to stress that the pope's overarching argument is that both kinds of rights are necessary in every society. The 1979 address was highly regarded as a clarion call to protect human dignity and to commit the members of the United Nations to implementation of the Declaration of 1948.

When John Paul II returned to the UN General Assembly in 1995 for the observance of the fiftieth anniversary of the United Nations Charter, he consciously developed his speech as a complement to the 1979 address. Then he spoke of the urgency to protect and promote the rights of the person in society. In 1995 he focused on the rights of nations, arguing that too little attention has been devoted to this theme. In a sense, the second address was a plea for a balanced view of nationalism. As a citizen of Poland, his voice carried special resonance in this argument. The pope was careful to acknowledge that nationalism has been an explosive idea in world politics, and he precisely noted that he was not arguing on a normative basis that every national claim necessarily deserved the status of sovereignty.[22] Neither UN address took up the idea of democracy directly, but both dealt with issues that can be argued to be prior to democracy. As noted above, human rights provide the moral claims that can be used to give preference to democracy as a mode of governance. The rights of nations is a topic that cuts across the internal life of states and the relationship of states in the international order.

Pope John Paul II did address democracy directly in the encyclical *Centesimus Annus* (1991), a text that surveyed a century of papal social teaching in light of the collapse of communism and the end of the Cold War. By 1991 John Paul II was a universally recognized leader of global significance. This recognition was uniquely tied to his acknowledged role (in tandem with others, to be sure) in bringing down the Communist order in Central and Eastern Europe. So there was widespread attention to the encyclical of 1991, expected not only to celebrate a century of social teaching, but also to offer reflections on the collapse of communism. Other theories were abroad in the world, tied principally to political, military, or economic factors. John Paul wove together distinct themes to account for the peaceful transition that ended the Cold War. He attributed the Communist failure, first, to its distorted view of the human person and the human rights violations that followed; second, to its inability to meet human economic needs; third, to the nonviolent opposition it faced from citizens; and fourth, to its atheistic orientation.[23]

The encyclical moved from a critique of communism to a narrative commentary about the Catholic vision of state, society, and culture. In this context, John Paul turned his attention to democracy. Strikingly, the title of the chapter was "State and Culture," not State and Society, the more likely linkage used in a Western context. It quickly became evident, however, why the pope linked state and culture: It fit his pervasive interest in analyzing the role of state.

The encyclical began its consideration of the state with the strongest explicit endorsement of democracy yet recorded in official Catholic teaching:

> The Church values the democratic system inasmuch as it ensures the participation of citizens in making political choices, guarantees to the governed the possibility both of electing and holding accountable those who govern them and of replacing them through peaceful means when appropriate.[24]

From Pius XII's acknowledgment that many believe democracy is a demand of nature, through *Pacem in Terris*'s thematic discussion of the elements of democracy, to the conciliar texts, there was a clear direction to Catholic teaching: coming to terms with a form of governance that Catholicism had approached skeptically in the past. But the explicit endorsement of democracy by a pope from the East was a new marker in the Church's social tradition. Quickly after the statement just quoted, the encyclical began to probe its meaning: "Authentic democracy," it said, is based on the rule of law and a correct conception of human nature. Then the step to culture was taken. In other places, I have written that the pope's belief in the political elements of democracy is clear cut and certain. But equally clear were his doubts about the cultural context often associated in the West with democracy. The critique was direct: "There is a tendency to claim that agnosticism and skeptical relativism are the philosophy and basic attitude which correspond to democratic forms of political life."[25] The Pope expresses his awareness that in Western societies, shaped by a secular conception of the state and pluralistic fabric of society, much public discussion and political commentary is premised on the idea of a "thin" theory of values a society should pursue. This idea may not be rooted in agnosticism or atheism, but in a belief that deeply rooted convictions about what constitutes "the good society" make consensus about law and policy very difficult. A "thin" theory of the good places much greater emphasis on tolerance, procedural rules, and individual freedom. An example, pertinent to this chapter, is debates about human rights. The debate goes back to the moment John Paul celebrated in his 1979 UN Address—the Declaration on Human Rights. Even in the human rights community of advocacy, debates about what counts as a right, the content of rights, and the relationship among rights, are relatively simpler than finding consensus on the foundation of rights, where they are rooted, and why. When *Centesimus Annus* speaks of "authentic democracy," the foundation of it is an understanding of human rights grounded in the dignity of the person. While the UN Declaration does cite human dignity as the basis of rights, John Paul has a much "thicker" conception of this idea than prevails in human rights discourse today.

John Paul did not remain, however, at the purely philosophical level when addressing the theme of democracy. Credited in part with the collapse of communism in Poland, and then in other states of the Communist system, in *Centesimus Annus* he turned to a critique of established democracies in the West. With his idea of "authentic democracy" in the background, he warned advanced democracies that failure to attend to foundational issues ran a huge risk, for, "as history demonstrates, democracy without values easily turns into open or thinly disguised totalitarianism."[26] At a more operational level, he criticized democratic societies that failed to create an effective consensus to take needed critical decisions.

In retrospect, there is no question that John Paul II tightened the bond between Catholicism and democracy. At the same time, some of his basic concerns remain debated to some degree inside the Church and more so in the wider civil society and international society. Yet, through his teaching and his pastoral ministry in countries throughout the world, John Paul II did strengthen the ties between Catholicism and democracy. From Poland to the Philippines, and from South Korea to Central America, John Paul II entered complex and conflicted political settings as a voice for human rights and democracy. Human rights advocates in the religious and secular communities came to see John Paul as a unique voice. This did not always mean they found his theoretical and/or theological arguments convincing. Willing to support the right to religious freedom with him, they did not necessarily see it as the anchor for human rights. After the collapse of communism there was broader agreement to support the full spectrum of rights found in the UN Declaration and Covenants; this was not necessarily based on the pope's 1979 Address about the unity and priority of rights. Finally, many remained unconvinced that a unified foundational view of rights could be achieved.

Benedict XVI

Benedict XVI strongly supported his predecessor's position that both human rights and democratic polity require a firm grounding in values and principles of the moral order.[27] In his 2008 Address to the United National General Assembly, Benedict noted positively that "human rights are increasingly being presented as the common language and the ethical substratum of international relations."[28] He then went on to stress in his own way the message of John Paul II about the necessary grounding of human rights:

> They are based on the natural law inscribed on human hearts and present in different cultures and civilizations. Removing human rights from this context would mean restricting their range and yielding to a relativistic conception, according to which the meaning and interpretation of rights could vary and their universality would be denied in the name of different cultural, political, social and religious outlooks.[29]

Benedict brought to the papacy his own distinctive characteristics, in some
ways complementary to the positions of John Paul II, and in other ways
shaped and expressed differently. He was a theologian with a distinguished
publication record reaching back before Vatican II. He had less experience
and engagement in the public arena than his predecessor and seemed less
suited to that dimension of the papal office. He was clearly more a teacher
than a diplomat or a prophetic voice on public issues. Looking back after
his historic resignation from the papal office, it is reasonable to assume
that Catholics will read his theological writings long after his papacy has
receded from public attention.

Pope Benedict XVI brought to the papal office two deeply held convictions, which remained prominent and persistent in his public role and related directly to his assessment of democracy. The first was a contemporary
conception of the traditional Catholic conviction that the world of faith
and the world of reason are complementary understandings of truth. They
are not adversarial or inimical positions. The second conviction may have
been Benedict's primary pastoral objective: to address the secularization
of public life and public policy that he saw in the postindustrial democracies of the West. Neither of these positions was missing in the pontificate
of John Paul II, but Benedict made them singularly important. Key texts
surveyed below highlight these themes.

Reason and faith were at the heart of one of Benedict's most publicized
addresses, his 2006 lecture at Regensburg University. Benedict had taught
in the theology faculty and his address was a homecoming in multiple ways.
It must be stated clearly that the pope's intention in giving the address
and its consequences were very different. The subject of the address, faith
and reason, initially became lost in a major controversy sparked by a quote
used by Benedict from a fourteenth-century Byzantine emperor that dispar-
aged Islam. The quote actually was not essential to the pope's intent or
primary audience. He addressed the gathering at Regensburg as representatives of the Western university world, and his message was a critique of
a narrow positivistic conception of reason, rooted in the physical sciences,
which excluded the classical conceptions of philosophy and theology. The
outcome of this postenlightenment definition of reason reduced the role
of religion and ethics to private status.[30] Theology and ethics in this conception were marginal disciplines in the university world and excluded
from influence in the world of public policy. His defense of a public role
for religion, for a fruitful collaboration of reason and faith, was stated

precisely: "We will succeed in doing so only if reason and faith come together in a new way, if we overcome the self-imposed limitation of reason
to the empirically falsifiable, and if we once more disclose its vast horizons."[31]
The missed opportunity of this address was that it not only pointed to instances in secular Western democracies where religion can be marginalized.
Beyond the pope's message, that secularity without religion can distort
what he called "the genuine dialogue of culture and religions so urgently
needed today,"[32] lay the other issue that religion without the disciplining
role of reason can easily become dangerous. A mischosen quote sacrificed
an opportunity to address the role of religion in Western democracies and
the role of religion in world politics.

Benedict XVI returned often and more effectively to questions of reason and faith, and did so in part because of his second major concern, the
secularization of society in the postindustrial democracies. The topic had
both pastoral and public dimensions to it. It also arose from the division
of faith and reason, particularly in Western Europe. Pastorally, Benedict
and many others believed the secularization of society led to the post–World
War II decline of participation in countries with historically strong Catholic cultures and populations. The consequences of the secularization of
the public arena marginalized the voice of religion, as just noted above.
Pope Benedict chose another German setting in 2011—that of the German
parliament—to address the consequences of secularization in the public
arena. In a tightly designed academic lecture, he traced the relationship of
biblical, philosophical, and legal sources as foundations of what he described as "a free state of law." To some degree, the address was about differences between a Natural Law conception of law and a legal positivistic
view represented (he noted) by Hans Kelsen. Beyond this theoretical debate, he argued that the complexity of public issues in Western democracies today is magnified by the power residing in human hands. "Man can
destroy the world. He can manipulate himself. He can, so to speak, make
human beings and he can deny them their humanity."[33] In the face of these
human stakes, "the decisions of a democratic politician, the question of
what now correspond to the law of truth, what is actually right and may
be enacted as law, is less obvious."[34]

Benedict's response was twofold. First, a call to recognize the secular
value of a Natural Law ethic for public policy, a language and criteria that
can be used across lines of cultures, different religions, and even between
the world's belief and unbelief. Second, while recognizing the essential

value of a public ethic rooted in "nature and reason as the true sources of law," Benedict also made a further point.[35] In a culture that marginalizes religion from its public discourse, there is a loss of both historical memory of religious insight and a voice that can complement nature and reason.

> At this point Europe's cultural heritage ought to come to our assistance. The conviction that there is a Creator God is what gave rise to the idea of human rights, the idea of the equality of all people before the law, the recognition of the inviolability of human dignity in every single person and the awareness of people's responsibility for their actions. Our cultural memory is shaped by these rational insights.[36]

Benedict's deep convictions, about faith and reason and about the danger of secularization for society, share two characteristics: They are faithful to a long Catholic tradition, and they are difficult to share with democratic societies on both sides of the Atlantic, and beyond, today. As noted, both convictions bear directly on one's conception of democracy. Benedict XVI offered his specific views of this theme in a historic setting: Westminster Hall in the United Kingdom. The background and the topic for the lecture were both significant. Benedict began by paying tribute to the role of the British Parliament and to the "common law tradition" which has influenced legal systems for centuries and throughout the world. His subject was "the proper place of religious belief within the political process." The address resonated with the two themes just discussed in this essay. In response to his own question of where can one find the ethical foundation for political choice, Benedict invoked the Catholic tradition, which "maintains that the objective norms governing right action are accessible to reason, prescinding from the content of revelation."[37]

He asked and answered his own question in a tone respectful of the gap that likely separated most of his audience from "the Catholic tradition." But then he moved beyond his initial answers, seeking to find common ground on the question of the proper place of religion in politics. Returning to the theme of reason and faith, he argued for a dialectical relationship of "purifying" discourse, with religion playing a purifying role in reason's development of moral norms, and then reason playing a purifying role within religious traditions. In Benedict's perspective, the world of religious belief and secular rationality need each other.[38] There is a religious potential for "corrective" action in the political arena, and a need for rational "corrective" critique within the religious traditions.

From *Pacem in Terris* (1963) through the retirement of Benedict XVI (2013), there has been a double dynamic at work around the theme of Roman Catholicism and democracy. The dominant note has been an increasing acceptance by the Church of the human rights and democratic traditions—indeed, beyond acceptance, a move toward identifying why the Catholic social tradition should find in these secular traditions reasons for support and complementarity. This dynamic has been the subject of this essay. But the narrative should not close without noting a counterpoint, voiced by both John Paul II and Benedict XVI, which is that the way in which specific topics in modern democracies are interpreted, decided in courts, and expressed in legislation in the twenty-first century (particularly a range of issues in bioethics, the understanding of marriage and family, and sexuality itself), has created quite specific conflicts for Catholicism, in spite of the more long-term reconciliation that has occurred between the Church and democratic regimes.

Notes

1. I draw on themes found in my previous articles, which include: "Catholicism and Democracy: Conflict, Change and Collaboration," in *Christianity and Democracy in Global Context*, ed. John Witte Jr. (Boulder, Colo.: Westview Press, 1993): 15–30; "Religious Activism for Human Rights: A Christian Case Study" in *Religious Human Rights in Global Perspective*, ed. John J. Witter and Johan D. van der Vyrer (The Hague: Martinus Nijhoff Publishers, 1996): 97–120; "The Modern Catholic Church and Human Rights: The Impact of the Second Vatican Council" in *Christianity and Human Rights*, ed. John Witte Jr. (Cambridge: Cambridge University Press 2011).

2. For the historical context, see: Owen Chadwick, *A History of the Popes 1830–1914* (Oxford: Clarendon Press, 1998): 1–95; Peter Steinfels, "The Failed Encounter: The Catholic Church and Liberalism in the Nineteenth Century" in *Catholicism and Liberalism: Contributions to American Public Philosophy*, ed. R. Bruce Douglass and David Hollenbach (Cambridge: Cambridge University Press, 1994): 19–44.

3. Paulo G. Carozzo and Daniel Philpott, "The Catholic Church, Human Rights and Democracy," *Logos* 15 (Summer 2012): 15–39.

4. John Courtney Murray SJ wrote six major articles before Vatican II that were close textual readings of Leo XIII's corpus on Church-State, religious

freedom, and democracy. A synthetic statement of this work was published during Vatican II (as a briefing paper for the American Bishops) under the title, "The Problem of Religious Freedom," *Theological Studies* 25 (1964): 503–75. In addition, he authored a series of scholarly commentaries on *Dignitatis Humanae* after the Council, and a number of these were edited by Leon J. Hooper SJ as *Religious Liberty: Catholic Struggles with Pluralism* (Louisville, Ky.: Westminster/ John Knox Press, 1993).

5. Murray saw Leo XIII as a transitional figure in Catholicism coming to grips with democracy. Leo XIII moved beyond his predecessors, but, Murray argued, was limited by the historical context (inside and outside the Church) in which he functioned; see "Leo XIII on Church and State: The General Structure of the Controversy," *Theological Studies* 14 (1953): 1–30.

6. Joseph N. Moody, "The Church and the New Forces in Western Europe and Italy," in *Church and Society: Catholic Social and Political Thought and Movements 1789–1950*, ed. Joseph N. Moody (New York: Art, Inc., 1953): 21–92.

7. Hehir, "Religious Activism for Human Rights," 99–100.

8. Robert A. Ventresca, *Soldier of Christ: The Life of Pius XII* (Cambridge, Mass.: The Belknap Press of Harvard University Press, 2013).

9. Pope Pius XII, Christmas Address 1944, §19, available at www.ewtn.com /library/papaldoc (accessed 14 January 2015).

10. Pope John XXIII, "Peace on Earth" in *Catholic Social Thought: The Documentary Heritage*, ed. David J. O'Brien and Thomas A. Shannon (Maryknoll, N.Y.: Orbis Books, 1992), 131, §1.

11. Paul Sigmund, "Catholicism and Liberal Democracy" in *Catholicism and Liberalism,* ed. Douglass and Hollenbach, 228.

12. "Declaration on Religious Freedom," in *The Documents of Vatican II,* ed. Walter M. Abbott (New York: America Press, 1996), 678–79, §2.

13. Murray, "Problem," 137–38.

14. Murray, "Problem," 144–45.

15. "Declaration on Religious Freedom," in Abbott, 684–85, §6.

16. "Pastoral Constitution on the Church in the Modern World," in Abbott, 285, §75.

17. Hehir, "Religious Activism," 106, 115.

18. There are two biographies of John Paul II, written at the outset and in the midst of his pontificate: George Huston Williams, *The Mind of John Paul II: Origins of His Thought and Action* (New York: Seabury Press, 1981); and George Weigel, *Witness to Hope: The Biography of John Paul II* (New York: Harper Collins Publishers, 1999).

19. Paul Kennedy, *The Parliament of Man: The Past Present and Future of the United Nations* (New York: Random House, 2006).

20. John Paul II, "Address to the 34th General Assembly of the United Nations," delivered 2 October 1979, available at: http://www.vatican.va/holy _father/john_paul_ii/speeches/1979/october/documents/hf_jp-ii_spe_19791002 _general-assembly-onu_en.html (accessed 14 January 2015), §19.

21. John Paul II, "Address to the 34th General Assembly of the United Nations," §14.

22. John Paul II, "Address to the 50th General Assembly of the United Nations" delivered 5 October 1995, available at http://www.vatican.va/holy _father/john_paul_ii/speeches/1995/october/documents/hf_jp-ii_spe_05101995 _address-to-uno_en.html (accessed 14 January 2015), §8.

23. John Paul II, "On the Hundredth Anniversary of *Rerum Novarum*" in *Catholic Social Thought,* ed. O'Brien and Shannon, 455–56, §§23–24.

24. John Paul II, "On the Hundredth Anniversary of *Rerum Novarum,*" 473, §46.

25. John Paul II, "On the Hundredth Anniversary of *Rerum Novarum,*" 474, §46; see also Hehir, "Religious Activism for Human Rights."

26. John Paul II, "On the Hundredth Anniversary of *Rerum Novarum,*" 474, §46.

27. For an analysis of Benedict XVI, see Joseph Komonchak, "The Church in Crisis: Pope Benedict's Theological Vision," *Commonweal* (3 June 2005): 11–14; Avery Dulles, "From Ratzinger to Benedict," *First Things* (February 2006): 24–29.

28. Benedict XVI, "Address to the General Assembly of the United Nations" delivered 19 April 2008, available at http://www.vatican.va/holy_father/benedict _xvi/speeches/2008/april/documents/hf_ben-xvi_spe_20080418_un-visit_en .html (accessed 14 January 2015).

29. Benedict XVI, "Address to the General Assembly of the United Nations," 3.

30. Benedict XVI, Papal Address at the University of Regensburg, "Three Stages in the Program of De-Hellenization," available at http://www.zenit.org /en/articles/papal-address-at-university-of-regensburg (accessed 14 January 2015), 5.

31. Benedict XVI, Papal Address at the University of Regensburg, "Three Stages in the Program of De-Hellenization," 6.

32. Benedict XVI, Papal Address at the University of Regensburg, "Three Stages in the Program of De-Hellenization," 6.

33. Benedict XVI, "Address to the German Parliament," *Origins* 41 (6 October 2011), 279.

34. Benedict XVI, "Address to the German Parliament," 281.

35. Benedict XVI, "Address to the German Parliament," 280.

36. Benedict XVI, "Address to the German Parliament," 282.

37. Benedict XVI, Meeting with the Representatives of British Society, "Address at Westminster Hall," delivered on 17 September 2001, available at http://www.vatican.va/holy_father/benedict_xvi/speeches/2010/september /documents/hf_ben-xvi_spe_20100917_societa-civile_en.html (accessed 14 January 2015), 2.

38. Benedict XVI, "Address at Westminster Hall," 2.

AN APOPHATIC APPROACH

HOW (NOT) TO BE A POLITICAL THEOLOGIAN

Stanley Hauerwas

Trying to Understand Where I Belong Politically

I have recently discovered I am numbered among those identified as "political theologians." I must be a political theologian because there is an article, a very good article by Rusty Reno, on my work in *The Blackwell Companion to Political Theology*.[1] Reno even begins his article with the astounding claim that "in the final decades of the twentieth century, Stanley Hauerwas articulated the most coherent and influential political theology in and for the North American context."[2] Rusty Reno is a theologian of rare intellectual judgment, so I assume he must know what he is talking about, but I confess for me the idea that I am a political theologian will take some getting used to.

I want to use this essay to explore why my identification as a political theologian takes, at least for me, some getting used to. To do so will require that I revisit some of the early developments in Christian ethics that shaped how I think about the fundamental political character of Christian theology. In short, I have always assumed that any theology reflects a politics whether that politics is acknowledged or not. Of course the crucial question is: What kind of politics is theologically assumed? In the tradition in which I was educated it was assumed that democratic politics was normative for Christians. Because I do not share that presumption, some think I have no politics.

In truth I have no stake one way or the other in being counted among those doing political theology. I have always resisted modifying theology with descriptors that suggest theology is the possession of certain groups or perspectives. For me nothing is more important than the fundamental task of theology to be of service to the Church; it belongs to the Church. I am well aware that time and place do and should make a difference for how theology is done. But too often I fear that, when theology is made subservient to this or that qualifier, it has inadequate means with which to resist becoming an ideology.

It is true, however, that there is no "method" that can protect theologians from engaging in ideological modes of thought, even when they claim to be doing theology qua theology. Theology stands under the permanent temptation to "choose sides," which means theology can become ideological long before anyone notices. I have no objection to calling theology "Christian," but that description does not ensure that theology that bears the name will be free of ideological perversion. "Christian" is no guarantee that theology can be safeguarded against being put at the service of political loyalties and practices that betray the Gospel.

I resist using the phrase "political theology" for many of the same reasons I try to avoid the phrase "social ethics." Ask yourself what kind of ethic would not be social? In a similar fashion I assume every theology, even theology done in a speculative mode, has been produced and reproduces a politics. If theology is done faithful to the Gospel it will not only be political but it will be so in a particular way. Thus, John Howard Yoder's observation in *The Politics of Jesus* that appeals to Jesus as "political" too often are only slogans that fail to indicate the *kind* of politics Jesus incarnated.[3]

Whether or not I am a political theologian depends on how "political theology" is understood. It is important to remember that the nomenclature, "political theology," has only recently been reintroduced into discussions in theology and political theory.[4] Indeed, as Elizabeth Phillips rightly reminds us, political theology did not originally come from Christian theology, but rather originated in Athens in which politics was understood as the art of seeking the common good of the polis.[5] Phillips observes that task was later taken up by Christian thinkers such as Augustine who compared and contrasted Christianity to what had been done in the name of political theology. The phrase, "political theology," however, has only recently been reintroduced into political and legal theory through the work of Carl Schmitt.

Schmitt maintained that all significant concepts that constitute the legitimating discourses of modern state formations are in fact secularized theological concepts.[6] Phillips observes that this claim has given new life to diverse approaches to "the political"—not the least being the discussions and ongoing debates around Schmitt's strong claim about the totalizing character of modern politics. Accordingly, political theology has become an attempt to identify how ideas concerning salvation and devotion to God migrated from Christian theology to the nation state. Schmitt's work is quite controversial not only because of his association with the Nazi party but because of his Hobbes-like contention that the sovereign is known as the one who decides on the exception.

Paul Kahn argues that Schmitt's understanding of sovereignty has structured an inquiry into the political that is a kind of mirror image of the political theory of liberalism. For Schmitt not the law but the exception, not the judge but the sovereign, not reason but decision determines the character of the political. Kahn argues that Schmitt's inversion of liberal presuppositions about politics is so extreme one "might think of political theology as the dialectical negation of liberal political theory."[7] Given my identification as a critic of liberal political theory, some might, with some justification, think I am rightly described as a political theologian.

I doubt, however, I deserve such a description. I confess it is tempting to claim that identity as a way to counter the oft-made criticism that I am a "sectarian, fideistic tribalist" who is trying to get Christians to abandon the task of securing justice through participation in politics.[8] It is true, moreover, that I find much of the work being done in political theology to be quite congenial to the way I think about the political challenges facing Christians in contexts such as America. But the path I have taken for how I understand the political stance Christians should assume in the world in which we find ourselves is quite different than those who now identify themselves with "political theology."

In order to explain that "path," as well as how I now think about the politics of Christian existence, I need to provide an account of how Christians in America became convinced they had a moral obligation to be political actors in what they took to be democratic politics. The expression "the politics of Christian existence" that I use to describe my position indicates my distance from the story I have to tell about how Christians came to ask themselves what political responsibilities they had as Christians. That question would often produce investigations into the relation of Christianity and politics. From my perspective that way of putting the matter—that is, "What is the relation between Christianity and politics?"—is to have failed to account for the political reality of the Church.

My point is not unlike John Howard Yoder's argument concerning the inadequacy of H. Richard Niebuhr's "method" in *Christ and Culture*. Yoder argued that the very way Niebuhr posed the problem of the relation of Christ to culture failed to be properly Christological just to the extent that the Christ who is Lord is separated from Jesus of Nazareth. Yoder argued that Niebuhr's account of Christ as the exemplification of radical monotheism failed to give adequate expression to the full and genuine human existence of the man Jesus of Nazareth. That Christological mistake from Yoder's point of view shaped the problematic character of Niebuhr's typology because recognition of Jesus's full humanity is necessary to recognize that Jesus himself is a "cultural reality." As a result, the Christ of *Christ and Culture* was assumed to be alien to culture qua culture, thus creating the problematic that shapes Niebuhr's book.[9]

What I must now try to do is to tell the story of the "and" that created the question of the relation of Christianity *and* politics. I hope to show that, just as Yoder suggests the "and" between Christ and culture reproduced a Christ that was less than fully human, so the "and" between Christianity and politics assumed a Church that was fundamentally apolitical. Because I have been so influenced by Yoder I am often accused of tempting Christians to withdraw from participation in politics. Yet neither Yoder nor myself have assumed it possible to "withdraw" from the world, or even if withdrawal were possible, that it would be a "good thing." Admittedly, as I will suggest in due course, Yoder changes how we as Christians are to understand "the political," but he does so because of how he understands "the politics of Jesus."[10] But to show the difference Yoder makes, I need to provide a brief account of how Rauschenbusch and Niebuhr understood democracy as the politics that is definitive for Christians.

How Christians Became "Political" in America

The story I have to tell is not unlike the story I planned to tell by writing a book on the development of Christian ethics in America. In a chapter in *A Better Hope* entitled, "Christian Ethics in America (and the *Journal of Religious Ethics*): A Report on a Book I Will Not Write," I explain why I did not write the book.[11] I did not write the book because I did not want to write about a tradition I thought had come to an end.[12] That the tradition had come to an end had everything to do with what I took to be the storyline of the book. The storyline is that the subject of Christian ethics in America was first and foremost America. That such was and still remains the case means: Just to the extent Christians got the politics they had identified as Christian—that is, democratic politics—they seemed no longer to have anything politically interesting to say as Christians.

Put differently, I suggested that the book I did not write would ask the dramatic question of how a tradition that began with a book by Walter Rauschenbusch entitled *Christianizing the Social Order* would end with a book by James Gustafson entitled, *Can Ethics Be Christian?* The story I sought to tell was meant to explore how that result came to be by concentrating on people such as Reinhold Niebuhr, H. Richard Niebuhr, Paul Ramsey, Jim Gustafson, and John Howard Yoder. Yoder, of course, did not stand in the same tradition as those from Rauschenbusch to Gustafson, but that was just the point: Namely, that only an outsider could offer the fresh perspective the mainstream theological tradition so desperately needed.

It is not quite true that I did not write the book I had planned. I did write a number of essays on Rauschenbusch, Reinhold and H. Richard Niebuhr, Paul Ramsey, and Jim Gustafson that developed some themes that the proposed book was to be about.[13] What I failed to do, and the failure was intentional, was to bring these essays and chapters together in one book. I do not regret that decision, but that I did not write the book means I can use this opportunity to make explicit how the development of Christian thinking about politics resulted in the loss of the politics of the Church.

A strange claim to be sure. The social gospel was, after all, largely a movement of churchmen to convince their fellow Christians that they had a calling to engage in the work of social reconstruction. Of course the central reality for the social gospel was not the Church but the Kingdom of God. Yet Rauschenbusch claimed that the Church is the social factor in salvation. The Church is so because it "brings social forces to bear on evil. It offers Christ not only many human bodies and minds to serve as ministers of his salvation, but its own composite personality, with a collective memory storied with great hymns and Bible moral feelings, and with a collective will set on righteousness."[14]

Rauschenbusch appealed to Schleiermacher and Royce to emphasize that the Church is the social organism that makes it possible for us to share in the consciousness of Christ. According to Rauschenbusch, the individual is saved by membership in the Church because the Church is necessary to make Christ's consciousness the consciousness of every member of the Church. It is not the institutional character of the Church, nor its continuity, its ministry, nor doctrine that saves, but rather the Church provides salvation by making the Kingdom of God present.[15]

According to Rauschenbusch the Kingdom of God is the heart of the revolutionary force of Christianity. It was the loss of the Kingdom ideals that put the Church on her path to abandon her social and political commitments. As a result, the movements for democracy and social justice were left without religious backing. In the process many Christians lost any sense that social justice might have something to do with salvation. Christians thus failed to emphasize the three commitments that the Kingdom entails: (1) to work for a social order that guarantees to all personalities their freest and highest development; (2) to secure the progressive reign of love in human affairs so that the use of force and legal coercion become superseded; and (3) the free surrender of property rights, which means the refusal to support monopolistic industries.[16]

All of which can be summed up by Rauschenbusch's claim that the social gospel is the religious response to the historic advent of democracy. For Rauschenbusch the social gospel sought to put the democratic spirit, which the Church inherited from Jesus and the prophets, once more in control of the institution of the Church.[17] Another word for salvation, Rauschenbusch asserts, is democracy, because Jesus's highest redemptive act was to take God by the hand and call him "our Father." By doing so Jesus democratized the conception of God and in the process not only saved humanity but "he saved God."[18]

The Christian's task is to work to extend this democratic ideal. Rauschenbusch thinks the ideal that has been largely achieved in the political sphere, but now the same democratic ideals must be applied to the economic realm. That means Christians must work to see that the brotherhood of man is expressed in the common possession of the economic resources of society. They must also seek to secure the spiritual good of humanity by insuring such a good is set high above the private profit interests of all materialistic groups.[19] Rauschenbusch was convinced, moreover, that these were not unrealizable ideals, but possible achievements Christians could bring to fruition if the gospel was recognized to be a social gospel.

It is tempting to dismiss Rauschenbusch as hopelessly naïve, but that would be a mistake. His rhetoric invites the judgment that he is far too "optimistic," but it should not be forgotten that after Rauschenbusch it was assumed by most people in mainstream Protestant denominations in America that Christians had a responsibility to be politically active in order to extend democratic practices. Reinhold Niebuhr will criticize Rauschenbusch for failing to account for the necessity of conflict and coercion for the establishment of justice, but Niebuhr never called into question Rauschenbusch's fundamental insight that Christians have to make use of politics to achieve justice. As critical of the social gospel as he may have been, Niebuhr simply assumed that Christians must be politically responsible. Niebuhr's chastened realism, to be sure, was a critical response to Rauschenbusch's far-too-optimistic presumption that justice was achievable, but in many ways Niebuhr's criticism of the social gospel was made possible by the achievement of that movement.

Of course it was sin that determined Niebuhr's fundamental perspective on the necessity of politics. Because we are sinners, justice can be achieved only by degrees of coercion, as well as resistance to coercion. Thus his oft-made claim that "the political life of man must constantly steer between the Scylla of anarchy and the Charybdis of tyranny."[20] That alternative, anarchy or tyranny, was the kind of dualism Niebuhr often confidently declared were our only choices if we did not strive to sustain democratic life and institutions. Thus his contention that democracy is the worst form of all governments, except all other forms of government, because democracy provides an alternative to totalitarianism or anarchy.

For Niebuhr, Christians have a stake in democratic societies because, given the realism that the Christian understanding of sin requires, Christians know "that a healthy society must seek to achieve the greatest possible equilibrium of power, the greatest possible centers of power, the greatest possible social checks of the administration of power, and the greatest possible inner moral check on human ambition, as well as the most effective use of forms of power in which consent and coercion are compounded."[21] Democracies at their best are, therefore, able to achieve unity of purpose within the conditions of freedom and to maintain freedom within the framework of order.

It is particularly important to note that for Niebuhr democracy is a system of government that does not require the governed to be virtuous.
Rather it is a form of social organization that limits self-interested men from
pursuing their interests in a manner that destroys community. Of course
a too-consistent pessimism concerning our ability to transcend our interests can lead to absolutist political theories. So Niebuhr is not suggesting
that democracies can survive without some sense of justice. Rather he is
reminding us that, as he puts it in what is probably his most famous epigram, "man's capacity for justice makes democracy possible; but man's inclination to injustice makes democracy necessary."[22]

The task of social Christianity for Niebuhr is not to advocate particular
solutions for economic or social ills, but to produce people of modesty and
humility about what can be accomplished given our sinful condition.[23] It
is equally important that some modesty be applied to the Church, which
is no less under the power of sin. In fact, from Niebuhr's point of view the
sins of the Church may be even more destructive given the temptation to
identify religious politics with the politics of God. For Niebuhr the task of
the Church is "to bear witness against every form of pride and vainglory,
whether in the secular or in the Christian culture, and be particularly intent upon our own sins lest we make Christ the judge of the other but not
of ourselves."[24]

The contrasts between Rauschenbusch and Niebuhr are clear, though
they share more than is immediately apparent. In particular, democracy
plays a very similar role in their respective positions. The question of the
relation of Christianity and politics is fundamentally resolved for Rauschenbusch and Niebuhr if the politics the Christian is to presume as normative is a democratic politics. Rauschenbusch and Niebuhr are vague about
what makes a democracy democratic, but I hope enough has been said to
show how the language of democracy became their way to assure Christians in America that they must "be political."

The Difference Yoder Makes

I simply assumed, as I suspect did almost anyone who worked in Christian ethics in the second half of the twentieth century, that Rauschenbusch's and Niebuhr's different understandings and justifications of
democracy were a given. Yet even before I had read Yoder I was beginning
to explore issues in democratic theory that would make me worry about the

assumption that democracy is normative for Christians. For example, in the earliest article I wrote on Christianity and politics, "Politics, Vision, and the Common Good," I began to worry about issues intrinsic to democratic practice and theory.[25] The civil rights movement, the protest against the war in Vietnam, and questions of economic inequality made me question pluralist justifications of democratic processes. Drawing on the work of Robert Paul Wolff, Ted Lowi, and Sheldon Wolin, I began to explore what alternatives there might be to Niebuhr's "realism."

The article on politics and the common good was paired with another chapter in *Vision and Virtue* entitled "Theology and the New American Culture."[26] "Theology and the New American Culture" is probably best described as an attempt at theological journalism. Reinhold Niebuhr was the master of this genre, as he ably helped us see that what seemed to be quite theoretical issues in political theory had concrete manifestations. In "Theology and the New American Culture," I was trying to suggest that the cultural despair that was so evident among many in the sixties was not accidentally related to some of the fundamental presumptions of liberal democratic theory and practice. Drawing on Philip Slater's *The Pursuit of Loneliness*, I tried to show there was a connection between our isolation from one another and our inability to discover goods in common through the political process.

Somehow, and it may have come from reading the Social Encyclicals, I began to think there was a deep tension between liberal political theory and accounts of politics that appealed to the common good. Niebuhr's political realism expressed in terms of interest group liberalism at best can give you an account of common interests. For Niebuhr, as well as more secular accounts of liberal democratic theory, there are no goods in common that can be discovered as well as serve democratic politics. The democratic state, as Ernst-Wolfgang Bockenforde has argued, is an order of freedom and of peace rather than an order of truth and virtue necessary for the recognition of common goods.[27] Accordingly, defenders of liberal democracies seek to establish institutions that make possible the achievement of relative justice without people themselves being just.[28]

I observed above that I was beginning to explore critical questions essential to issues in democratic theory. That way of putting the matter is, I think, important because it indicates I was not calling into question the presumption that some account of democracy is important for Christians if we were to be politically responsible. *A Community of Character: Toward a Constructive Christian Social Ethic,* a book published in 1981, included a chapter entitled "The Church and Liberal Democracy." In that essay I began to try to distinguish democratic practice from liberal political theory.[29] Drawing on the work of C. B. Macpherson, I tried to show how liberalism, particularly in its economic modes, subverted the democratic commitment to sustaining a common life necessary to make possible lives of virtue.[30] Accordingly, I argued, just to the extent the Church is or can be a school for virtue, Christians can be crucial for the sustaining of democratic social and political life.

By the time I wrote *A Community of Character* I had read and begun to absorb the work of John Howard Yoder. What I learned from Yoder meant I was to be labeled a sectarian, fideistic tribalist because I was allegedly tempting Christians to withdraw from political engagement. Nothing could have been further from the truth. In fact the attempt to distinguish democratic practice from liberal political theory reflected my conviction that Christians could not and should not withdraw from serving their neighbor through political engagement. Some suggested the book I wrote with Rom Coles, *Christianity, Democracy, and the Radical Ordinary: Conversations between a Radical Democrat and a Christian,* represented a more positive approach to the political than my previous work.[31] That may be true of the tone of the book, but I understood the conversation between Coles and myself to be the continuation of my attempt to find a way to talk about forms of democratic life that were not shaped by liberal presuppositions.

That is not to say, however, that Yoder did not make a difference in how I thought about Christian political engagement. Prior to reading Yoder I had the sense that my emphasis on the virtues meant that the Church was crucial to politics for the formation of lives of virtue. The Church became the *polis* that Aristotle knew had to exist but, in his case, did not. Accordingly Yoder's ecclesiology supplied the politics I needed to make intelligible the stress on the virtues. That meant, as Dan Bell argues, that I had to resist any politics that portrays the Church as apolitical in a manner that leaves the formation of the body to the state. I refused any reduction of politics to statecraft in order to emphasize the political character of the Church as a political space in its own right.[32]

From such a perspective the moral emptiness at the heart of liberalism could be construed as an advantage for Christians if the Church was capable of producing lives that are not empty. Liberalism as a practice for organizing cooperative arrangements between moral strangers could be good for Christians, though I think it bad for liberals. Indeed I thought my critiques of liberalism were charitable because my criticisms were an attempt to suggest to liberals that there are alternatives to a liberal way of life. Of course one of the difficulties with that way of conceiving the political mission of the Church is that too often Christians had policed their Christianity to make it compatible with liberal tolerance. The other difficulty being that the alleged indifference of liberal states concerning formation of "citizens" was anything but "neutral." In fact, the liberal state is quite good at the formation of people with virtues to sustain war.

I do not mean to suggest that Yoder's influence on me made little difference. In fact it made all the difference. Thus his claim:

> To ask, "What is the best form of government?" is itself a Constantinian question. It is representative of an already "established" social posture. It assumes that the paradigmatic person, the model ethical agent, is in a position of such power that it falls to him to evaluate alternative worlds and to prefer the one in which he himself (for the model ethical agent assumes himself to be part of 'the people') shares the rule.[33]

Yoder's challenge, interestingly enough, made me wonder—given my interest in exploring issues in democratic theory—whether, in fact, rather than being a "sectarian," I did not continue to be a Constantinian.

Of course, if Alex Sider is right, and I certainly think he is, it is very hard to avoid being Constantinian. That it is hard to avoid being Constantinian is clear because, as Sider argues, even Yoder was unable to avoid that fate. According to Sider, Constantinianism is not so much a "problem" as it is a totalizing discourse. That means that the resources one has to map a way out of Constantinianism will themselves likely be implicated in Constantinianism.[34] In short, Constantinianism conditions the possibility for its own investigation just to the extent it determines what is to count as history.[35] That is why Sider argues that more fundamental than the distinction between transcendental and empirical uses of the description, "Constantinianism" is the distinction between historicist and eschatological discourse. That means for Yoder "the true meaning of history is in the church. And this history is, at least in part, one of disavowal and apostasy."[36] But the very narration of Constantinianism as apostasy reproduces a Constantinian view of history.

Sider's account of the unavoidability of Constantinianism makes clear how, in spite of what I have learned from Yoder, I have in many ways remained a Constantinian. Yet I have never pretended that everything associated with Constantinianism is to be rejected.[37] Certainly Yoder did not think such a rejection warranted or required because he often saw much good in some developments associated with Christendom arrangements. It is, moreover, important to note that Yoder's observation about the question of what is the best form of government is one made in the context of his chapter, "The Christian Case for Democracy." With his usual analytical power Yoder explores in that essay the limits and possibilities of appeals to the rule of the people, observing that it is by no means clear why rule by the people is a good; and how would we know it to be good if the people did rule?[38]

Yoder worries that the glorification of democracy as the rule of "the people," as well as the presumption that democracy represents a form of government that does not suffer from the disabilities of other forms of government, results in uncritical support for wars fought in the name of democracy. So his strategy in his chapter on democracy can almost be described as Niebuhrian, just to the extent he seeks to humble the rhetoric surrounding the uncritical celebration of democracy by Christians. Yet he argues that if Christians accepted our minority status in societies, like those in North America, we would be free to hold rulers to account by asking them to rule consistent with the rhetoric they use to legitimate their power. What we dare not forget, however, is that the assumption that "we" the people are governing ourselves is actually not the case. We are governed by elites. Democracies are no less oligarchic than other forms of government, but it is true, according to Yoder, that democratic oligarchies tend to be the least oppressive.[39]

For Yoder the task is not to justify "democracy." Rather he simply accepts the fact that we are told we live in a democracy. He is not convinced we know what that entails. But drawing on A. D. Lindsay's argument in his *The Modern Democratic State*, that the origins of democracy were in Puritan and Quaker congregations where the dignity of the adversary made dialogue not only necessary but possible, Yoder argues the Church can serve democratic orders in a similar fashion by being a community that continues to respect the adversary both within and outside of the Church. From Yoder's perspective the Church best serves the social orders that claim to be democratic by taking seriously the internal calling of the Church rather than "becoming tributary to whatever secular consensus seems strong at the time."[40]

That is the strategy I have tried to adopt in my work. It is a strategy that makes any identification as a "political theologian" doubtful. There is much to learn from work in political theology, but the way I think about Christian political engagement is less grand than most of what is identified as work in political theology. For example, I think calling attention to the work of Jean Vanier has a political purpose. For it must surely be the case that the existence and support of the work of Vanier to secure homes for the mentally disabled indicates the kind of moral commitment necessary to sustain a politics capable of recognizing the dignity of each human being.[41] But to hold up the work of Vanier as politically significant I am sure seems to many simply a way to avoid the primary political challenges before societies like the United States of America. That may be the case, but that is the way I have learned to think theologically about politics.

In *The First Thousand Years: A Global History of Christianity*, Robert Wilken observes that Christianity is a culture-forming religion. Consequently the growth of Christian communities led to the transformation of the cultures of the ancient world, which meant the creation of several new civilizations. At the heart of that process was language because, as Wilken suggests, "culture has to do with the pattern of inherited meanings and sensibilities embedded in rituals, institutions, laws, practices, images, and the stories of people."[42] Wilken's description of the conceptual revolution brought about by Christianity rightly directs attention to the significance of language as the heart of politics. That is why I resist any attempt to suggest that the Church is one thing and politics something else.

Luke Bretherton puts this well when he suggests that "doing church" and "doing politics" are both about the formation of shared speech and action that forms a common world. Therefore, according to Bretherton, politics and ecclesiology name two mutually constitutive locations where a *sensus communis* can be forged.[43] I take it to be that one of the characteristics of the culture currently described as democratic is the loss of elegant speech. It is not simply the loss of elegance that I lament, but the language used in politics is intended to obscure rather than illumine. If, as Bretherton suggests, ecclesiology is politics by another name, then the Church can serve the world in which we find ourselves by attending to our speech. Well-formed sermons may turn out to be the most important contribution Christians can make to a politics that has some ambition to be truthful.

To conceive Christian witness in this manner may seem insignificant and to require patience we do not have, but that is why Jean Vanier is so important. He is the culture Christianity produces.

The Church as Foot-Dragging

I am aware that these last suggestions may seem far too abstract, so let me try to suggest the kind of concrete politics I think they entail, at least for Christians in advanced capitalist societies, by calling attention to James C. Scott's recent book, *Two Cheers for Anarchism: Six Easy Pieces on Autonomy, Dignity, and Meaningful Work and Play*.[44] I am well aware that to identify with Scott's account of anarchism will only confirm for many I am a "sectarian, fideistic, tribalist," but I have long given up on any attempt to counter that charge. That I am directing attention to Scott's book is not meant to suggest that he provides the only way to think about the political character of the Church—in fact, I am quite sympathetic to Luke Bretherton's more robust account of what a Christian politics might look like.[45]

One of the attractions of Scott's account of anarchy is his reticence about any account of anarchy that tries to be comprehensive. Accordingly he describes his "method" as an "anarchist squint" that is intended to help us see what we might otherwise miss.[46] Scott does not deny that Proudhon's description of anarchism as "mutuality or cooperation without hierarchy or state rule" certainly captures some of what may pass as anarchy, but that description may not adequately suggest the anarchist tolerance for confusion and improvisation that accompanies social learning.[47] Scott has no reason to try to nail down a definition of anarchism, being content to use anarchism to describe a defense of politics, conflict, and debate, along with the perpetual uncertainty and learning they entail. That means that, unlike many anarchists, Scott does not believe the state is always the enemy of freedom.

Scott's project might be called an exercise in small politics. For example, he writes about his stay in Germany when he was trying to learn German by forcing himself to interact with fellow pedestrians in the small town of Neubrandenburg. He tells the story of crossing the street to get to the train station in obedience to lights that indicated when it was legal to cross the street. He reports that fifty or sixty people would often wait at the corner for the light to change even though they could see no traffic was coming. He reports after five hours of observation he saw no more than two people cross against the light. Those two who would cross against the lights had to be willing to receive from those that waited gestures of disapproval. Scott reports he had to screw up his courage to cross the street against their disapproval. He did so, justifying his law-breaking performance by remembering that his grandparents could have used more of the spirit of breaking the law in the name of justice. But because they had lost the practice of breaking small laws, they no longer knew when it really matters to break the law. Scott calls such practice of law breaking "anarchist calisthenics," implying that Germans could use the practice.[48]

Scott observes that, under authoritarian regimes, subjects who are denied public means of protest have no recourse but to resort to "foot-dragging, sabotage, poaching, theft, and, ultimately, revolt." Modern forms of democracy allegedly make such forms of dissent obsolete. But Scott argues that the assumed promise of democracy that makes "foot-dragging" no longer necessary is seldom realized in practice. He argues that what needs to be noticed is that most of the political reforms that have made some difference for democratic change have been the result of disruption of the public order. Accordingly, Scott argues that anarchism at least is a reminder that the cultivation of insubordination and law breaking is crucial for the political developments we call democracy.[49]

Yet Scott observes that proponents of liberal democratic theory seldom attend to the role of crisis and institutional failure that lead to political reform. That liberal democracies in the West are generally run for the top 20 percent of those that possess wealth no doubt is one of the reasons for the occlusion of crisis to account for democratic developments. Indeed, Scott observes the greatest failure of liberal democracies is the lack of protection they give to the economic and security interests of their least-advantaged citizens. As a result, Scott argues, the contradiction between the renewal of democracy by major episodes of extra-institutional disorder and the promise of democracy as the institutionalization of peaceful change is seldom noticed.[50]

Scott's book is an account of episodes of foot-dragging and disruption. In particular he directs attention to matters not often considered "political" to illumine our political landscape in advanced industrial societies. For example, he pokes fun at the use of quantitative measures of productivity in the academy in order to show how democracies like the United States have embraced meritocratic criteria for the elite selection and distribution of public funds to create "a vast and deceptive 'antipolitics machine' designed to turn legitimate political questions into neutral objective administrative exercises governed by experts."[51] This strategy to depoliticize protest masks a lack of faith in the possibilities anarchists and democrats have in the mutuality and education that can result from common action.

Scott's defense of anarchy, therefore, turns out to be a defense of politics. He observes that "if there is one conviction that anarchist thinkers and nondemagogic populists share, it is faith in the capacity of democratic citizenry to learn and grow through engagement in the public sphere."[52] Yet he argues that the formation of bodies wrought through populist politics is often defeated by something as simple as the SAT exam. For that exam serves as a way to convince middle-class whites that affirmative action is a choice between objective merit and favoritism. As a result, the SAT robs us of the public dialogue we need to have about how educational opportunity ought to be allocated in a democratic and plural society. Cost-benefit analysis often functions in a similar way to make the conflict needed seem petty.[53]

Scott ends his book by directing our attention to the role of history in modern politics. The purpose of enunciating histories is to summarize major historical events, making them understandable as a single narrative. As a result, the "radical contingency" of history is domesticated in an effort to underwrite the assumption that the way things turned out is the only way they could be. Such condensations of history, which fulfill the need of elites to project an image of control, create a blindness to the fact that "gains for human freedom have not been the result of orderly, institutional procedures but of disorderly, unpredictable, spontaneous action cracking open the social order from below."[54]

I confess that it is with some hesitancy that I use Scott's account of anarchy to exemplify what a Christian politics might look like. I worry that "anarchy" may suggest that I have no use for institutions that inevitably involve hierarchies of authority. I assume it is never a question of whether hierarchies of authority should or should not exist, but rather how authority should be understood as an aid for the discovery of the common good of a community. Indeed I am in deep agreement with Victor Lee Austin's argument in *Up with Authority* that, because the common good of communities is not one isolated goal, "authority is needed because it is desirable that particular goods should be taken care of by particular agencies."[55] The irony is that such an account of authority stands as a challenge, a challenge that may appear to threaten anarchy, in a liberal social order in which common goods by design are reduced to common interest.

The Church is rightly a hierarchical institution. It is so because the Church is a community that believes the truth matters. Accordingly, the saints and martyrs stand as authorities necessary to test the changes that the Church will undergo if it is to remain faithful to the gospel. Those singled out for office in the Church (to insure that the Church attends to the saints) must recognize that the exercise of their authority can never be an end in itself. But it is "political" in the most basic sense of what it means to be political and accordingly can serve as an example for the exercise of authority beyond the Church. If that is a Constantinian strategy, then I am a Constantinian.

Above I referred to Sider's suggestion that Yoder's anti-Constantinianism is best expressed in terms of the Church being the true meaning of history. That is an extraordinary claim, requiring a people to exist who know how to drag their feet when confronted by those who think they know where history is headed—which, I hope, is one way to say that the Church does not have a politics, but rather the Church is God's politics for the world. If Christians are well-formed by that politics, they hopefully will serve the world well by developing an "ecclesial squint." By doing so they might just be able to serve their neighbor by helping us see that "it did not have to be." That, moreover, is the most radical politics imaginable.

Notes

1. Rusty Reno, "Stanley Hauerwas," in *The Blackwell Companion to Political Theology* (Oxford: Blackwell Publishing, 2004), 302–16.

2. Reno, "Hauerwas," 302.

3. John Howard Yoder, *The Politics of Jesus: Vicit Agnus Noster*, 2nd ed. (Grand Rapids, Mich.: Eerdmans, 1995), 3.

4. For an extremely informative overview of the history of Christian engagement with politics, see C. C. Pecknold, *Christianity and Politics: A Brief Guide to the History* (Eugene, Oreg.: 2010).

5. Elizabeth Phillips, *Political Theology: A Guide for the Perplexed* (London: T & T Clark, 2012), 4.

6. Carl Schmitt, *Political Theology: Four Chapters on the Concept of Sovereignty* (Chicago: University of Chicago Press, 1985), 36.

7. Paul Kahn, *Political Theology: Four New Chapters on the Concept of Sovereignty* (New York: Columbia University Press, 2011), 31.

8. For a summary of James Gustafson's description of my work and my response, see Stanley Hauerwas, Introduction to *Christian Existence Today: Essays on Church, World, and Living In-Between* (Grand Rapids, Mich.: Brazos Press, 2001), 1–21. This book was originally published in 1988.

9. John Howard Yoder, "How H. Richard Niebuhr Reasoned: A Critique of *Christ and Culture*," in *Authentic Transformation: A New Vision of Christ and Culture*, ed. Glen Stassen, D.M. Yeager, and John Howard Yoder (Nashville, Tenn.: Abingdon Press, 1996), 68.

10. For a fascinating reading of the implications of Yoder for political theology, see Daniel Barber, *On Diaspora: Christianity, Religion, and Secularity* (Eugene, Oreg.: Cascade, 2011), 117–22.

11. Stanley Hauerwas, *A Better Hope: Resources for a Church Confronting Capitalism, Democracy, and Postmodernity* (Grand Rapids, Mich.: Brazos Press, 2000), 55–70.

12. Hauerwas, *Better Hope*, 67.

13. See, for example, the chapter on Rauschenbusch entitled, "Walter Rauschenbusch and the Saving of America" in *Better Hope*, 71–108. I follow that chapter with another on John Courtney Murray and his role in drafting the encyclical of the Second Vatican Council, *Dignitatis Humanae*. Murray and John Ryan are part of the story I wanted to tell about Christian ethics as they represented the Catholic alternative to mainstream Protestantism. I have written numerous essays on Reinhold Niebuhr, but the two that are most relevant to this paper appear in Stanley Hauerwas, *Wilderness Wanderings: Probing Twentieth-Century Theology and Philosophy* (Boulder, Colo.: Westview, 1997), 32–62. The same book also includes my essays on Jim Gustafson and Paul Ramsey. The essays I have written on Yoder are too numerous to list.

14. Walter Rauschenbusch, *A Theology for the Social Gospel* (Nashville, Tenn.: Abingdon Books, 1917), 119.

15. Rauschenbusch, *Theology*, 129.

16. Rauschenbusch, *Theology*, 142–43.

17. Rauschenbusch, *Theology*, 5.

18. Rauschenbusch, *Theology*, 174–75.

19. Rauschenbusch, *Theology*, 224.

20. Harry Davis and Robert Good, eds., *Reinhold Niebuhr on Politics* (New York: Scribner, 1960), 182. This volume organizes Niebuhr's writing on politics in an extraordinary helpful way.

21. Davis and Good, *Reinhold Niebuhr*, 182.

22. Davis and Good, *Reinhold Niebuhr*, 186. This famous epigram is from Niebuhr's *Children of Light and Children of Darkness*, a book he wrote after the Second World War to chasten what he regarded as the uncritical celebration of democracy.

23. It is to Charles Mathewes's great credit that he develops what I take to be a Niebuhrian theme by suggesting that Christian engagement in politics is itself a discipline for the shaping of the Christian life. Christians must have virtues that will prepare them politically, but those same virtues will be honed through political engagement. I am sure Mathewes is right about that, but I suspect the ambiguity that is, according to Mathewes, intrinsic to political involvement can be learned from singing in the church choir—and I suspect Mathewes would agree. See Charles Mathewes, *A Theology of Public Life* (Cambridge: Cambridge University Press, 2007).

24. Davis and Good, *Reinhold Niebuhr*, 205.

25. Stanley Hauerwas, *Vision and Virtue* (Notre Dame, Ind.: Fides Press, 1974), 222–60.

26. Hauerwas, *Vision and Virtue*, 241–60.

27. This is Rhonheimer's characterization of Bockenforde's views in Martin Rhonheimer, *The Common Good of Constitutional Democracy* (Washington, D.C.: Catholic University Press, 2013), 74–75. It is extremely important to note that Rhonheimer argues against Bockenforde by suggesting that a modern democratic state's attempt to secure peace is itself a good in common. Rhonheimer does not contest Bockenforde's contention that truth is not the aim of democratic constitutionalism, but Rhonheimer argues that constitutional democracies rightly seek to secure a minimum morality, to ensure people can live together in peace. The institutions of societies so ordered, Rhonheimer argues, compensate for the deficit in individual morality. Rhonheimer's is a powerful argument but I remain doubtful that peace is possible without truthfulness.

28. Some may think this an unfair characterization but John Rawls is admirably candid that his project is an attempt to give an account of justice that does not require those that enjoy the system of justice so created to be just. See John Rawls, *A Theory of Justice* (Cambridge, Mass.: Harvard University Press, 1971), 54–65.

29. I am quite well aware that a phrase like "liberal political theory" does not do justice to the many forms of liberal theory. For the best account I know of the diversity of liberal theory, see Paul Kahn, *Putting Liberalism in Its Place* (Princeton: Princeton University Press, 2005). Kahn argues that liberalism's greatest deficit is its failure to account for the place of the will (and thus of love) in the politics of modern nation states. Kahn distinguishes between a liberalism of interest and a liberalism of reason. The former emphasizes the centrality of the market while the latter attempts to ground political life in a compelling foundation comparable to the sciences. Both these forms of liberalism fail to do justice to the will as the source of love necessary to ground politics. See Kahn's chapter, "The Faculties of the Soul: Beyond Reason and Interest," in *Putting Liberalism*, 145–82.

30. Stanley Hauerwas, *A Community of Character: Toward a Constructive Christian Social Ethic* (Notre Dame, Ind.: University of Notre Dame Press, 1981), 72–88. I cannot believe I used the phrase "social ethic" in the title of this book. The use of that phrase is problematic because it cannot help but reproduce the presumption that there is another area of ethics that is not social. I am aware that Macpherson's account of "possessive individualism" has been the subject of aggressive critique. I remain convinced, however, that the principal lines of his argument remain valid. For an insightful analysis of the question of the relationship of democracy to liberalism in my work, as well as Stout's critique of my identification of democracy with liberalism, see William Cavanaugh, "A Politics of Vulnerability: Hauerwas and Democracy" in *Unsettling Arguments: A Festschrift on the Occasion of Stanley Hauerwas's 70th Birthday* (Eugene, Oreg.: Cascade, 2010), 89–111. In Aristotle Papanikolaou, *The Mystical As Political: Democracy and Non-Radical Orthodoxy* (Notre Dame, Ind.: University of Notre Dame Press, 2012), the author observes I have never "really taken the time to nuance what I mean by liberalism" (135). I do not think that a fair characterization. The problem is not I have not taken the time to give more nuanced accounts of liberalism. The problem is I have done so too occasionally. I should say I am quite sympathetic to Papanikolaou's emphasis on the importance of spirituality for democratic politics and in particularly the politics of truth.

31. Stanley Hauerwas and Romand Coles, *Christianity, Democracy, and the Radical Ordinary: Conversations Between a Radical Democrat and a Christian* (Eugene, Oreg.: Cascade, 2008). For a very enlightening analysis of the relation of liberal political theory and democracy, see Alan Ryan, *The Making of Modern Liberalism* (Princeton: Princeton University Press, 2012), 21–107. Ryan rightly identifies liberalism as a "theory of the good life for individuals that is linked to a theory of the social, economic, and political arrangements within which they may lead that life" (15). He suggests that Rawls failed finally to separate his account of liberalism from a view of the good life. His account of liberal anxiety is particularly telling, as Ryan observes "liberals suffer a self-inflicted wound: they want the emancipation that leads to disenchantment, but want the process that emancipates us to relocate us in the world as well. Nietzsche and Weber are only the most eloquent among the voices that say it cannot be done in the way the liberal wants" (78).

32. Dan Bell, "State and Civil Society," in *The Blackwell Companion to Political Theology*, 433–34.

33. John Howard Yoder, *The Priestly Kingdom: Social Ethics as Gospel* (Notre Dame, Ind.: University of Notre Dame, 1984), 154.

34. Alex Sider, *To See History Doxologically: History and Holiness in John Howard Yoder's Ecclesiology* (Grand Rapids, Mich.: Eerdmans, 2011), 120.

35. Sider, *To See*, 121.

36. Sider, *To See*, 121.

37. In a number of essays I have tried to suggest that the polarization of Constantinianism and non-Constantinianism is often not very helpful in helping us to discern how Christians must attempt to find ways to serve their neighbor. Several chapters in Hauerwas, *Better Hope* were attempts to defy the assumption that anti-Constantinianism means that Christians have nothing useful to say to the politics of the world. Stanley Hauerwas, *The State of the University: Academic Knowledges and the Knowledge of God* (Oxford: Blackwell, 2007) may be more relevant.

38. Yoder, *Priestly Kingdom*, 151.

39. Yoder, *Priestly Kingdom*, 157–58.

40. Yoder, *Priestly Kingdom*, 168.

41. I have written about Vanier a number of times, but I was honored to collaborate on Stanley Hauerwas and Jean Vanier, *Living Gently in a Violent World: The Prophetic Witness of Weakness* (Downers Grove, Ill.: IVP Press, 2008). I suspect, however, that the work of my students is more indicative of how to proceed than anything I myself have completed. See, for example, Charles Pinches, "Hauerwas and Political Theology: The Next Generation," *Journal of Religious Ethics* 36, no. 3 (September 2008), 513–42. Pinches directs attention to Cavanaugh, Long, Toole, Bell, McCarthy, Shuman, Lysaught, and Johnson as representatives of this way of doing "political theology."

42. Robert Wilken, *The First Thousand Years: A Global History of Christianity* (New Haven: Yale University Press, 2012), 2.

43. Luke Bretherton, "Coming to Judgment: Methodological Reflections on the Relationship Between Ecclesiology, Ethnography, and Political Theory," *Modern Theology* 28, no. 2 (April 2012), 177.

44. James C. Scott, *Two Cheers for Anarchism: Six Easy Pieces on Autonomy, Dignity, and Meaningful Work and Play* (Princeton: Princeton University Press, 2012).

45. Luke Bretherton, *Christianity and Contemporary Politics* (Oxford: Wiley-Blackwell, 2010). Indeed, I think much of what Bretherton does in his book is compatible with Scott's understanding of anarchy. For example, commenting on the significance of "ordinary time" Bretherton observes that attention to ordinary time "enables the valuation of the micro-political as just as important for conceptualizing faithful political witness as the set-piece relationships between church and state, and ordinary political actor as just as significant as 'heroic' figures such as Martin Luther King" (213).

46. Scott, *Two Cheers*, xii.

47. Scott, *Two Cheers*, xii.

48. Scott, *Two Cheers*, 3–7.

49. Scott, *Two Cheers*, 16–17.
50. Scott, *Two Cheers*, 18–19.
51. Scott, *Two Cheers*, 111.
52. Scott, *Two Cheers*, 121–22.
53. Scott, *Two Cheers*, 123–24.
54. Scott, *Two Cheers*, 141.
55. Victor Lee Austin, *Up with Authority* (London: T&T Clark, 2010), 31. The quoted sentence is from Yves René Marie Simon, *A General Theory of Authority* (Notre Dame, Ind.: University of Notre Dame Press, 1980), 72. Austin's account of authority draws quite rightly on Simon.

Contributors

Timothy D. Barnes is currently an honorary professorial fellow at the University of Edinburgh's School of Divinity and School of History, Classics, and Archaeology, as well as a fellow of the British Academy. Previously, he spent the whole of his teaching career at the University of Toronto until retiring in 2007. He was awarded both the Philip Schaff Prize by the American Society of Church History for *Constantine and Eusebius* (Harvard University Press, 1981) and the Charles Goodwin Award of Merit by the American Philological Association. His recent projects and publications include *Funerary Speech for John Chrysostom: Translated Texts for Historians*, in collaboration with George Bevan (Liverpool University Press, 2013), and *Constantine: Dynasty, Religion and Power in the Later Roman Empire* (Wiley-Blackwell, 2011).

Luke Bretherton is professor of theological ethics and a senior fellow of the Kenan Institute for Ethics at Duke University. Before joining Duke he was reader in theology and politics and convener of the Faith & Public Policy Forum at King's College London. His books include *Hospitality as Holiness: Christian Witness amid Moral Diversity* (Ashgate, 2006), *Christianity & Contemporary Politics: The Conditions and Possibilities of Faithful Witness* (Wiley-Blackwell, 2010), and *Resurrecting Democracy: Faith, Citizenship and the Politics of a Common Life* (Cambridge University Press, 2014).

Rev. Emmanuel Clapsis is Archbishop Iakovos Professor of Orthodox Theology at Hellenic College and Holy Cross Greek Orthodox School of Theology. Fr. Clapsis has served as the vice-moderator of the Faith and

Order Commission of the World Council of Churches (1991–98) and commissioner of the Faith and Order Commission of the US National Council of Churches (1985–91). He has also participated in the theological dialogues of the Orthodox Church with the Evangelical Lutheran Church (USA) and the Roman Catholic Church. He is author of *Orthodoxy in Conversation: Orthodox Ecumenical Engagements* (Holy Cross Press, 2000) and editor of *The Orthodox Churches in a Pluralistic World* (WCC Publications, 2004).

George E. Demacopoulos is Fr. John Meyendorff & Patterson Family Chair of Orthodox Christian Studies and codirector of the Orthodox Christian Studies Center at Fordham University. He specializes in the history of Christianity in late antiquity, the early medieval West, and Byzantium. His monographs include *Gregory the Great: Ascetic, Pastor, and First Man of Rome* (University of Notre Dame Press, 2015), *The Invention of Peter: Apostolic Discourse and Papal Authority in Late Antiquity* (University of Pennsylvania Press, 2013), and *Five Models of Spiritual Direction in the Early Church* (University of Notre Dame Press, 2007).

Mary Doak is currently associate professor of theology at the University of San Diego. She received her PhD from the University of Chicago. Her research interests include public theology, religious freedom, eschatology, and ecclesiology. She has published *Reclaiming Narrative for Public Theology* (SUNY Press, 2004) as well as various articles on aspects of Christian faith, especially in relation to US culture and politics. Her current book project is an exploration of the mission of the Church in the face of the challenges of the twenty-first century, especially the feminization of poverty, worldwide migration, and ecological degradation.

Eric Gregory is professor of religion at Princeton University. He is the author of *Politics & the Order of Love: An Augustinian Ethic of Democratic Citizenship* (Chicago 2008), and numerous articles related to his interests in ethics, theology, political theory, law, and the role of religion in public life. In 2007, he was awarded Princeton's President's Award for Distinguished Teaching. A graduate of Harvard College, he earned an MPhil and diploma in theology from the University of Oxford as a Rhodes scholar, and his doctorate in religious studies from Yale University. Among his current projects is a book tentatively titled *What Do We Owe Strangers? Globalization and the Good Samaritan*, which examines secular and religious perspectives on global justice.

Perry T. Hamalis is the Cecelia Schneller Mueller Professor of Religion and director of the Office of Academic Opportunities at North Central College in Naperville, Illinois. He earned his PhD in religious ethics at the University of Chicago in 2004, under the mentorship of William Schweiker. Dr. Hamalis's primary areas of research and teaching include Eastern Orthodox ethics, religion and politics, and applied ethics. He also serves as a consultant to the World Council of Churches. In addition to his forthcoming book *Formed by Death: Insights for Ethics from Orthodox Christianity* (University of Notre Dame Press, 2014), his works have been published in the *Journal of Religion*, the *Greek Orthodox Theological Review*, and in several edited volumes, including *The Orthodox Christian World*, edited by Augustine Casiday (Routledge, 2012), and *Thinking through Faith*, edited by Aristotle Papanikolaou and Elizabeth Prodromou (St. Vladimir's Seminary Press, 2012).

Father Capodistrias Hämmerli is an Orthodox theologian at the University of Fribourg, Switzerland. His main research interests are theology, law, and political sciences, articulated around issues concerning the display of religious symbols in the public sphere, but he is equally interested in topics such as secularization, ethnicity, and nationalism. His PhD thesis is on "The Freedom to Exclude: A Theological Perspective on the Concept of Non-Discrimination."

Stanley Hauerwas is the Gilbert T. Rowe Professor of Theological Ethics at the Divinity School of Duke University. In addition to reclaiming the importance of character and the virtues for the display of Christian living, he has also drawn attention to the importance of narrative for explicating the interrelation of practical reason and personal identity, and correlatively the significance of the Church as the necessary context for Christian formation and moral reflection. His recent writings include *Working with Words: On Learning to Speak Christian* (Cascade, 2011), *War and the American Difference: Theological Reflections on Violence and National Identity* (Baker Academic, 2011), and *The Work of Theology* (Eerdmans, 2015).

Rev. J. Bryan Hehir is the Parker Gilbert Montgomery Professor of the Practice of Religion and Public Life at Harvard University's John F. Kennedy School of Government. He is also the secretary for health care and social services in the Roman Catholic Archdiocese of Boston. Previously, he served as distinguished professor of ethics and international affairs at Georgetown University's School of Foreign Service. Rev. Hehir's academic and policy work have focused upon Catholic social teaching and social policy, the role of religion in world politics and in American society, and the role of ethics in international politics and US foreign policy. His writings include "The Moral Measurement of War: A Tradition of Continuity and Change," "Catholicism and Democracy," and "Social Values and Public Policy: A Contribution from a Religious Tradition."

Peter Iver Kaufman is George Matthews & Virginia Brinkly Modlin Chair in Leadership Studies at the University of Richmond and professor emeritus at the University of North Carolina at Chapel Hill. The author of six monographs, Dr. Kaufman specializes in the intersection of religion and politics in the cultures of late antiquity, the middle ages, and the early modern period. He is also the founder of the Scholars Latino Initiative, which has five chapters in North Carolina and Virginia.

Aristotle Papanikolaou is professor of theology and Archbishop Demetrios Chair in Orthodox Theology and Culture at Fordham University. He is also codirector of Fordham's Orthodox Christian Studies Center. He has expertise in contemporary Eastern Orthodox theology, Trinitarian theology, and political theology. Most recently, he is author of *The Mystical as Political: Democracy and Non-Radical Orthodoxy* (Notre Dame University Press, 2012) and is co-editor of *Orthodox Constructions of the West*, published with Fordham University Press in the *Orthodox Christianity and Contemporary Thought* series (2013). His current book project is on violence and virtue in relation to theological anthropology.

James C. Skedros is the dean and the Michael G. and Anastasia Cantonis Professor of Byzantine Studies and Professor of Early Christianity at Hellenic College and Holy Cross Greek Orthodox School of Theology, Brookline, Massachusetts., where he has been on faculty since 1998. Professor Skedros received his ThD from Harvard Divinity School in the history of Christianity. From 1996 to 1998 he was assistant professor of Orthodox studies at the Graduate Theological Union in Berkeley, California. His teaching and research areas include popular religious practices in late antiquity, Byzantine Christianity, the lives of early Christian and Byzantine saints, pilgrimage, and Christian-Muslim relations.

Kristina Stoeckl is assistant professor in the Department of Sociology at the University of Innsbruck and principal investigator of the ERC-funded research project "Postsecular Conflicts." A member of the Young Academy of the Austrian Academy of Sciences, she has been fellow at the University of Vienna and the Institute for Human Sciences (IWM) and visiting fellow at the Robert Schuman Centre for Advanced Studies of the European University Institute in Florence, as well as a Marie Curie Fellow at the University of Rome Tor Vergata. She holds a PhD in social and political sciences from the European University Institute. Her fields of interest include the intersection of religion, society, and politics with a specific focus on Russian Orthodox Christianity. She is the author of *The Russian Orthodox Church and Human Rights* (Routledge 2014).

Nathaniel Wood is completing a doctorate in systematic theology at Fordham University and is a graduate fellow of Fordham's Orthodox Christian Studies Center. He does constructive Orthodox theology with an ecumenical focus and has interests in modern Russian theology and philosophy, political theology, and Christian responses to modernity and secularization. His dissertation, "Deifying Democracy: Liberalism and the Politics of Theosis," explores the relationship between incarnation, deification, and liberal democracy in the Russian Orthodox tradition and Radical Orthodoxy.

INDEX

commonwealth, 133; Christian doctrine and, 135; civil obedience and, 134–35; religious fears and, 135; sovereignty and, 133–34
communion: power structure and, 85. *See also* divine-human communion
Communism, religion after collapse, 46
Communist countries, secularism, 43–44
Communist Revolution, 1–2
community: freedom and, 115; *versus* society/association, 74n4
A Community of Character: Toward a Constructive Christian Social Ethic (Hauerwas), 261–62
complex space, Mount Athos, 62
Conciliar Era, democracy and, 235–38
Confessions (Augustine): first narrative philosophy, 208; the Manichees, 207–8; Simplicianus, 209
conflict, 84; power and, 84–90
connected critics, 122–23
consensus seeking, 92
consociationalism, 64–66; authoritarianism and, 67–68; Church as distinct community, 71; CST (Catholic Social Teaching), 67–68; English Pluralists and, 66; Maritain, Jacques, 67–68; millet system of Ottoman Empire, 76n16; Orthodoxy and, 2, 68; saeculum and, 71; sovereignty, 65–66
Constans (Emperor), 178
Constantine: Alexander and, 176; Caecelian and, 203–4; conversion, 4; God's favor beliefs, 205; proclaimed emperor, 175–76; "Shadow of Constantine," 127
Constantinian triumphalism, 99
Constantinianism, 4–5, 167, 273n37; secular and, 6; Sider on, 263–64
Constantius (Emperor), 176
constitutional democracies, 271n27
constitutional federalism, sovereignty and, 65
constitutional state, 237
cosmic social imagination, 68
cosmopolis, 76n22
Council of Antioch: Gregory of Nazianzus and, 181; Paul's deposition and, 180
Council of Constantinople, 182; homoean creed, 180. *See also* Second Ecumenical Council
Council of Europe, *Lautsi v. Italy*, 31–32
Council of Nicaea, Paul's election and, 176
Council of Serdica, 178
creation, the incarnation and, 158–59
the Crucifix Case. *See Lautsi v. Italy*
CST (Catholic Social Teaching), 67, 95n20
cultural development, human rights and, 11–12

cultural pessimism, 114–15
culture of subjectivity, 113–14

de Mesquita, Bruce Bueno, 80
death: decamegamurderer regimes, 137–38; democide, 137–38; by government, 137–38; limits of politics, 144–47; mortality, 138–39; social contract and, 133–35; sovereignty and, 136–37; spiritual, 138–39, 151n34. *See also* dynamics of death
Death by Government (Rummel), 137
decamegamurderer regimes, 137–38
Declaration on Human Rights and Dignity (Tenth World Council of Russian People), 12, 19–20
The Declaration on Religious Freedom *(Dignitas Humanae)*, 235, 237
deification of humanity, 159–60
Delikostantis, Konstantinos, 17
Demacopoulos, George, 276
democide, 137
democracy: Augustinianism and, 98; authentic democracy, 242; Benedict XVI and, 243–47; Catholicism and, 232–47; Christianity and, 1–2, 6–7; Conciliar Era, 235–38; consociational, 64–66; constitutional democracies, 271n27; as counterculture, 80; death of citizens, 137–38; definition, 62–64; divine purposes and, 99; divine-human communion and, 81–84, 129; glorification as rule of the people, 264; Gregory XVI and, 232–33; human rights and legal system, 237–38; individuals and, 63–64; John Paul II and, 238–43; Leo XIII and, 233; listening as political act, 71–72; in modern political thought, 63–64; Niebuhr, Reinhold and, 259–60; Orthodox and, 6; Pius XII and, 232–34; pluralism and, 33; political power representing people, 34; Rauschenbusch, Walter, 6; relationships and, 63–64; social gospel and, 258–59; theory gap, 128; *theosis*, 128–29; Vatican II, 6
democratic action as idolatry, 103
democratic citizenship, 63–64
democratic despotism, 64
democratic peace thesis, 137
democratic practice *versus* liberalism, 262
Demophilus, 180–81, 187
demos, 64
Despotate of Epiros, 225
despotism, 64
diakonia, 117
dialogue, unity and, 122

Gregory I (pope), desecularization, 203
Gregory of Nazianzus, 181–82, 187; Last Will
and Testament, 189–95
Gregory XVI (pope), democracy and, 232–33
guild socialists, 75n10
Guriouan, Vigen, 17
Gustafson, James, *Can Ethics be Christian?*,
257
Gvosdev, Nikolas, 128

Hamalis, Perry, 3, 277
Hämmerli, Capodistrias, 2, 277
Hauerwas, Stanley, 6, 277; *A Better Hope*,
256–57; *The Blackwell Companion to
Political Theology*, 253; *A Community of
Character: Toward a Constructive Christian
Social Ethic*, 261–62; "Politics, Vision, and
the Common Good," 261; "Theology and
the New American Culture," 261
The Healing of the Two Blind Men (von
Carolsfeld), 12
Hehir, J. Bryan, 6, 277
Hellenism, 226
Henkin, Louis, 13–14
heresy: Byzantine emperors and, 220; secular
politics as, 155–66
hierarchy: Marian laity and, 86; the Trinity
and, 86–87
Hilarion Alfayev (metropolitan): on Universal
Declaration of Human Rights, 22
*Historical Dialogue of Palladius, Bishop of
Helenopolis, on the Life and Conduct of the
blessed John, Bishop of Constantinople, called
Golden Mouth*, 183–84
history: God's entry into time, 100; time as,
72–73
Hobbes, Thomas: commonwealth, 133–34;
dynamics of death, 130–38, 143; on
government, 132–33; *Leviathan*, 131–32,
135–36; Orthodoxy and liberal tradition, 3;
political legitimacy, 136–37; politics, 132;
purpose of, 139–44; sovereignty, 132–34;
state of nature, 131–32, 134–35
homoean Reichskirche, 180
hope, God's gift of, 120–21
human dignity: *Basic Teaching*
and, 23; human rights and, 14; morality
and, 24; religious understanding, 14
human rights: acceptance-through-rejection
strategy, 17; Catholic Church endorsement,
15–16; cultural development and, 11–12;
East-West divide, 2; French Revolution and,
15–16; John II and, 239–43; Kirill on, 11–12;
Lautsi v. Italy interpretations, 40–41; legal

system of democracy, 237–38; Makrides on
Orthodox theological engagement, 17;
Patriarch Alexei II on, 22; Pollis, Adamantia,
on, 16; religion's suspicion, 14–15; religious
inspiration theory, 14; ROC (Russian
Orthodox Church), 1, 14; sacralization of the
person and, 15–17; as supplemental theology,
14; United Nations Declaration on Human
Rights, 236; Universal Declaration of
Human Rights, 11–12. *See also* ROC (Russian
Orthodox Church)
humanism of liberal democracy, 168
humanitarianism, 104–6

identity: sovereign self and, 117. *See also*
national identity
idolatry: democratic action as, 103; of politics,
101–2
imperial power, 79–80; Byzantium, 221
imperialist globalization, Christianity and, 80
the incarnation: creation and, 158–59; inward
overcoming, 156, 164–65; as political task,
157–61; pure nature and, 158–59; theandric
operation, 162–63; *theosis* and, 159
individual *versus* community, 14–15
individualization of Orthodox faith, 117
individuals, democracy and, 63–64
inward overcoming, 156, 164–65; the
incarnation and, 164
Irenaeus of Lyons (Saint), 140–41
Isidore, 182–83

Joas, Hans, sacralization of the person, 15–17
John Chrysostom, 187–88
John of Damascus, *Exact Exposition of the
Orthodox Faith*, 162
John Paul II (pope), 238; authentic democracy,
242; *Centesimus Annus*, 239, 241–43; United
Nations addresses, 239–40
John XXIII (pope): constitutional state, 237;
Pacem in Terris, 235–36
Julian the Apostate, 180
juridical pluralism: Europe and, 35; *Lautsi v.
Italy* and, 40–41
just behavior, political practice and, 210
justice: charity and, 105; divine-human
communion, 88–89; politics' use, 259
The Justification of the Good (Soloviev), 158
Justinian I (emperor): Church-related
legislation, 220; emperors and the law,
223–24; *Sixth Novella*, 4, 57n54

Kaufman, Peter Iver, 5, 106–7, 278
kenosis, 163, 165

Orthodox Christianity and Contemporary Thought

SERIES EDITORS
George E. Demacopoulos and Aristotle Papanikolaou

Ecumenical Patriarch Bartholomew, *In the World, Yet Not of the World: Social and Global Initiatives of Ecumenical Patriarch Bartholomew*. Edited by John Chryssavgis. Foreword by Jose Manuel Barroso.

Ecumenical Patriarch Bartholomew, *Speaking the Truth in Love: Theological and Spiritual Exhortations of Ecumenical Patriarch Bartholomew*. Edited by John Chryssavgis. Foreword by Dr. Rowan Williams, Archbishop of Canterbury.

Ecumenical Patriarch Bartholomew, *On Earth as in Heaven: Ecological Vision and Initiatives of Ecumenical Patriarch Bartholomew*. Edited by John Chryssavgis. Foreword by His Royal Highness, the Duke of Edinburgh.

George E. Demacopoulos and Aristotle Papaniklaou (eds.), *Orthodox Constructions of the West*.

John Chryssavgis and Bruce V. Foltz (eds.), *Toward an Ecology of Transfiguration: Orthodox Christian Perspectives on Environment, Nature, and Creation*. Foreword by Bill McKibben. Prefatory Letter by Ecumenical Patriarch Bartholomew.

Lucian N. Leustean (ed.), *Orthodox Christianity and Nationalism in Nineteenth-Century Southeastern Europe*.

John Chryssavgis (ed.), *Dialogue of Love: Breaking the Silence of Centuries.*
Contributions by Brian E. Daley, S.J., and Georges Florovsky.

George E. Demacopoulos and Aristotle Papaniklaou (eds.), *Christianity, Democracy, and the Shadow of Constantine.*